Dr. John's
HEALING
PSORIASIS
COOKBOOK...Plus!

by Dr. John O.A. Pagano
Chiropractic Physician

Foreword by:
Annemarie Colbin

Published by:
The Pagano Organization, Inc.
35 Hudson Terrace
Englewood Cliffs, NJ 07632

Dr. John's
P HEALING SORIASIS
C O O K B O O K...Plus!

By Dr. John O.A. Pagano
Chiropractic Physician

Published by:
The Pagano Organization, Inc.
35 Hudson Terrace
Englewood Cliffs, NJ 07632 USA
Telephone: 201-947-0606
Fax: 201-947-8066
www.psoriasis-healing.com

DISCLAIMER: This book was created to assist the psoriatic, eczema and psoriatic arthritic patient regarding food selection and cooking which may be conducive to healing. Although the purpose of this book is to help alleviate, control and heal the above-named conditions, it does not constitute a guarantee for success. No two patients are alike, some may react differently. Therefore, no dietary plan for a specific condition should be embarked upon without the approval of your personal physician.

Copyright © 2000 by John O.A. Pagano - Second Printing 2008

Printed in India

Library of Congress Cataloging-in-Publication Data: Pagano, John O.A.
Dr. John's Healing Psoriasis Cookbook...Plus!

Includes Index

1. Cookbook 2. Psoriasis 3. Eczema 4. Skin Diseases 5. Natural Healing 6. Holistic Medicine 7. Alternative Medicine

I. Title

Library of Congress Control Number 00-090456

ISBN 978-0-9628847-2-6 Hardcover

Dr. John's
HEALING
PSORIASIS
COOKBOOK...*Plus!*

"Dr. Pagano has provided a new perspective in the management of psoriasis–one that justifies serious consideration by the scientific community."

Harold Mermelstein, M.D.
(Dermatologist)
New York, New York

"Dr. John's Healing Psoriasis Cookbook...Plus! is a godsend for anyone suffering from psoriasis or eczema."

James Ferlisi, M.D.
Concord, Ontario, Canada

The Pagano Organization, Inc.
35 Hudson Terrace
Englewood Cliffs, NJ 07632
www.psoriasis-healing.com

For Ordering Only:
1(800) 919-4001
9:00-6:00 [E.S.T.]

Editor:
Johanna R. Bayati
Ridgewood, NJ

Typography:
JoAnne MacBeth
Shakespeare Computer & Graphics, Inc.
Clifton, NJ
Elsa Reinhardt, Elsa Reinhardt Enterprises
Hackensack, NJ
Johanna R. Bayati

Photographs and Illustrations:
John O.A. Pagano

Printing and Assembly:
Thomson Press India, Ltd.

Cover Design:
The Morris Group
Henderson, NV

To Psoriasis and Eczema Sufferers Everywhere

May this book
And all contained herein,
Fulfill your dream
Of beautiful skin.
May it lift your hearts
From the depths of despair,
To a state of joy
Beyond compare!

Dr. John

Acknowledgments

Without the support of my family, my mother Nettie, my sisters Carol and Maria, and the many close friends I am honored to know and love, this book may never have been created. My business manager, Elsa Reinhardt, my editor, Johanna Bayati, my secretaries, Marie Diehl and Jennifer Velardo, all loaned their support to the completion of this work in ways I can never repay.

I appreciate the many patients, some of whom I never met, who expressed their desire for such a book and spurred me on through the years. It is my ardent desire that they now feel it was worth the wait.

To Harry K. Panjwani, M.D., Ph.D., Harold Mermelstein, M.D. (Dermatologist), James Ferlisi, M.D., Zoltan P. Rona, M.D., M.Sc., Andrej Strauss, M.D., Norman F. Childers, Ph.D., Rona Weiss, Ph.D., MS., Annemarie Colbin, Author and Founder of The Natural Gourmet Institute of Food and Health, and to all the many people who have written or e-mailed me expressing their joy of accomplishment in healing the psoriasis they had been plagued with, my sincere thanks for your continued vote of confidence.

Dedication

To the memory of my beloved Mother

Nettie Pagano

January 16, 1907 - December 30, 1999

Through diet and excercise, the greater portion of all disturbances may be equalized and overcome, if the right mental attitude is kept.

Edgar Cayce #262.109

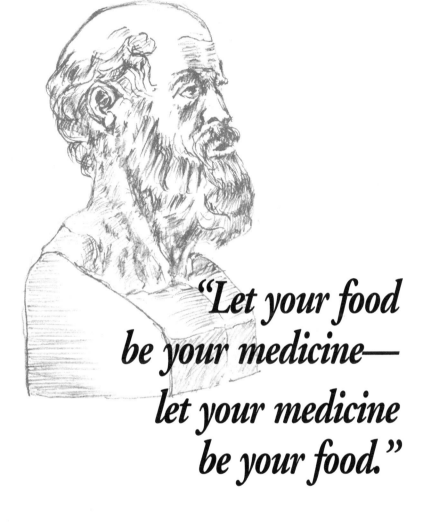

*"Let your food
be your medicine—
let your medicine
be your food."*

—*Hippocrates*
The "Father of Medicine"

Foreword

What makes us sick? There are many factors, and the answer to that question depends on who you ask. A molecular biologist will say it's our genes. A physician will say its the virus or bacteria. Ask a shaman and you'll hear about evil spirits, the anger of the gods. In the Middle Ages it would have been bad humors or miasms.

One way in which we can look at sickness is by separating the causes into two camps: contagion or toxicity. Catching the flu would be an example of contagion. A disease such as psoriasis, which is not considered catching, would then have to be classified as caused by toxicity. As this is not exactly a widespread notion, John Pagano's approach has to be considered revolutionary. His discovery that the nightshade vegetables are contributors to this toxicity builds on the fine work done by Professor Norman Childers, of the Arthritis Nightshades Research Foundation, who has been warning the world about these common vegetables for many years.

Dr. Pagano's ground-breaking book **HEALING PSORIASIS: The Natural Alternative** shows, in dramatic photographs and case histories, his success in healing this difficult disease through dietary changes and cleansing. In **Dr. John's Healing Psoriasis Cookbook...Plus!** he continues to provide psoriasis sufferers tools for improving and even healing themselves. This is a comprehensive and practical book, with simple, easy recipes and lots of information. Rather than adding to their toxicity with further unhealthy foods and useless drugs, readers of this book have the opportunity to reverse the course of their disease and take charge of their lives. It is not easy—nothing worthwhile is—but embarking on the healing path of healthy eating is the beginning of an empowering and life-affirming journey.

Annemarie Colbin, M.A., CHES
Author, **Food and Our Bones** (Dutton/Plume)
New York City, January 2000

Preface

(Updated 2008)

Seventeen years have passed since my book, HEALING PSORIASIS: *The Natural Alternative* was first published in 1991. It has been the #1 Bestseller in its category from 1998 to the present time with both Amazon.com and Barnesandnoble.com. It is now in its 6ᵗʰ updated and expanded printing. Orders come from virtually every corner of the earth: the USA and Canada, Australia and the Philippines, from India to Israel to Iceland, from the British Isles to Kodiak Island. The book is also available in Russian, Italian, Finnish and Japanese.

I have appeared as a featured guest on several radio and TV talk shows, among them: NBC's *Unsolved Mysteries*, CNBC's *America's Talking, The Dr. Ronald Hoffman Show*, Gary Null, Jeff Donagan, The Gourley Group, *Alternative Medicine*, and at The Natural Gourmet Institute for Food and Health in New York. In 2001 I addressed the World Health Conference on Psoriasis sponsored by the National Psoriasis Foundation.

The word is getting out! And what is that word? It is that there IS another approach toward the healing of psoriasis and eczema, a natural one that can bring about successful results in many, many people. This approach can, and has, transformed the life of many a psoriasis and eczema sufferer from one of misery, pain and disfigurement to one of joy, relief and beauty.

My approach views psoriasis and eczema as an external manifestation having an internal cause; one that begins in the intestinal tract and ends in the integument, namely, our skin! My initial reference came from the works of Edgar Cayce, a medical intuitive known as the Sleeping Prophet. This internal cause has since become known as *The Leaky Gut Syndrome*. (See "The Principles Behind the Regimen" in the pages that follow). [For the reader who may be interested in studying this underlying cause I refer you to my newest book on The Leaky Gut Syndrome published in 2008 by the ARE Press in Virginia Beach, Virginia. To order a copy, call 1-757-428-3588, or visit their website at www.edgarcayce.org.]

The results obtained by patients who faithfully followed the regimen were complete in most, partial in some and unremarkable in a few. Indispensable, in practically every case, was *the patient's own commitment* to the regimen (especially in regard to the DIET) coupled with persistence and determination. In this natural approach to healing these diseases, I have found DIET and ELIMINATIONS to be the principle factors involved. The many unsolicited letters and e-mails I receive, from people whom I have never met but who have on their own faithfully followed the suggestions to a successful outcome, serve as testimony to the effectiveness of the protocol. I extend my deep appreciation to the wonderful people who write expressing their joy of accomplishment. Their lives have been changed and they are sharing this vital information with others suffering from these diseases.

After a few years of the book being out, something more had to be done. Since diet plays the key role in this approach to the disease, it followed naturally that a *cookbook* designed for such people was in order. It was my good fortune to interest talented cooks in working with me to produce the cookbook you now hold in your hands. It took seven years to complete from start to finish. Several other people contributed to help this volume come into being. No effort was spared to ensure that it contains a well rounded array of dishes that are nourishing, delicious and easily prepared. Practically every measure in it follows the dietary selections I have found to be most helpful in controlling, alleviating and even healing the disease. In a few cases, it became necessary to bend a little in order to have some ingredients hold together better, or to make it more palatable, but these are few and far between.

The purpose of this book is to take a step toward making your everyday life just a bit easier. I believe a psoriatic sufferer needs all the help he/she can get. Such people are often told, "Diet has nothing to do with it". I beg to differ! In my experience with patients **DIET is the key factor in healing psoriasis and eczema in a natural way!** I have never been able to help or heal a person with psoriasis and/or eczema who *failed* to follow these dietary guidelines for an *adequate period of time*. When they do follow through, seeming miracles can happen. (See evidences in the Photographic Section of this book). Without such commitment, all efforts are fruitless. However, it must be understood, that following this diet does not necessarily *guarantee* success. I am merely providing recipes that follow the rules of food selection that I have found to be beneficial to most of my own patients. Whole families have successfully used this diet, which is of course easier for the chef. Incidentally, a side benefit quite pleasing to most people is the healthy weight loss they experience on this diet. I have seen patients lose 35-40 pounds of fat they didn't need, and most reported that they never felt better in their life!

If you are committed to getting well, this book will help you take the guesswork out of cooking and enable you to concentrate your energies on the other helpful measures that can lead to success. Keep in mind what I call the **"3 D's"—Diet, Detoxification, Determination** - for these are what I have found to be the cornerstone to healing psoriasis and/or eczema. Also, keep your mind focused on the *healing* of the disease, not the disease itself. By doing this, you will be practicing the Art of Visualization, a powerful tool in the attainment of your goals. **It can be done, because it has been done!** And with that, dear reader, what can I say other than:

Bon Appétit!

Dr. John O.A. Pagano
Englewood Cliffs, NJ
January 16, 2008

Table of Contents

PART I
Basic Principals—Building a Foundation

Part II
The Recipes

PART III
Eye on Nutrition

Part I
Basic Principles

Part I
Basic Principles

PART I

Basic Principles

Building a Foundation

PSORIASIS
The Basic Concept

The most important thing to grasp about psoriasis is that it is *one disease that the patient does not necessarily have to live with!* It is possible for a patient to rid himself of every scale, lesion or irritation caused by the disease in a natural way, regardless of its extent or location.

In its most simple terms *psoriasis is caused by an overabundant accumulation of toxins (poison) in the body.* In psoriasis, what the skin is doing is trying to help the body rid itself of those toxins through the sweat glands, thus the external manifestations of the disease—the lesions, scales, rash and irritation. If the normal channels of elimination are open and working properly, and further toxins (derived primarily from eating the wrong foods) are halted from entering the system in the first place, the psoriatic lesions can gradually disappear, enabling the skin to completely renew itself. The evidence of increasing numbers of patients proves it not only CAN be done— IT HAS BEEN DONE!

Questionnaire

Before getting into the heart of the matter, take a few minutes to read through these questions with pencil in hand, and check off the box that best describes your present day diet selections. At this point there is no right or wrong answer. It is just *your* answer. As time goes on, you can refer back to these questions and answers and see how far you have progressed and how much you have learned. The Chinese have an old saying: "The journey of a thousand miles begins with a single step." This is your first step.

When you are shopping—

1. Do you avoid buying refined foods such as white flour or sugar?   Yes ☐   No ☐

2. Are you aware that locally grown foods are better for you than those that must be shipped?   Yes ☐   No ☐

3. Do you avoid buying canned foods whenever possible?   Yes ☐   No ☐

4. Do you regularly check labels for preservatives and other chemicals?   Yes ☐   No ☐

5. Do you choose natural foods rather than processed foods?   Yes ☐   No ☐

6. Do you have a good variety of foods in your diet as well as experiment with new wholesome recipes? Yes ☐   No ☐

7. Do you buy fresh fruits and vegetables often?   Yes ☐   No ☐

When you are cooking—

1. Do you serve your fruits and vegetables nearest to their natural state, i.e. cooking as little as possible in order to preserve their nutrients?   Yes ☐   No ☐

2. Do you avoid cooking in aluminum ware?   Yes ☐   No ☐

3. Do you steam your vegetables rather than boil them?   Yes ☐   No ☐

4. Do you wash fruits and vegetables before cooking?   Yes ☐   No ☐

5. Do you avoid frying foods?   Yes ☐   No ☐

When you are eating—

1. *Do you chew your food well before swallowing?*
   Yes ☐ No ☐

2. *Do you avoid getting up once you've sat down to eat and enjoy your meal?* *Yes ☐ No ☐*

3. *Are you calm and relaxed rather than angry or upset?*
   Yes ☐ No ☐

4. *Do you know that vitamins and minerals derived directly from foods are more easily assimilated and better for you than those from manufactured products? Yes ☐ No ☐*

5. *Are you aware that some foods should not be combined at the same meal although they may be good for you if eaten separately? [Ex.: a) Citrus with whole-grain products, such as cereals or breads.; b) Starches with sweets; c) Coffee with cream or milk or sugar.]*
   Yes ☐ No ☐

Your answers thus far should be "Yes." If you answered "No" to some questions, you are not practicing ideal dietary habits.

Psoriatic, psoriatic arthritic and eczema cases, in particular, should strongly consider the following:

As a part of your regular diet—

1. *Do you eat foods high in animal fats, e.g. beef and beef products, pork and pork products, cold cuts or processed meats such as salami, ham and bologna? Yes ☐ No ☐*

2. *Do you include shellfish, e.g. shrimp, lobster, clams, mussels, crabs, etc. or sauces made from shellfish?*
   Yes ☐ No ☐

3. *Do you eat any of the nightshades, e.g. tomatoes, tomato products, eggplant, white potatoes, peppers, paprika?*
   Yes ☐ No ☐

4.   *Do you include junk foods, e.g. packaged, cream-filled, sugary pastries, as well as fast-foods, e.g. hamburgers, hot dogs, fries, pizza, potato chips, pretzels, soda?*
Yes ☐   No ☐

5.   *Do you drink alcoholic beverages: gin, vodka, whiskey, beer, wine coolers, etc.?*   Yes ☐   No ☐

6.   *Do you eat fried foods?*   Yes ☐   No ☐

7.   *Do you smoke, chew tobacco, or "do drugs"?*
Yes ☐   No ☐

The answer to this last set of questions should be "No." If you answered "Yes" you are **aggravating** your psoriatic condition!

HEALING PSORIASIS:
The Natural Alternative

The Principles Behind the Regimen: An Overview

My approach to the healing of psoriasis and eczema has its origin in the works of the late Edgar Cayce (1877-1945). The information provided through Cayce gave me the "clue" as to the cause of psoriasis and eczema, and the procedure to follow for its alleviation, control, and even total healing. Since modern medicine admits that it has been, and still is, in the dark concerning the cause and cure of psoriasis, it comes as no surprise that their results are temporary at best, dangerous at worst, and extremely expensive, with an annual price tag of over three billion dollars in the USA alone! Cayce described psoriasis and/or eczema as a *process* taking place in the body; a *process* attempting detoxification manifesting through the skin. If this is true, logic dictates that it will take another process to clear the condition, the reverse of that which started the problem. This is what I have done for thirty years, working on a regimen to help those afflicted with the disease, with results that have beautified many patients, amazed dermatologists, and thrilled me. *For those people who have followed through*, with few exceptions, the results showed marked improvement or complete healing, and to this day they are in control of their condition.

This is not to say that I have never met with failure. I most certainly have, but, it was the dramatic successes, especially with young people, that kept me going. There is an old saying "Success requires no explanation; failure permits no alibis." This, on the surface, appears to be largely true—but, a thinking person would still probe the reasons for both as best he could in order to find a possible common denominator. I have found the common denominator for success to consistently be the *patient's commitment to the regimen*. In most cases, the common denominator for failure was the patient's lack of patience, persistence, and commitment to the regimen. While this does not always hold true, it is by far the most common reason for failure. But—mind you, there have been cases when the patient returned, after failing the first or second time, and resumed the regimen to a successful outcome. So if a patient does not succeed the first time, he very well may do so on the second or even third attempt.

The Regimen *I speak of is based on six principles:*

1. **Internal Cleansing**: *Eliminating the toxins and poisons that have been accumulating, particularly in the colon, for years.*

2. **Proper Diet and Nutrition**: *Concentrating on a high alkaline/low acid forming diet–the key, in this approach, to the natural healing of psoriasis.*

3. **Specific Herb Teas**: *Taking Slippery Elm Bark Powder in the morning, or Omega-3 fish oil and/or Flaxseed oil for the healing of the intestinal walls. Taking American Yellow Saffron Tea in the evening to help flush out the system. (For variety you may substitute watermelon seed, mullein, or chamomile tea for the saffron tea.)*

4. **Adjustments of the Spine**: *Adjusting of the spine, particularly the 6th and 7th dorsal vertebrae; as well as the 3rd cervical, 9th dorsal and 4th lumbar vertebrae, which will help rebuild thin intestinal walls and improve eliminations by insuring proper nerve impulses to these visceral organs.*

5. **Natural External Applications:** *Applying primarily Hydrophilic Ointment or any good proven moisturizer such as Aveeno Moisturizing Lotion, Vaseline Intensive Care Lotion, Lubriderm, or Aquaphor, combined with an olive/peanut oil mixture, or castor oil in the case of heavy lesions. Epsom salts and Dead Sea salts baths have also proven very helpful when applicable.*

6. ***Right Thinking and Sound Emotions****: Realizing it can be done because it has been done; guarding against negative emotions which turn the blood acid, and concentrating on and practicing positive emotions that turn the blood alkaline.*

Coupled with time and patience, these are the principles of healing psoriasis and/or eczema that I have used with extremely encouraging results.

In order to understand how and why the process works, the patient must grasp the theory behind the therapeutic regimen. My years of research dealing with the subject convince me that **psoriasis is the external manifestation of the body's attempt to throw off internal toxins.** The idea behind the therapeutic procedure is twofold: 1) eliminate, as much as possible, the toxic (poison) elements that have built up within the system by insuring good eliminations, and, 2) do not add more of the same toxins to the system found primarily in the foods you eat.

This is the two-pronged secret to the natural healing of psoriasis—*a carefully selected diet and proper elimination!* If patients and their physicians refuse to believe this, they are fighting a losing battle. I have never been able to help a psoriasis sufferer who did not follow the proper rules of diet and nutrition as they pertain to psoriasis and eczema. Without it, patients remain in misery, torment and pain, constantly seeking answers. Their lives are dominated by the disease, and *it need not be so!*

Orthodox medicine has never seriously considered diet as having anything to do with psoriasis or eczema. Yet doctors will freely admit that they remain baffled as to the cause and cure of the disease, even after 200 years of research, therefore, it is classified as unknown and incurable. From *their* point of view they are absolutely correct. But, when viewed from the inside-out rather than from the outside-in, a whole new approach to the disease emerges. We see psoriasis as a defense mechanism on the part of the body to throw off poisons and acids that would cause irreparable harm to the internal cells and structures of the body if they were not adequately drained from the system.

This toxic accumulation takes place when the body's natural organs of elimination, primarily the bowels and the kidneys, cannot discharge the toxic elements as quickly as they are building up. In no uncertain terms, the blood is overloaded with pollutants that must be eliminated. The skin steps in and "comes to the rescue" by trying to eliminate this toxic accumulation through the sweat glands. In this it is doing a job it is not primarily designed to do. It is acting as a backup system, since the main organs of elimination are overloaded and cannot effectively keep up with the vast accumulations.

What happens is these acids and waste products become so great that they begin to actually seep through the intestinal walls and are absorbed by the lymphatic system. The lymphatic system then dumps the toxins into the blood circulatory system. This seepage of toxins is technically referred to as Intestinal Permeability, otherwise known as *"The Leaky Gut Syndrome."* The blood is constantly filtered and purified by the liver and kidneys primarily, but sooner or later, the workload becomes so great that the liver and kidneys can no longer handle the job. So, the skin, a secondary organ of elimination, kicks in and helps the body throw off these poisons, thus causing the rash, irritation, scales and lesions. In other words, in cases of psoriasis, eczema, and probably many other skin diseases, the skin is doing what the bowels and kidneys should be doing—removing toxic waste.

The secret then is to remove the toxins present, don't add more, and eventually the body can handle the accumulations normally. The skin can then relax and drop back to normal, in many cases not even leaving a trace of the disease. I have seen it happen time and time again. Admittedly, patients must follow through for at least six months after they have cleared to help insure better healing of the intestinal walls—but by that time they are usually so satisfied that they wouldn't think of reverting to their old way of living, especially where diet is concerned. The bottom line however is time and patience. There is no substitute for persistence and determination. It took a long time to pollute the body; it will take a reasonable amount of time to purify it. What I said in my Preface is worth repeating:

Keep in mind what I call the **3D's** as they apply to the healing of psoriasis and eczema:

- **Diet**

- **Detoxification**

- **Determination**

The three go hand-in-hand and have convinced my patients and me that they are the principles to the healing of this devastating dermatological enigma.

The photos in the Photographic Portfolio graphically demonstrate the results that many patients have obtained by strictly adhering to the regimen outlined above.

[For an extensive and comprehensive treatment of this subject, you may order Dr. Pagano's award-winning book **HEALING PSORIASIS: *The Natural Alternative***, using the ordering information at the back of this book.]

DISCLAIMER: This book was created to guide the psoriatic, eczema and psoriatic arthritic patient regarding food selection and cooking which may be conducive to healing. Although the purpose of this book is to help alleviate, control and heal the above named conditions, it does not constitute a guarantee for success. No two patients are alike, some may react differently. Therefore, no dietary plan for a specific condition should be embarked upon without the approval of your personal physician.

To My Readers

Make no mistake about it, according to my research, DIET PLAYS THE MOST IMPORTANT ROLE IN HEALING PSORIASIS!

It took you just seconds to read that statement, it took me over thirty years to prove it—to myself and to my patients!

Adhering to the nutritional guidelines outlined in this section will greatly enhance your chance of success in ridding yourself of psoriasis or eczema. All the other measures I have used in treating these diseases, i.e. internal cleansing, spinal adjustments, external applications, specific herb teas, and developing a proper attitude, are adjuncts to the healing process. While these are important components of the regimen, they truly play a secondary role in comparison to the importance of proper diet. The success ratio in healing my patients of these afflictions is in direct proportion to their conscientiously following the dietary guidelines contained herein.

Along with commitment, there must be *patience* and *persistence* in order to achieve results. Our bodies must be given *time* to go from a diseased, polluted state to one of cleansed, vitally energetic health. It is of paramount importance that the patient be convinced that healing is possible; secondly, it is indispensable that *adequate time* be devoted to the regimen. Most of my patients see changes within three to six months. It is my contention that the disease *begins to reverse itself* on the very day that the patient begins to follow the proper diet.

Basic Dietary Rules

1. **Dietary Balance:** It is most important to establish a dietary balance of foods. The daily diet should consist of 70-80% alkaline forming foods and 20-30% acid forming foods. The desired proportion should be 4 vegetables (especially green leafy and carrots) and 2 fruits to 1 protein and 1 starch.

2. **Acid vs. Alkaline:** One must guard against having too much of the same type of food at the same meal, especially the acid formers. More alkaline reacting foods should be eaten particularly if the patient does not engage in exercise, manual activity, or if he or she is under exceptional emotional stress.

3. **Food Combinations:** Certain combinations of food can be very detrimental to the body, whereas these same foods, if consumed separately, are beneficial. Desirable and undesirable combinations are included elsewhere in the book.

4. **Vitamins:** If there is a proper balance of food in the diet, supplementary vitamins are usually not necessary. However, the recommended daily allowance (RDA) of vitamins A combined with D, B-1, and B-Complex is advised for those patients who desire or require added nutrition. Modern research concurs that a diet high in fresh fruit and vegetables (sources of vitamins A and C), whole grains (for B-Complex, vitamin E, Selenium and Fiber), and a reduced intake of animal proteins and fats, will help to promote a healthy, clear skin.

5. **Lecithin** (granular, soy-balanced preferred) should be part of the daily diet five days out of the week. I recommend that my patients take 1 tablespoon of lecithin in the morning, 1 at noon, and 1 in the evening each day, until the condition clears. Lecithin may be added to any liquid, salad, or cereal; or, if preferred, it may be taken by itself.

6. **Fruits and Vegetables:** Eat a great deal of fruits and vegetables that are yellow and/or green in color, such as lemons, grapefruits, yellow peaches, yellow cooked apples, yellow corn, oranges, carrots, Romaine lettuce, celery, spinach, broccoli, watercress, parsley, etc. [Avoid citrus fruits and their juices in cases of eczema and/or psoriatic arthritis.]

7. **Juices:** Invest in a juicer as well as a blender for making fresh fruit and vegetable juice. Drinking freshly made juice is one of the most effective measures to take for good nutrition and internal cleansing.

8. **Water:** It is impossible to overemphasize the importance of drinking plenty of pure water daily. In addition to all other beverages, the recommended amount of water consumption is 6-8 glasses, unless contraindicated due to some underlying medical condition of the bladder or urinary tract.

The "Why Me?" Syndrome

I have frequently observed that those patients do better who do not delve too deeply into the reasons why they are plagued with psoriasis or eczema, compared to patients who expect an answer to all their questions before they embark on the program. It may never be known why a particular patient is afflicted with one of these diseases. Admittedly, it would be wonderful to have all the right answers, but it is not necessarily a prerequisite for the start of therapy, nor is it essential for a successful outcome. Anyone suffering from what I call the "Why Me?" Syndrome would benefit more by simply getting on with it. I suggest that you simply proceed with the program, knowing that others have succeeded with it when all else had failed.

Part of "right" thinking is to eliminate "wrong" thinking. To dwell too much on seeking the answer as to *why* one is afflicted is practicing wrong thinking. It is a waste of precious time and energy. I am convinced that one should just make a new beginning and give the regimen an opportunity to work—this should be the new goal. Once patients are cleared of the disease, they no longer occupy themselves with the question "Why?" but are instead happy and content to find that they have succeeded. Should there be a recurrence, they know how to control it.

70%-80%
of the Daily Diet

70%-80% **of the Daily Food Intake** should be selected from the following, most of which are **Alkaline** formers:

WATER: 6 to 8 glasses of pure water daily.

LECITHIN: (granular) 1 tablespoon 3 times per day, 5 days per week.

FRUIT: (Fresh preferred, frozen is permitted, packed in water in glass jars on occasion.) Stewed fruits are highly recommended whenever possible.

Allowed: Apples (cooked), Apricots, Most Berries, Cherries, Dates, Figs (unsulphured), Grapes, Grapefruit, Lemons, Limes, Mango, Nectarines, Oranges, Papaya, Peaches, Pears, Pineapple, Prunes (small), Raisins, Kiwi, etc.

Permitted in lesser quantities are: Avocado, Cranberries, Currants, Large Prunes and Plums.

Note: Raw Apples, Bananas and Melons are permitted provided they are eaten alone and sparingly.

VEGETABLES: Vegetables should be consumed more than fruits. To 2 to 3 fruits per day, 5 to 6 vegetables should be eaten. (Daily intake should be 3 that grow above the ground to 1 that grows below the ground. Fresh preferred, frozen is permitted, packed in glass jars on occasion.)

Allowed: Asparagus, Beets, Broccoli, Brussel Sprouts, Cabbage, Carrots,* Celery,* Cucumbers, Garlic,* Lettuce* (Romaine in particular), Onions,* Olives, Parsnips, Scallions, Soy Beans, Spinach*, Sprouts*, String Beans, Squash, Sweet Potatoes, Watercress*. [Note: Those followed with (*) are particularly important.]

Permitted in lesser quantities are: Corn (White Corn preferred), Dried Beans, Peas, Lentils, Rhubarb and Mushrooms. Almonds are the only nuts that are alkaline. Eating five to ten raw almonds a day is suggested. Filberts are permitted occasionally.

JUICES: Vegetable and fruit juice daily (freshly made preferred) is highly recommended. A juicer is the most valuable kitchen appliance a patient should invest in.

20%-30% of the Daily diet

20%-30% of the Daily Food Intake should be selected from the following, most of which are **Acid** formers:

GRAINS: All grains should be natural whole grain products such as: Breads, Bagels, Muffins, Cereals with very little, if any, preservatives or artificial sweeteners. Rice: Brown and/or Wild preferred. No White Flour Products.

MEATS: Fish (not shellfish) salt or fresh water (fresh or frozen). If canned, water or oil packed is permitted. Fish is beneficial, but, dark-fleshed oily fish carries the most Omega-3 fatty acids which are highly desirable.

Fowl (Poultry): Chicken, Turkey, Cornish Hen, Non-fatty Wild Fowl. (All skinless, white meat preferred)

Lamb: Trimmed of all fat before cooking, well done, once or twice a week.

Note: The above listed meats are never to be fried. No more than 4 to 6 oz. is permitted at a serving, once a day, unless the person has a heavy work load or is very large in stature.

DAIRY: Only Low Fat/Low Sodium products are permitted: Skim or Low Fat Milk, Cheese, Buttermilk, Yogurt, etc. (No Ice Cream, Cream Toppings or Whole Milk Products). Do not have Citrus Fruits or Citrus Juices with Dairy products or Cereals at the same meal.

> **Note:** In cases of Eczema, substitute Goat's Milk & Soy Milk.

> **Butter (unsalted):** is permitted but only occasionally and in very sparing amounts. (Even though it is a saturated fat, a little butter is better than margarine and other hydrogenated products).

> **Eggs:** are permitted, 2 to 4 per week, prepared any way but fried.

OILS: Permitted: Olive oil, Canola, Safflower, Cottonseed, Soy Bean, Sunflower, Sesame and occasionally Peanut. One teaspoon of Olive oil three times per day is suggested for most patients unless there is a gallbladder problem.

It is important to adhere to the 70-80% / 20-30% food selection in order to maintain a proper acid/alkaline balance. If this is too difficult, at least try to consume as much as possible from the 70%-80% list.

AVOID

1. *Almost all saturated fats, such as: Red Meats (except Lamb), Beef, Pork, Veal, Sweetbreads, etc.; Processed meats: Sausage, Salami, Bologna, Frankfurters, Hamburgers; Hydrogenated products: Margarine.*

2. *The Nightshades: Tomatoes (& Tomato Sauces and products), Tobacco (smoking), Eggplant, Peppers (all types), White Potatoes, Paprika. Avoid hot spices of all kinds.*

3. *Shellfish: Lobster, Shrimp, Clams, Crabs, etc., and sauces made with shellfish.*

4. *Junk food: Soda (diet & regular), Sweets, Candy & Pastries, Chocolate (and all products made with chocolate), Potato Chips, French Fries, etc.*

5. *Yeast or yeast laden foods, if there is an underlying yeast infection (Candidiasis); or gluten in cases of Celiac disease.*

6. *Miscellaneous: All Fried Foods, Pizza, Alcohol (& Beer), Sugary Cereals, Wine or Grain Vinegar, Pickled and Smoked Foods, Hot Spices, Gravies, Coconut, Coconut Oil, Palm Oil, and too many Starches.*

Note: In every case of psoriatic arthritis, avoid Citrus Fruit, Strawberries and adding Salt to foods. Salt in particular should be avoided at all costs. The salt (sodium) found naturally in the daily diet is quite adequate.

Your Shopping List

It goes without saying that if recipes must be of a certain nature, it is equally important that the consumer be aware of what to buy and what not to buy. It is not uncommon that whole families sometimes go on the same diet (for the most part) as the patient with psoriasis. Of course, it is easier if there are only two people to consider, such as husband and wife. It is even easier if the patient lives alone. Whatever the case may be, the refrigerator should be stocked with as many of the permitted food items as possible, and absent of the foods to be avoided.

The following foods and beverages should constitute your shopping list. With very few exceptions, my patients learn to truly enjoy the diet, lose weight in a healthy manner, increase proper eliminations, and experience an overall sense of well-being with their energy level rising to peak efficiency. Needless to say, this will include the gradual disappearance of psoriasis and eczema lesions.

Make copies of the following pages in this section and bring them with you when you go food shopping. Soon you will memorize them, and selecting the right foods will become second nature to you.

Your Shopping Guides

"Go For It!"

ENJOY!

The message each chef holds in his hand tells you the whole story as to which things to buy, and which things not to buy.

"No!" "No Way!"

AVOID!

Food Items To Always Have On Hand

Essentials

- Almonds, raw
- Gelatine, unflavored
- Olive oil
- Bottled spring water
- Lecithin (granular)

Pantry Items

- Apple cider vinegar
- Beans, dried
- Coffee
- Seltzer water
- Sardines, canned, unsalted
- Beans, canned
- Canola oil
- Honey
- Salmon, canned
- Tuna, canned, white albacore

Cereals, Flour, Grains, Pasta, Rice

- Barley
- Brown Rice
- Bran
- Fat-free Whole Wheat Crackers
- Flour (whole wheat or other whole grain flours)

- Oatmeal
- Pastas
  - Jerusalem artichoke
  - Vegetable pastas other than tomato
- Wheat germ
- Wheat grain bread and rolls
- Wild rice

Herb Teas

- American yellow saffron*
  (or substitute watermelon seed, mullein or chamomile)
- Slippery elm bark powder*
  (or substitute Omega-3 fish oils, or Flaxseed Oil)

Spices, Herbs and Seasonings

- Basil, sweet (dried)
- Bay leaf
- Black or white
  pepper, ground
- Cinnamon, ground
- Dill weed, dried
- Garlic powder
- Parsley, dried
- Sage, dried
- Sea salt
- Thyme, dried
- Vegetable seasoning blend

---

* See page 531 for ordering information to obtain these teas.

Food Items To Purchase As Needed

Fresh Vegetables

- Beets
- Carrots
- Cucumber
- Lettuce
- Parsley
- Romaine lettuce
- Sweet potatoes
- Broccoli
- Celery
- Garlic
- Onions
- Parsnips
- Spinach

Fruits and Fruit Products

- All fresh fruits
- Dried fruits (unsulphured)
- Jelly or preserves
- Applesauce
- Frozen fruit
- Products sweetened with fruit juice

Dairy Products

All should be no fat or low fat

- Buttermilk (light)
- Cottage cheese
- Milk (skim or 1%)
- Cheese, white
- Goat's milk
- Yogurt, plain

Meat, Poultry, Eggs

- Eggs
- Chicken
- Lamb
- Turkey
- Wild fowl

Fish

- Fresh fish fillets, assorted varieties, particularly dark-fleshed (see list in "Fish" section)

Vegetarian Protein Products

- Soy
- Textured vegetable proteins
- Tempeh
- Tofu

Vegetables: The Builders of the Body

Alkaline Forming Vegetables—Enjoy!

- Acorn Squash*
- Artichoke (including Jerusalem [sunchoke])
- Beets*
- Broccoli
- Brussels Sprouts
- Carrots*
- Cabbage
- Chard
- Chives
- Collard Greens
- Dandelion*
- Endive (French)
- Fennel
- Garlic*

- Alfalfa Sprouts*
- Asparagus
- Bamboo Shoots
- Beet Greens
- Broccoli Rabe*
- Butternut Squash*
- Cauliflower
- Celery*
- Chicory Greens*
- Cilantro
- Cucumbers
- Dulse
- Escarole*
- Finocchio
- Ginger

- Green Beans
- Hubbard Squash*
- Kohlrabi*
- Konnyaku
- Lettuce*
  (particularly Romaine)
- Mung Bean
- Okra
- Parsley*
- Pumpkin
- Rutabaga (Yellow Turnip)
- Scallions*
- Shiitake Mushroom
- Spinach*
- String Beans
- Sweet Potato*
- Turnip Greens*
- Water Chestnuts
- Winter Squash*
- Zucchini
- Green Peas
- Kale*
- Kombu*
- Leeks
- Lotus Root
- Mustard Greens
- Mushrooms
- Onions*
- Parsnip
- Radish
- Salsify (Oyster Plant)
- Sea Kelp
- Soy Beans
- Sprouts*
- Summer Squash*
- Turnips
- Wakame
- Watercress*
- Yams*

---

*Most desirable

Acid Forming Vegetables—Eat sparingly!

- Corn (White preferred)
- Lentils
- Dried Beans & Peas
- Rhubarb

Keep in Mind: Fresh vegetables are preferred; frozen are permitted; canned (with the exception of beans) are generally prohibited. More vegetables than fruits should be part of the daily diet.

Dr. John's "3/1" Super Salad

The ideal combination of raw salads is to combine three vegetables that grow above the ground to one that grows below the ground. As an aid to the chef, I have formed a chart showing, at a glance, many of the vegetables that grow above and below the ground. The recipes are as simple as they can be:

For a Small Salad: combine six vegetables that grow above the ground, with two that grow below. Toss and serve with olive oil, lemon juice and a splash of apple cider vinegar.

For a Large Salad: combine twelve vegetables that grow above the ground, with four that grow below. Toss and serve with olive oil, lemon juice and a splash of apple cider vinegar.

Observe the following *(vegetables which are prohibited have not been listed):*

- Artichoke
- Beans (soy, lentils, peas)
- Brussels Sprouts
- Cauliflower
- Chicory
- Cucumber
- Endive
- Leek
- Olive
- Pumpkin
- Watercress

- Asparagus
- Broccoli
- Cabbage
- Celery
- Chives
- Dandelion
- Fennel
- Lettuce (all types)
- Parsley
- Spinach
- Zucchini

Above ground (3)

Ground Level

Below ground (1)

- Beets
- Garlic
- Onions
- Parsnips
- Sweet Potatoes
- Yams

- Carrots
- Jerusalem Artichoke (Sunchoke)
- Oyster Plant (Salsify, Goatsbeard)
- Radishes
- Turnips

From this you can glean the most nutritious, tasty tossed salad possible.

The Nightshades*— Avoid!

- **Tomatoes**—Raw and cooked, and all tomato preparations and sauces, such as spaghetti sauce, pizza, ketchup, barbecue sauce, taco sauce, hot sauce, etc.
- **Peppers**—All varieties, except black
- **Potatoes**—All varieties, including white, red, new, russet, Idaho, etc.
- **Eggplant**
- **Tobacco**
- **Paprika**

Note: Sweet potatoes and yams are NOT nightshades, are very nutritious, and are highly recommended on the psoriasis and eczema diet.

---

* Patients often ask what it is about the nightshades that makes them undesirable especially to the psoriatic arthritic patient. To answer, I turn to the monumental work of **Dr. Norman F. Childers,** professor at the University of Florida (Gainesville), founder of The Arthritis Nightshades Research Foundation, and author of *Arthritis: Childers' Diet that Stops It!* Dr. Childers is the leading authority on the nightshades and the devastating

effect they can have on some individuals, especially those prone to psoriasis, psoriatic arthritis, and eczema. In his "Nightshades Newsletter" of Spring 1984 he explained:

> *"There is an enzyme in muscles that gives us agility of movement, known as cholinesterase. Any chemical or factor that inhibits this enzyme will cause stiffness and soreness when it builds in our system to a critical level. Older people seem unable to counter this situation as well as younger people, but the latter are not entirely exempt. Cholinesterase inhibitors in the nightshades are:* **solanine** *in potato and eggplant,* **tomatine** *in tomato,* **capsicum** *in peppers and* **nicotine** *in tobacco."*

[Note: There is no question that tomatoes carry one of the most valuable of all antioxidants, namely, lycopene. However, since tomatoes are to be avoided, you can still have a supply of lycopene from other sources, such as red or pink grapefruit *and their juices.*]

[Dr. Childers' book can be ordered directly by calling 1-888-501-8822 or by writing to him at: Dr. Norman F. Childers Publications, 3906 NW 31st Place, Gainesville, FL 32606]

Fruits: The Cleansers Of The Body

Alkaline Forming Fruits—Enjoy!

- Apples (especially red or golden delicious)
- Bananas (sparingly eaten alone)
- Cherries
- Dates
- Gooseberries
- Grapefruit*
- Huckleberries
- Kumquat*
- Limes*
- Mango
- Melons (all varieties eaten alone)
- Olives

- Avocado (sparingly)
- Apricots
- Blackberries
- Cantaloupe
- Citrangedin*
- Figs
- Grapes
- Guava
- Kiwi
- Lemons*
- Litchi
- Mandarins*
- Mulberries
- Nectarine*
- Oranges*

- Papaya
- Pears
- Pineapple
- Pomelo*
- Pummelo*
- Raspberries
- Tangerine*

- Peaches
- Persimmon
- Pomegranates
- Prunes (Small)
- Raisins
- Shaddock*
- Tangelo*

---

* *Citrus* (to be avoided in cases of eczema and/or psoriatic arthritis)

Acid Forming Fruits—Eat sparingly!

- Blueberries
- Currants
- Plums

- Cranberries
- Large Prunes

Keep in Mind: Dried fruits such as figs, dates, raisins, apricots, peaches, etc., make ideal snacks. Frozen fruit (unsweetened) is permitted. Stewed fruits are highly recommended. Remember, fruits constitute sweets for the body in the form of fructose, which is still a form of sugar and therefore should not be overdone. To every 2-3 fruits taken per day, 4-5 vegetables (especially green, leafy vegetables) should be taken.

Fruits And Combinations To Avoid!

- Strawberries often cause an adverse reaction with some people. If you are one of them, avoid strawberries.

- Do not combine citrus fruits or their juices with dairy products or cereals at the same meal.

- Do not combine raw apples, bananas, and melons (all varieties) with any other foods, although they may be eaten alone as a snack between meals. (Cooked apples may be eaten at any time and as often as desired.)

- Citrus fruits and their juices are to be avoided in cases of psoriatic arthritis and eczema. (Refer to list of citrus on previous page.)

- Avocados are to be avoided if there is also an underlying condition of gout.

Meats to Enjoy & Avoid

Fish
- Cold water
- Fresh water
- Salt water
- White flesh
- Dark, oily flesh

Poultry
- Chicken
- Turkey
- Cornish hens
- Non-fat wild fowl

Lamb

Beef
- Steaks
- Hamburgers

Pork
- Ham
- Bacon

Veal

Sweetbreads

Shellfish
- Lobster
- Crabs

All Processed meats
- Sausages
- Bologna

- Shrimp
- Clams, etc.

- Salami
- Frankfurters, etc.

Acceptable Breakfast Cereals

The following is a **partial list** of some dry and cooked cereals each of which contain approximately 5 grams of sugar per one-cup serving. Sugar content is indicated in grams [g] after each product. Check the nutrition label for sugar content before you purchase. All cereals are best served with skim or 1% milk, soy or goat's milk, or even plain water.

Dry cereals

- General Mills *Multi-Grain Cheerios* [6g]
- General Mills *Cheerios,* low fat [1g]
- General Mills *Wheaties* [4g]
- Health Valley *Organic Fiber 7* [5g]
- Health Valley *Amaranth Flakes* [5g]
- Health Valley *Organic Blue Corn Flakes* [5g]
- International Home Foods *Wheatena* [0g]
- Kashi Company Breakfast Pilaf *Kashi* [0g]
- Kashi Company *Kashi* [5g]

- Kashi Heart to Heart Cereals [5g]
- Kellogg's *Crispix* [2g]
- Kellogg's *Rice Krispies* [3g]
- Kellogg's *Product 19* [4g]
- Kellogg's *Special K* [4g]
- Post *100% Bran* [7g]
- Post *Honey Bunches of Oats*, with Almonds [6g]
- Post *Grape Nuts* [7g]

Hot cereals

- Maltex [1g]
- Maypo *Maple Flavor* [3g]
- McCann *Oatmeal* [0g]
- Nabisco *Cream of Rice* [0g]
- Nabisco Regular and Instant *Cream of Wheat* [0g]
- Pillsbury *Farina* [0g]
- Quaker *Old Fashioned Regular and Quick Oats* [0g]
- Quaker *Oat Bran* [0g]
- Quaker *Instant Oatmeal* [0g]
- Quaker *Whole Wheat Hot Natural Cereal* [0g]
- Quaker *Instant Grits* [0g]
- Quaker Regular and Quick *Grits* [0g]
- Ralston *High Fiber Hot Cereal* [0g]
- Total *Quick Oatmeal* [0g]
- Wheatena [0g]

Snacks

Snacks are always a concern with patients. Although they do not constitute a meal, they should be carefully selected as part of the daily menu. The following is a list of snacks which will help thwart hunger pains between meals, but which also adhere to the rules of proper diet and nutrition for the psoriasis and eczema patient.

- Fresh or dried fruit (unsulphured)
- Fresh vegetables: carrot, celery, broccoli florets, etc. (plain lowfat yogurt as dressing)
- Chopped fruit or vegetables in a plain gelatine mold
- Frozen fruit bars or pops (100% natural)
- Lowfat frozen yogurt
- Baked apple with honey and cinnamon
- Baked fruit, i.e. apples, pears, bananas, peaches, etc., with some raisins and almonds, sprinkled with some nutmeg, cinnamon, grated lemon or orange rind
- Frozen grapes (seedless)
- Fresh or frozen blueberries with plain lowfat yogurt and a teaspoon of honey
- Breadsticks (fat free varieties are best)
- Cottage cheese, lowfat

- Canned tuna, salmon, or sardines (salt removed) on whole-grain rice cakes or pita
- Almonds (4-12 a day) or 100% natural almond cookies
- Raisins
- Stewed fruit (figs, prunes, apricots, etc.)
- Applesauce (homemade or commercial 100% natural)
- Cookies, crackers (whole grain/natural)
- Rice cakes (whole grain, with a little honey or 100% natural fruit preserves)
- Toasted shredded wheat squares with a little grated Parmesan cheese
- Frozen pulp of cantaloupe or honeydew melon (make it a sorbet)
- Whole wheat or sourdough pretzels, unsalted
- Green leafy salad with olive oil and lemon juice dressing
- Fruit salad
- Tortilla chips, baked not fried
- Bagel chips (whole grain with Silken Tofu spread)
- Popcorn (plain, air popped) 1 cup
- Baked sweet potato or vegetable chips
- Roasted, unsalted soy nuts
- Almond butter on whole grain crackers

Remember, these are snacks to hold you over between meals. Do not overdo it. Don't do what one of my patients did when I told him that almonds were allowed—he ate an entire pound in one evening! When I asked why he did such a thing, his answer was, "Well, Doc, you said I could eat almonds!" Needless to say, I am careful now to spell it out by recommending four or five a day, but no more than ten or twelve. Moderation in all things is the key to successful living—*and eating!*

Almond Butter—An Ideal Snack

Kids love peanut butter, as do many adults, but it is not permitted on the diet. Not only is it high in fat content, but it is acid reacting and in many cases causes an allergic response in people sensitive to peanuts. Hydrogenated peanut butter is particularly prohibited.

Is there an effective substitute that may even be better in all its essence than peanut butter? There most certainly is: *almond butter*!

Although it is available in many stores, people can easily make their own, with excellent results, devoid of any preservatives, hydrogenated processes, artificial colors, etc.

1. *Place 1 pound of raw, shelled almonds in a blender.*

2. *Add ⅓ cup of either olive oil, canola oil or some other vegetable oil (except corn oil).*

3. *Grind on a heavy crush cycle until smooth in the container.*

4. *Place in a plastic container, refrigerate and use as desired.*

It makes an ideal spread on a whole grain cracker or slice of toasted whole grain bread. It is highly alkaline, rich in calcium and fiber, and kids love it! In addition to the above benefits is the fact that whole grains combined with olive oil or canola oil make for a "healthy heart!" Unless you are allergic to almonds, try almond butter remembering however, not to overdo it. A snack means one or two, not five, six or eight!

Beverages

1. **Water:** *6-8 glasses a day.*

2. **Soda (Soda Pop) Substitute:** *For those who simply like the taste of soda, a most effective and nutritious substitute is easily created. To ½ glass of pure 100% fruit juice, add ½ glass of seltzer (not club soda). This is far more beneficial than regular "soft drinks" or even diet sodas. Although this is not to be taken too often because of the carbonation of the seltzer, it can be taken occasionally if the desire for "soda" is overwhelming. The chances are you will never want to revert to canned or bottled sodas again. There can be as much as 10-12 teaspoons of sugar in a 12 ounce can of commercial soda!*

3. **Coffee:** *One to three cups per day, without cream or sugar, is permitted if desired.*

4. **Tea:** *American Yellow Saffron Tea, chamomile tea, mullein tea, watermelon seed tea, and green tea are the most beneficial. Green tea, combined with a teaspoon of honey and a teaspoon of Korean ginseng, makes a powerful antioxidant beverage.*

5. **Milk:** *No more than 1% fat, or, if you are allergic, goat's milk or soy milk often makes an acceptable substitute.*

6. **Vegetable juice:** *The most desirable of all drinks, but excluding the nightshades. Most beneficial are fresh carrot, celery, and lettuce juice made in a juice extractor.*

7. ***Fruit juice:*** *May be diluted with water if too tart and should be consumed less than the vegetable juices because of their high fructose (sugar) content.*

Caution:

Alcohol: According to a study of 94 male patients with psoriasis published in the *Journal of the American Academy of Dermatology*, heavy drinkers of alcohol had significantly less improvement after (conventional) treatment than their counterparts who drank less. Patients on my regimen are not permitted any alcohol during the healing period, which averages 3 - 6 months. A little (2 - 4 oz.) dry red wine is permitted late in the afternoon with a slice of dark, coarse bread provided there is no after-effect. Occasionally a white wine spritzer (white wine with seltzer on the rocks) may be permitted, but, again, if a reaction such as itching, irritation, or painful joints takes place, even this is to be avoided. If a patient is on any kind of medication, alcohol of any kind is completely prohibited.

The Taking of the Teas

Although mentioned earlier in "The Principles Behind the Regimen," the importance of taking specific herbal teas in this approach to healing psoriasis cannot be overemphasized. The purpose of taking the teas is twofold: 1) The healing of the inner walls of the intestines, and 2) The flushing out or cleansing of the alimentary canal.

Slippery Elm Bark Powder is used for healing the walls of the intestines. It is prepared by putting ¼ to ½ teaspoon of the powder in a cup of warm water and allowing it to steep for about 15 minutes. Stir occasionally and sip down. This is to be done in the morning, 30 minutes before breakfast. If for any reason this timing is not possible, it may be taken just before retiring the night before. It is taken five days of the week for about 10 days, then every other day until the condition clears. If it seems difficult to take, add ice to the mixture—the colder the better. The slippery elm is also available in the form of capsules or Thayer's Lozenges, and they now come in different flavors which children prefer. In the event that the slippery elm bark powder is difficult to take, the capsules or lozenges are an acceptable alternative. Taking Omega-3 Fish Oils or Flaxseed Oil is an excellent substitute in the healing of the intestinal walls. (see below)

(Note: Pregnant women or those anticipating pregnancy are to avoid both Slippery Elm Tea and American Yellow Saffron Tea.)

The American Yellow Saffron Tea (not Spanish) is used for the purpose of flushing out the liver and kidneys. About ¼ to ½ teaspoon of the Saffron Tea is placed in a cup and hot water is added. Let it steep for about 10 to 15 minutes, then drink it. It is best taken between meals or on a relatively empty stomach. Two or three cups can be had if desired–but there is one hard and fast rule to follow: **Do not drink the Slippery Elm Bark Powder Tea and the American Yellow Saffron Tea too close to each other. They should be taken at opposite ends of the day from each other.**

[See list of Suppliers on page 531 to find out where to obtain Slippery Elm Bark Powder and American Yellow Saffron Tea, which are two essential components of the regimen.]

Saffron Water: A very cleansing and healthful measure is to prepare a gallon of Saffron Water and keep it in the refrigerator at all times. Bring a gallon of pure mountain spring or distilled water to a boil. Turn off the heat and add one full teaspoon of the saffron to the water and allow it to steep for about 20-30 minutes. Strain it and return it to the container the water originally came in, then refrigerate it. At least one full glass of this water is taken each day as part of your 6-8 glasses of water. It is a most effective way to flush out the system.

The taking of Omega-3 Fish Oils and/or Flaxseed Oil five days out of the week has been added to my regular regimen in the past few years, since these oils have been recognized as being very effective in the regeneration and reconstruction of the intestinal walls, thus helping to repair the "leaky gut." These, as well as L-Glutamine, may help considerably in this function, particularly when the breakdown of these walls can be traced to excessive use of antibiotics or drugs used in psoriasis such as Methotrexate (MTX).

These items, the teas and oils, should be kept refrigerated at all times while in their packages. They may be obtained from any well-supplied natural health food store. The American Yellow Saffron Tea is the most difficult to obtain, therefore, I suggest my readers go straight to the product suppliers listed at the back of this book and order from them directly.

NOTE: *These teas may be taken provided they do not interfere with the absorption of any medication such as heart medication or diabetes. Always seek the advice of your licensed health practitioner for any contraindication before taking these teas.*

Juicing

Whenever a patient asks me to recommend the most important kitchen appliances they should buy, my answer is unequivocally, first a juicer, and secondly a blender. No household should be without these handy helpers, especially where there is psoriasis or eczema involved.

Juicing brings nutrients directly into the blood stream without their having to go through the breakdown process. True, the fiber of the fruits and vegetables is largely removed by juicing, but they can easily be replaced since raw fruits and vegetables are a mainstay of the overall psoriasis/eczema diet.

Juicing is extracting the juice of fresh vegetables and fruits. Of the two, it is of greater value to juice vegetables, especially green leafy ones, due to their desirably high chlorophyll and Omega-3 content, and due to the undesirably high sugar (fructose) content of fruits. Chlorophyll is highly effective in purifying the blood. Sugar, even fruit sugar, in general should be kept at a minimum, especially in cases of diabetes, hypoglycemia, or any other underlying condition where sugar is to be avoided. I tell my patients that they should consume 4-5 vegetables to every 2-3 fruits in their daily diet. This is a healthy balance and also conforms to the latest guidelines established by the USDA.

Remember to avoid the nightshades in preparing your juices. In other words, no tomatoes, eggplant, white potatoes and peppers (all kinds), and do not spice with hot pepper flakes.

As far as the best unit to buy, most of them on the market can do the job, perhaps some better than others, but in general they are all good these days. Prices range from under $80.00 to over $300.00. Depending on your circumstances, select the one that best fits your budget and your needs. In my opinion, a major factor to consider is how easy it is to clean. The unit must be cleaned after each use, and the extracted juice should be consumed within ten minutes of preparation in order to absorb the live nutrients at their peak. If you store it for any length of time, even in the refrigerator, the molecules will oxidize and lose their potency.

Fresh juicing each time is the best route to take, but at times it is simply not convenient and the patient must resort to store-bought juices. If that is the case, I often advise my patients to add the actual fruit to the juice, not only to enhance the flavor and liven it up a bit, but also to replace some of the fiber that was lost in the commercial juicing process. For instance, if you buy pear juice, cut up a fresh pear (after washing the skin), put the pear juice in a blender and add the fresh pear. Delicious! If you buy juice blended of two or three different fruits, select one of them and add a fresh one to the fruit juice and blend until smooth. For example, if you buy juice consisting of peach, mango, and kiwi, cut up a fresh peach or mango or kiwi and blend it together with the commercially prepared juice.

Remember, however, that in the case of fruit juicing the sugar content soars, so diabetics or others with a sugar problem should avoid such "smoothies." There are times when you may wish to cut down on a high sugar juice, such as grape juice. This is easily done by adding water (as much as 50%) to the juice you wish to dilute.

Rather than go into an array of juice combinations which can easily be found in any number of "juicing" books currently on the market, suffice it here to list a few rules to follow in concocting your own juices.

- Avoid the nightshades in juicing [tomatoes, eggplant, white potatoes, peppers] and do not add hot spices to your drink.
- Try to avoid mixing apples, bananas and melons with other fruits in the mix. Avoid strawberries if there is an adverse reaction to them.
- Wash all fruits and vegetables thoroughly before juicing, or buy the special fruit and vegetable wash now available in supermarkets.
- Organically grown fruit is most desirable and may be juiced with the peels; but if organic fruit and vegetables are not available, peel them before juicing.
- The base of most juices should be those products that have a high water content, such as carrots, cabbage, grapes and simply water. Produce with a strong flavor should be used in small amounts, e.g. garlic, onions, scallions, turnips, etc.

Some practitioners who advocate juicing for health suggest taking four glasses per day for "speed healing" and two a day for maintenance. If this is practical, I see nothing wrong with it, but I have found it a workable practice to have at least one 6-8 ounce glass of freshly made juice per day.

Below are examples of juice mixtures, fruit and/or vegetable, that I most often recommend to my patients. These formulas give you an idea of some good combinations for juicing. Try them, enjoy them, and experiment to develop your own. They can go a long way in getting you well, especially if you have at least one glass a day.

- Watercress, carrot (one pound makes one glass), dandelion, cucumber

- Turnips, cabbage, carrot

- Apples (5 apples make one glass)

- Beets (one pound makes one glass)

- Romaine lettuce (2 hearts), celery (2-3 stalks), beet (1 medium), alfalfa sprouts (wrap sprouts in one of the lettuce leaves and place in juicer)

- Orange juice (4 parts) combined with lemon juice (1 part)

- Grapefruit juice and lemon

- Orange, peach, and mango

- Romaine lettuce, carrots, celery, beet and parsley

Food Combining

The reason one should develop an awareness of beneficial versus detrimental food combinations is because of the importance of maintaining a proper acid/alkaline balance within the body, as already mentioned. Most people are not aware that certain foods should not be combined at the same meal, but may, if desired, be eaten separately. This is because some food combinations may cause havoc within the body that sooner or later show their deleterious effect in the form of poor digestion as well as improper utilization and assimilation of vital nutrients. When this occurs, the end result is intestinal discomfort, malnutrition and poor elimination. Add the over-abundance of acid formers and you have the breeding ground for a generalized toxic buildup.

The following food combinations are listed for your consideration for the very reasons just stated. However, do not consider them "hard and fast" rules, they are rather helpful guidelines or warnings. When preparing meals, the proper 70-80% alkaline—20-30% acid ratio should always be kept in mind. I advise my patients to keep it simple. Rather than weigh out or measure each portion, simply make it 3 to 1. That is, at least triple the amount of alkaline to acid formers and you will be on target. Do not agonize over it if, for some reason, you find it difficult to follow this rule 100% at each meal. If, by the end of the day, your alkalines exceeded your acid formers, you are dieting in the healthy zone. Once you have learned to identify those foods that are alkaline and those that are acid formers, the process will become automatic.

Some "Do Not's" Of Food combining

- **Do not** combine too many acid forming foods (proteins, starches, sugars, fats and oils) at the same meal with milk or cheese.

- **Do not** combine citrus fruits or their juices with dairy products such as yogurt, etc.

- **Do not** combine whole-grain products, i.e., cereals, breads, etc. with citrus fruits, citrus juices, or stewed and dried fruits.

- **Do not** combine any type of fruit with white flour products, such as bread, crackers, cereals, pasta, etc.

- **Do not** combine melons (any variety), raw apples or bananas with other foods. These fruits may, however, be eaten separately between meals as a snack.

- **Do not** add milk, cream or sugar to coffee or tea.

- **Do not** have combinations where corn, rice, spaghetti (even Jerusalem Artichoke) and the like are taken all at the same meal. Individually these foods are permitted, but together they make for too much starch, especially if meat is eaten at the same meal.

- **Do not** eat large quantities of starch with proteins or meats. Starches are inclined to have an acid reaction.

- **Do not** eat large quantities of breads with sweets.

- **Do not** take large quantities of fats and sugars as they are acid forming.

- **Do not** drink beverages during meals. A glass of pure water 30 minutes before a meal and 30 minutes after a meal will not interfere with proper enzyme action in the digestive tract during breakdown and absorption (assimilation). A little dry red wine is permitted before or after a meal as well, but not during.

Remember: The diet should be more bodybuilding, that is, less acid foods and more alkaline reacting is best.

Keep in mind the most valuable foods to consume are green leafy vegetables, particularly Romaine lettuce, celery, spinach, sprouts, watercress, parsley, and the like; also, carrots, onions, leeks, scallions, beets, and garlic. The most valuable fresh fruits to consume are apricots, berries, cherries, figs, grapes, mango, nectarines, papaya, peaches, pears, prunes, and citrus (if you are not arthritic).

Red meats and processed meats, except those permitted in recommended quantities, are to be avoided because of high saturated fats, and because of additives, preservatives and sodium. Lamb is the only red meat permitted.

Not permitted are the Nightshades, especially tomatoes, and all tomato derivatives such as ketchup, sauces, tomato juice, salad dressings with tomato, pizza made with tomatoes and peppers. Also avoid soup and dip mixes which may contain dehydrated peppers, tomatoes and white potato starch. Be sure to check the label for ingredients.

Pizza, one of America's favorite foods, spells disaster to the psoriatic or eczema patient. Hot spices, and foods prepared with hot spices, are to be avoided at all costs, such as spicy Italian, Mexican, Indian, Chinese and Cajun-style recipes where these products are used. It is equally important to avoid sweets, chocolate, too many starches and too much salt. No fried foods!

A good weight loss measure is to have ½ a glass of 100% pure grape juice in ½ a glass of water 30 minutes before each meal. However, this may not apply to diabetics.

The most valuable beverage is water. It is imperative that six to eight glasses of pure water (not distilled) be consumed daily, unless medically inadvisable. I do permit seltzer water, plain or with a touch of flavor but not too often since it is carbonated and may be rather harsh on the kidneys. You will appreciate the importance of clean water intake when you fully grasp the fact that psoriasis, as well as eczema, is not rubbed off, it is not burned off, it is flushed out! Sodas, both regular and diet, as well as alcoholic beverages, number among the most important beverages to avoid.

From this list you can readily discern what types of foods and beverages are permitted and which types are not. Since we obviously cannot provide a listing of every food item available, it is not too difficult to recognize the type they belong to, and consequently judge whether a particular item is permitted or not. If in doubt, however, look it up in a good book on nutrition—or avoid it altogether. You will find there is still plenty of good nutritious food and drink to choose from.

Note: 80% alkaline to 20% acid formers, found on pages 15-18, is the ideal combination of food selection, however, there are times when people must alter this ratio due to physical demands, especially young children. Therefore, it is permitted to alter the list to 60-70% alkaline to 30-40% acid formers. The most important thing to adhere to is that the alkaline formers exceed the acid formers.

Proteins and Starches

The following lists will help you identify the most common proteins and starches, thereby making it easier for you to formulate beneficial food combinations. Proteins and starches should not be combined too often. They all tend towards building up the acidity of the body, which in turn can be detrimental to the kidneys. The average person needs no more than 45 to 65 grams of protein per day. This may be increased if the individual's level of activity calls for it.

Proteins

- Fish, fowl and lamb
- Eggs
- All types of Grains (especially when eaten with legumes, beans or vegetables)
- Avocado
- Tofu

- Cheese
- Milk
- Nuts
- Dried beans, peas, soybeans, lentils
- Olives

Starches

- All cereals
- Dry beans and peas
- Breads and Crackers
- Bran
- Corn and Rice

- Syrups & sugars (use only those permitted)
- Winter squash, pumpkin, yams
- Grains: *(acid)* barley, buckwheat, oats, rye; *(alkaline* or close to *alkaline)* millet, spelt
- Vegetables: *(alkaline)* beets, carrots, burdock, parsnips, rutabaga, salsify, water chestnuts

Fiber

The word fiber is derived from the Latin word *fibra* which means "internal strength; toughness." Fiber should constitute a very important aspect of our daily diet. Research over many years indicates that proper fiber is a major preventative of colon cancer as well as other diseases that form by waste accumulations in the inner linings of the small and large intestines. The National Cancer Institute says we should be eating 25-35 grams of fiber a day. Presently, the average American consumes only 12 grams a day. Fiber-rich foods include fruits and vegetables, green beans, mangoes, blackberries, figs, okra, broccoli, cauliflower, Brussels sprouts, cabbage, bok choy, kale, and turnips. Almonds contain 3.9 grams of fiber in a ¼ cup serving.

The August 1999 issue of *Consumer Reports on Health* states, "In particular fiber helps reduce cholesterol, blood pressure, and body weight; it may also help the heart by warding off blood clots and reducing insulin levels."

Here is a list of foods which provide the highest fiber for each category, with the number of grams of fiber listed in parentheses beside each item.

Fruits
Pear (4g)
Apple (3.7g)
Orange (3.1g)
Banana (2.7g)

Vegetables
½ cup cooked peas (4.4g)
1 medium sweet potato (3.4g)
½ cup cooked Brussels sprouts (3.4g)
½ cup cooked spinach (2.8g)

Grains
1 cup Kellogg's Raisin Bran (8g)
1 cup cooked oatmeal (4.0g)

¼ cup wheat germ (3.7g)

2 slices whole wheat bread (3.0g)

Legumes

½ cup lentils (7.8g)

½ cup black beans (7.5g)

½ cup kidney beans (7.3g)

½ cup chickpeas (5.3g)

As you eat more fiber, drink plenty of fluids, particularly water, since constipation may develop. Recommended daily intake of water is 8 glasses.

Remember, meat does not contain fiber. It is found only in fruits, vegetables, whole-grain products, nuts, seeds and legumes. Perhaps the greatest benefit relative to the psoriatic, eczema or psoriatic arthritic patient is the cleansing effect fiber-rich foods have on moving along the contents of the alimentary canal thereby helping to avoid "backup" pressure in the intestines, a prime consideration in the healing of these diseases.

Cookery

The foundation of this dietary regimen is a carefully selected diet in which raw fruits and vegetables dominate. As important as it is to choose your foods carefully, the manner in which cooked foods are prepared is of equal importance. The reason is twofold:

- to cut down on saturated fat in cooking as much as possible

- to retain the vital nutrients contained in the foods consumed

Only in recent years have the dangers of consuming saturated fats been fully established as the leading cause of heart disease as well as being highly suspect in other degenerative diseases, such as rheumatoid arthritis and various forms of cancer. With this in mind, the following information should prove helpful when deciding on which method of cooking to use. You will be pleasantly surprised to find the methods permitted far exceed those that are not.

Permitted Cooking Methods

- Baking
- Barbecuing
- Boiling
- Clay cookery
- Microwaving
- Pressure cooking
- Sautéing/stir-frying
- Broiling
- Cooking in paper
- Poaching
- Roasting
- Steaming

Baking

Baking is cooking by dry heat at various temperatures in a confined space, usually in an oven. The dry heat surrounds the food and causes it to become more contracted. When this method is used to cook meats, it is called roasting. When baking, be sure to check the correct oven temperature recommended for each recipe you choose, the type and size of pans needed, and specified baking time.

Barbecuing

Barbecuing refers to foods cooked over an open fire, over coals, in a pit or on a spit in front of a fire. Meats are usually brushed with a basting (moistening) sauce or marinade before and during cooking to prevent them from drying out. Grills with a handle are designed to hold food firmly in place which prevents it from curling and also allows food to be easily turned while cooking. Foods that have a tendency to fall apart easily (fish, chicken, turkey, rolls, vegetables, etc.) are sometimes grilled with these hand-held units.

I personally do not advocate barbecuing foods since recent studies indicate that toxic emissions from charcoal briquettes and gas grilling can permeate foods and may be harmful to one's health. If one chooses to grill, however, it should be remembered that barbecuing with an electric grill or over gas-fired lava rocks is preferable to charcoal grilling, unless one has a sensitivity to hydrocarbons produced by gas grilling.

Boiling

Boiling means cooking foods in liquid in which bubbles rise constantly to the surface and break. Boiling too long can destroy the vital nutrients which usually end up going down the drain as the water is discarded, therefore, it is the least desirable of the cooking techniques. If boiling is the method of choice for any particular food, do so, but only as long as is necessary.

Broiling

Broiling is cooking directly under or above a source of radiant heat which may be gas, electricity, charcoal or an open fire, the most recommended of which is electricity. In England, it is referred to as "grilling." It is cooking food on a rack, especially meats, by very hot direct heat. Many of the natural fats cook out and drain, therefore it is ideal for weight-watchers. It is excellent for meats (lamb), chicken or fish.

Since broiling is cooking with very dry heat, basting (moistening) with a marinade is necessary in order to prevent food from drying out as well as adding flavor. When broiling chicken or fish, baste with lemon or lime juice, or a little butter or olive oil. A glaze made from natural fruit preserves can be used over chicken or lamb.

Clay cookery

A clay cooker is a unit that permits you to cover meats (fish, fowl and lamb) with assorted vegetables and bake them together. A clay cooker comes glazed or unglazed. If unglazed, soak the cooker in water. The wet clay will steam the meat and will retain all the flavors of the vegetables.

Cooking in paper

Cooking in paper, also known as Vegetable parchment or Patapar Paper, is a form of steaming and is by far the most valuable way to cook food. There are two distinct features about it that makes it most desirable: 1) It preserves the vitamins and minerals of the food being cooked, and 2) It avoids messy clean-up.

Cooking in paper is nothing new. The Chinese have been using this method for centuries and it is a favorite among health-minded individuals of all nations. The paper is nontoxic and actually can be rinsed out and reused many times.

The foods to be cooked (vegetables, fruits and even meat) are washed, chopped and placed in a dampened sheet of parchment. The corners of the paper are folded around the food and tied together with a natural cotton string. The pouch is then placed in a pot filled with two to three inches of boiling water, covered and simmered at a low to medium temperature. It may also be baked in a glass container in the oven. Be careful not to overcook as that will destroy its vitamin/mineral content.

The juices formed in the pouch should be retained, served with the meal or actually drunk immediately to obtain the maximum benefits from these powerful juices.

Many health-minded people feel this is superior even to regular steaming because it prevents oxidation by sealing out light and air to a great extent. For those readers who want to go the whole nine yards in natural food preparation, I highly urge them to study this technique and put it to use when appropriate. This may very well be classed as a habit worth practicing.

Microwave Cooking

Microwave cooking is a method in which the electromagnetic waves heat the food by agitating the molecules within the food, without heating the oven or the dish holding the food. Speed is the chief advantage to this method. Preheating the oven is not required and it consumes less energy than conventional cooking methods. Speed thawing is another benefit that makes electronic cooking popular. There are those who either like this cooking method or those who are opposed. Whatever the case, there is no denying that the microwave oven has become an essential appliance in the modern kitchen.

Microwaving advocates claim that this method of cooking is beneficial because it retains nutrients, eliminates the use of fats and sodium, enhances flavor and retains moisture without the use of oil, and is ideal for people with busy schedules. Opponents of microwaving claim that it doesn't brown roasts or cook foods as well as traditional methods do, dispute whether microwaved foods are tastier, and are concerned about possible effects from radiation. There is no doubt that the microwave is ideal for defrosting, and for quick cooking or reheating of small quantities, but for larger portions, a gas or electric range or oven is still better.

Microwaving meat or poultry prior to outdoor grilling is an effective way to save time and assure that the meat is thoroughly cooked without being dried out. It also liquefies fat which can then drain away over the barbecue. Some people barbecue meat first to get the flavor, then put it in the microwave to assure that it is thoroughly cooked.

Poaching

Poaching is simmering food in a moderate amount of liquid. It differs from steaming in that poaching is placing the food directly in the liquid, while steaming is placing the food on a rack suspended above boiling water. Poaching can be accomplished by simply using a skillet or wide saucepan and a slotted spoon. For special dishes, however, it is advisable to purchase an egg or fish poacher.

The liquids used in poaching vary widely depending on whether you are cooking a main dish, side dish or dessert. The type of cooking liquid to be used then depends on whether your choice is meat, chicken, fish, eggs, vegetables or fruits. Obviously, water is the most common poaching liquid, but for soups and main dishes, milk, broth, stock (chicken or fish), dry wine, or fresh lemon juice, which will help to maintain the shape of the food, and even vegetables may be used. In the case of desserts, use fruit juice or milk. Flavor is added by using various mild spices, not harsh.

Poaching has been used for centuries. Again, by varying foods and liquids, you can poach anything from main dishes to desserts. Simple techniques on poaching are easily found in many reputable cookbooks. It's easy, quick, and again requires no fat—a most important factor for psoriatic and eczema patients to consider.

Pressure Cooking

A pressure cooker is a utensil that consists of a pan, a sealing ring or gasket, a lid that fastens tightly to the pan, and an air vent or safety fuse with a weight that prevents dangerous or excessive pressure buildup within the pan. Before using a pressure cooker, it is imperative to read and follow the manufacturer's instructions, especially pertaining to the air vent and safety fuse. The cooker may be either electric or nonelectric. Pressure cooking cuts cooking time by as much as two-thirds. It also conserves flavors and nutrients which may be lost in conventional stove-top or oven cooking methods.

Roasting

Roasting and baking are the same; they are methods of cooking by exposing the food to low, dry heat.

As I mentioned, cooking meats in this fashion is called roasting, and, when cooking other types of food, this method is called baking. Roasting is perhaps the oldest method of cooking in the world. It was primitive man's most common cooking practice. Food would be buried in hot ashes or placed on sticks or spits. Today, oven roasting is the procedure most often used in a range oven, top of the stove oven, or portable electric oven. Rotisserie roasting is the modern equivalent of spit roasting. Electric rotisseries, both indoor and outdoor, are quite popular today.

Sautéing and Stir-frying (Wok cooking)

These cooking methods involve cooking food in an uncovered shallow pan over brisk heat, using just enough fat to keep the food from sticking. Once only used for meats and vegetables, today, it is used more extensively in preparing anything from main dishes to desserts.

The French call it sautéing, the Chinese call it stir-frying. In essence, they are one and the same, and incorporate the same principle in cooking—foods are cooked quickly in a small amount of oil or broth.

To adhere as closely to the diet as possible, cook foods in 1 or 2 tablespoons of olive oil, peanut oil, or plain water. Meat or poultry should be cut into thin slices before sautéing. The cooking oil should be hot but not smoking.

This type of cooking not only lends variety to food preparations, but is also a time saver, easy on the budget, and helps keep the waistline trim since very little fat is used. In addition, the fact that the flavors and nutrients are most effectively preserved, makes this a desirable form of cooking.

Wok cooking is extremely versatile in its use, yet remarkably simple in design. It can be used for steaming, simmering, and parboiling—which are all acceptable methods of cooking for the psoriatic/eczematic patient. Wok cooking is done quickly. In a few minutes, ingredients are stirred and tossed with a turner until things are "just done." The best type of wok is made of rolled tempered steel. Sizes range from 12-24 inches. The largest are used in restaurants or barbecues. The most practical type for a couple or family is the 12-14 inch wok.

Steaming

Steaming is a method of cooking by exposure to the vapor of boiling water. It is by far the most desirable form of cooking for anyone interested in preserving nutrients, retaining natural taste and watching calories. Foods may be placed in special paper such as vegetable parchment or patapar paper. This method steams vegetables so that they cook in their own juice.

Another very popular and convenient technique is the use of a steamer-basket in which food can be suspended over boiling water and consequently the steam from the water cooks the food.

Steaming is ideal for cooking vegetables, lamb, poultry, fish, fruits, and even breads. To cook frozen vegetables for maximum nutrition, heat quickly by steaming in as little water as possible. When steaming fish, wrap in cheesecloth, allowing the long ends of the cheesecloth to hang out on either side of the pan. Bring up the ends of the cheesecloth over the top of the lid and tie them together loosely. When the fish is cooked, untie the cheesecloth, and lift out the fish by the holding the ends of the cloth. A fish steamer should have a rack which holds the fish above the level of boiling water. Foods cooked in this manner retain their shape, texture and nutrients. A big plus is that no fat has been used for cooking.

There are different techniques to learn for effective steaming, but once mastered, this method will prove to be a favorite with your friends, family and most importantly, yourself.

Cooking Methods To Avoid

- Frying (Shallow or deep-fat frying)
- Smoke-house cooking (Home or commercial processing)

Basic Cooking Equipment

- Steaming basket
- Poaching pans such as a shallow poaching pan and an egg poacher
- Pressure cooker
- Clay cooker
- Barbecue grill
- Pot, saucepan, skillet, wok
- Broiling and baking pans, glass pie plates, racks, etc.
- Ovens—standard and microwave

Pots And Pans Should Ideally Be Made Of

- Cast-iron

- Heat-resistant glassware (Pyrex, etc.)

- Stainless steel

- Nonstick pans (Silverstone, Teflon, etc.)

- Porcelain or porcelain-coated steel

- Avoid aluminum and copper ware of any kind. Because of the softness of the metal, these can dissolve into food and be ingested. In the case of Teflon-coated pans, be very careful NOT to scratch the surface while cleaning because tiny teflon chips can break off and possibly get into the food.

Food Storage- Refrigeration

As is the case with many discoveries in man's world, refrigeration was found to be effective in preserving foods quite by accident. The story is told that it was Sir Francis Bacon who came upon the earliest form of refrigeration when he accidently dropped a whole chicken in the snow, recovering it only days later. When it thawed out naturally, he found the quality of the meat apparently unaffected by the freezing, and he proceeded to cook and eat it to his satisfaction. Thus, the first unplanned experiment at refrigeration was successfully carried out.

Today, one cannot fathom living without a refrigerator for the preservation of so many food items. It pays, therefore, to know a little about foods that are refrigerated and/or frozen, and the temperatures that best maintain them. The following chart includes only those foods acceptable for patients with psoriasis and/or eczema.

Food Item	Refrigerator (Maintain at 40°F)	Freezer (Maintain at 0°F)
Ground turkey, lamb, stew meat	1-2 days	3-4 months
Lamb chops and roasts	3-5 days	6-9 months
Whole chicken or turkey	1-2 days	1 year
Chicken or turkey pieces	1-2 days	9 months
Cooked poultry dishes	3-4 days	4-6 months
Open packages of lunch meat	3-5 days	1-2 months
Unopened packages of lunch meat	2 weeks	1-2 months
Lean fish (such as cod)	1-2 days	6 months
Fatty fish (such as blue, perch, salmon)	1-2 days	2-3 months
Soups and stews	3-4 days	2-3 months
Fresh eggs in shell	3 weeks	Don't freeze

Storing Fresh Fruits and Vegetables

The following, stored in the coldest part of the refrigerator, will keep for less than a week:

- All berries
- Broccoli
- Cauliflower
- Leafy & Iceberg lettuce
- Ripe Summer Fruits
- Sweet Corn
- Asparagus
- Brussels Sprouts
- Green Onions
- Mushrooms
- Spinach
- Watercress

The following, stored in the coldest part of the refrigerator, will keep for a week or more:

- Artichokes
- Beets
- Cabbage
- Celery
- Parsley
- Romaine lettuce

- Apples
- Blueberries
- Carrots
- Leeks
- Radishes
- Turnips

The following should be stored in the warmest part of the refrigerator, at 45-55°F, and will keep there for less than a week:

- Green Beans
- Ripe Avocados

The following should be stored in the warmest part of the refrigerator and will keep there for a week or more:

- Cucumbers
- Ripe Melons
- Zucchini

- Oranges
- Summer Squash

The following should be stored at cool room temperature (50-60°F) and will keep there for a week or more:

- Grapefruit
- Limes
- Winter Squash (uncut)

- Lemons
- Sweet Potatoes

Bananas should be stored at room temperature (65-70°F) and will keep for less than a week. Dry onions and garlic should be stored at room temperature (65-70°F) and will keep for one week or more.

Photographic
Portfolio

Photographic
Portfolio

Photographic Portfolio

The following represents a cross-section of different cases of psoriasis the author was privileged to have as patients. They show what kind of results were obtained when the patient followed through with the regimen long enough, particularly where food selection and preparation were concerned. They committed themselves, did not try to set a time limit, persisted, and let Nature do the rest. Initials only are used in keeping with patients' right to privacy.

Turn to these pages if doubt
or impatience creeps in,
and say to yourself:
"If they could do it, so can I!"

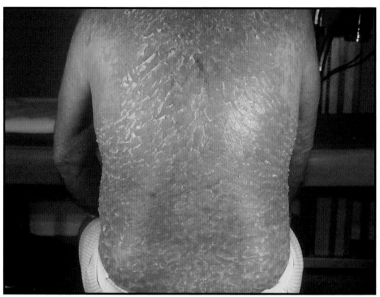

Figure 1-1: Patient: W.H. [age 56], afflicted 24 years

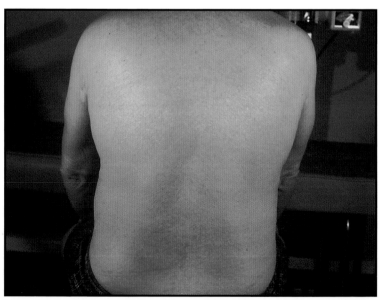

Figure 1-2: Patient: W.H.—7 months after starting regimen

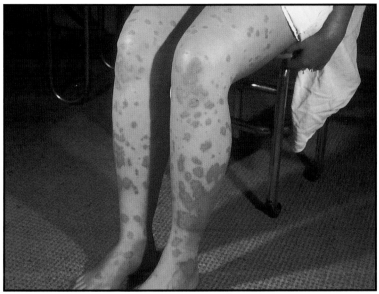

Figure 2-1: Patient: I.C. [age 19], afflicted 4 years

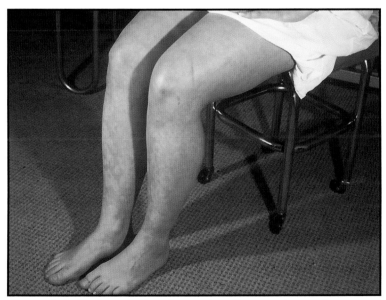

Figure 2-2: Patient: I.C.—4 months after starting regimen

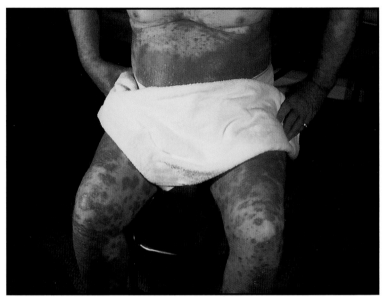

Figure 3-1: Patient: M.E. [age 64], afflicted 46 years

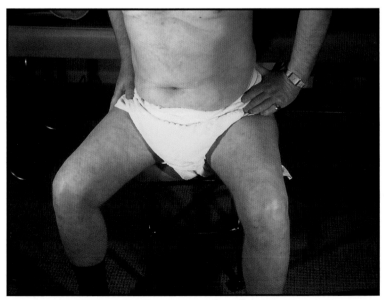

Figure 3-2: Patient: M.E.—7 months after starting regimen

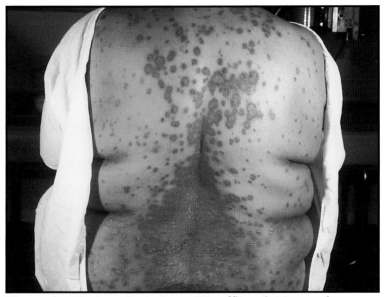

Figure 4-1: Patient: R.A. [age 60], afflicted 11 months

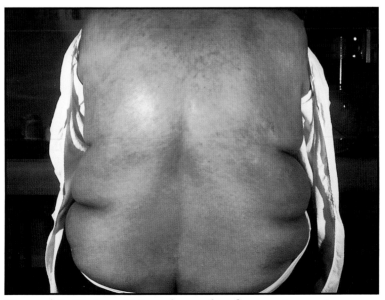

Figure 4-2: Patient: R.A.—4 months after starting regimen

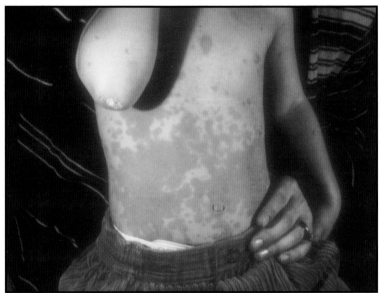

Figure 5-1: Patient: L.S. [age 3], afflicted at 9 weeks of age

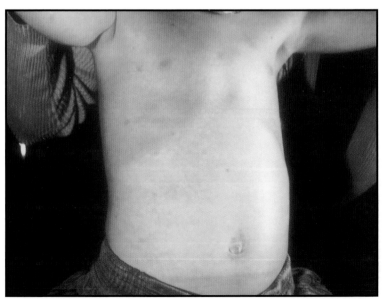

Figure 5-2: Patient: L.S.—3 weeks after starting regimen

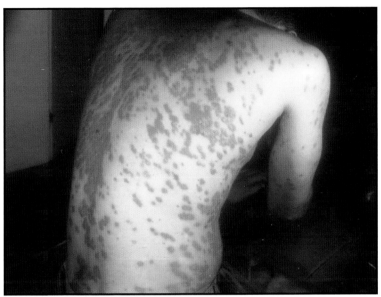

Figure 6-1: Patient: F.V. [age 21], afflicted 6 years

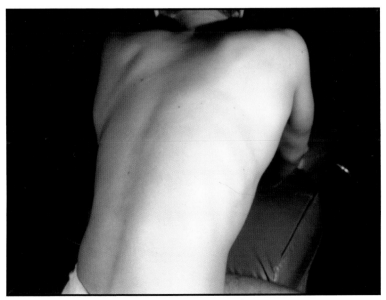

Figure 6-2: Patient: F.V. —7 months after starting regimen

The 3 Stages of Healing:
A Classic Example

This patient, P.J., was afflicted with guttate psoriasis over all portions of his body for five years. After conventional methods failed, he turned to the Pagano Regimen. Emphasis was placed on changing his diet, ensuring proper eliminations, and using external applications of Castor Oil, Olive/Peanut Oil and Hydrophilic Ointment. He remained faithful to the regimen and achieved remarkable results in three months.

Figure 7-1 shows the Initial Stage at the start of the Pagano Regimen. Figure 7-2, four weeks later, shows the Inflammatory (Purge) Stage, known as the Herxheimer Reaction. Figure 7-3 shows the Healing Stage, three months from the beginning of the regimen.

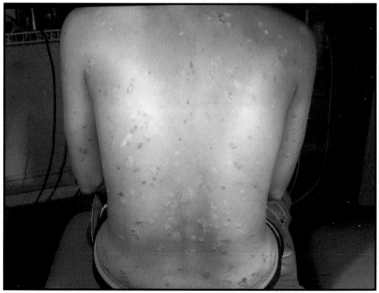

Figure 7-1: Patient: P.J.[age 36], afflicted 5 years

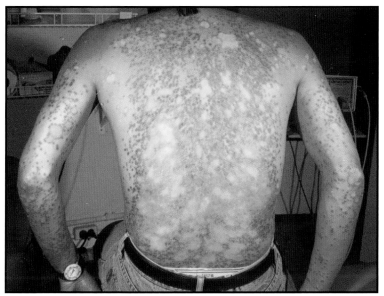

Figure 7-2: Patient: P.J. —4 weeks after starting regimen

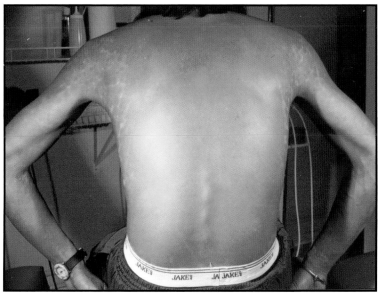

Figure 7-3: Patient: P.J. —3 months after starting regimen

The Healing of J. J.

This photographic account is that of a young boy, J. J., age 8, who suffered with psoriasis for five years. It is included here to emphasize the various stages he went through which eventually brought about a complete healing. He followed the regimen to the letter, especially the diet and the avoidance of gluten products, with the total commitment and support of his mother, father and brother. They followed through in spite of advice and criticisms to the contrary. When the breakthrough finally occurred, they realized they had made the right decision. From then on it was simply a matter of time. Without his parents' total devotion to their son's welfare, this result may never have taken place.

The initial photographs were taken by Dr. Pagano on J. J.'s first visit on November 14, 1999. Because of the great distance between patient and doctor, all subsequent photos were taken by his parents throughout the stages of detoxification and healing while at home.

It is J. J.'s and his parents' hope that his story will serve as an inspiration to all people, especially children, suffering with the disease. (See *"A Story That Needs Telling"* on page 516.)

Phase I – Start of Regimen
J. J., Age 8, Afflicted 5 years
Diagnosis: Common (Plaque type) Psoriasis

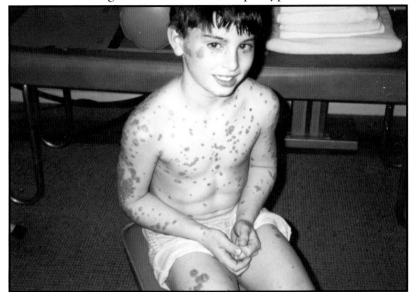

Figure 8-1: J. J. starts the regimen   November 14, 1999

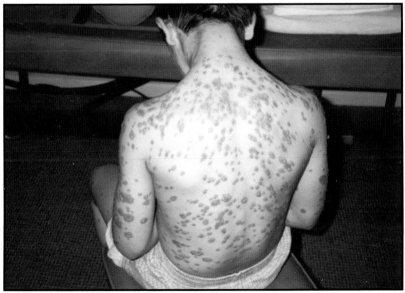

Figure 8-2:   November 14, 1999

Phase II – The Purge (Detox) Period Begins

Note: This purge period does not necessarily happen in every case. When it does, however, know that it is the body's way of throwing off all the internal toxins.

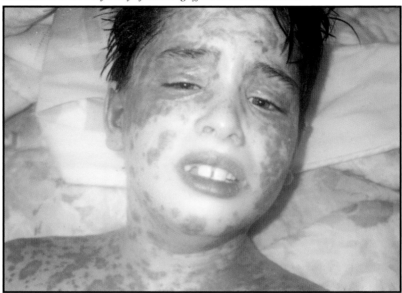

Figure 8-3:   One month later   December 15, 1999

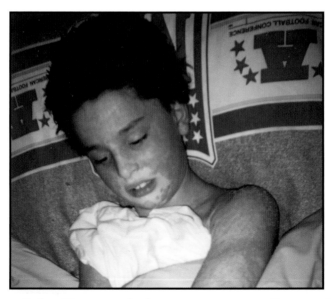

Figure 8-4:   Two months later   January 16, 2000

Purge continues to the healing crisis (Herxheimer Reaction)

Phase III – The Healing Period
Proceeds from January 16 – May 7, 2000

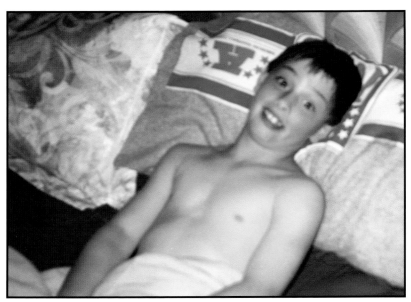

Figure 8-5:   The look of joy   June 29, 2000

Figure 8-6:   June 29, 2000

Healing time: approximately 6 mos. from start

J. J.'s Back – Close-up

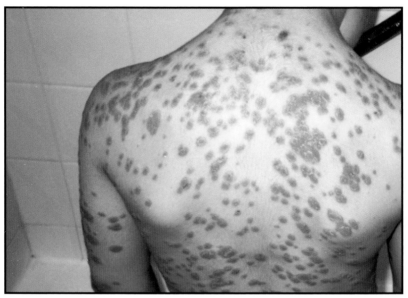

Figure 8-7:   November 15, 1999

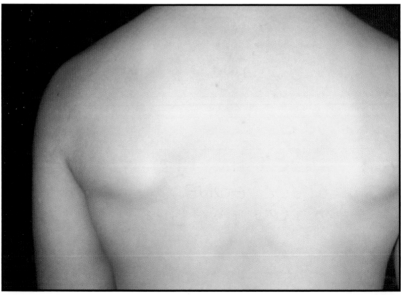

Figure 8-8:   June 29, 2000

A letter from J. J.

WHEN I HAD PSORIASIS I FELT NO ONE UNDERSTOOD. THE KIDS MADE FUN OF ME BECAUSE I LOOKED DIFFERENT. WHEN WE MET DR. PAGANO I WAS ITCHING IN PAIN AND BLEEDING. **I WAS SAD.** ALL THE OTHER DR.'S PUT ME ON MEDACINES BUT DR. PAGANO REALLY HELPED ME. IT WASN'T EASY. IT TOOK ALOT OF HARD WORK. IT WAS <u>VERY</u> WORTH IT. MY PSORIASIS IS COMPLETELY GONE. DR. PAGANO, I OWE YO YOU MY LIFE.

THANK YOU

J. J.

At the present time, October 1, 2000, over 5 months after healing, J.J. remains 100% clear. Pictured are J. J. and Dr. Pagano.

"I consider it the ultimate mark of success when a patient draws from my experience, achieves the desired goal and as a result, no longer has need of me."

Dr. John O.A. Pagano

Part II
The Recipes

Part II
The Recipes

PART II

The Recipes

Introducing
The Cooks

Monique Hill, a noted authority on cooking, is also a food stylist and consultant. After living in Europe for eight years (during which time she studied with several French chefs) she returned to the United States and studied in New York with Jacques Pepin, Guilliani Bugialli, and Lydie Marshall, among others. Monique has been teaching privately for many years and was a chef in the Executive Dining Room at a major U.S. corporation for ten years, providing world-class cuisine to top executives and business leaders from around the world. Recipes created by Monique are indicated with a "‑☞" in the front of each recipe section.

Pria Senaratne lends a touch of Far East cooking to our array of dishes. She studied Ayurvedic Nutrition in her native Sri Lanka where she was honored with the highest scholastic achievement in nutrition. In the United States she studied macrobiotic cooking and Dr. Anne Wigmore's Living Food Program. Pria had her own newspaper column on cooking in Dayton, Ohio before relocating to Perth, Australia. Pria teaches cooking and brings to her students a vibrant love and creative spirit for cooking with a wealth of experience as an Ayurvedic nutritionist, macrobiotic counselor, and western trained herbalist.

Maribel Steinmann, before moving to California, was a patient of Dr. Pagano suffering from psoriasis. For six to eight years she had been seeking answers to this disfiguring disease. Within four months after starting the regimen, she was completely clear of all psoriasis lesions, and also lost 37 unwanted pounds! Her energy level reached highs she never thought possible. In the process of following the regimen, Maribel, a very talented cook, developed several recipes which she graciously offered to share with other patients suffering from the same disease.

Mr. Wok (Nouvelle Chinese Cuisine) Located in the heart of Tenafly, New Jersey, Mr. Wok Restaurant offers delectable Chinese cooking at its best. The management prepared special dishes at Dr. Pagano's request for this publication following the rules of food selection and preparation as closely as possible. Watch for these special recipes as they appear periodically throughout the book.

Other Contributors

In addition to the above featured cooks, the author gratefully acknowledges the following individuals for the help and contributions they made in the preparation of this volume:

Nettie Pagano, Carol A. Miller and Maria Pagano, Justine Skiba, Mildred DeLuca, Adele Miller, Linda Cutrupi, Johanna Reinhardt Bayati, Barbara Reinhardt, Jennifer Velardo, Sheilah B. Galanti, Michele Cislo, Camilla Mork, Haricleea Pena, Dolores Sullivan, Mari Fettke and Doris Stauffer.

Special Note

There are many talented cooks in the world, be they housewife or professional chef, who may have created recipes based upon the principles set forth herein. If that describes you, you may wish to share your creations with fellow psoriasis/ eczema sufferers. We invite you to submit such recipes to us for possible inclusion in later supplements to or future editions of this book. Please send them to us in the format of the recipes which follow. Any recipes sent will be kitchen-tested. If your recipe is approved, you will receive full credit as the contributor for each recipe we publish. Please include a note granting permission for the Pagano Organization to use your recipe. Further, please include your name, address and telephone number in the event we need to contact you regarding your recipes. Mail recipes to: The Pagano Organization, 35 Hudson Terrace, Englewood Cliffs, NJ 07632.

About The Recipes

The recipes that follow are designed by specialists or simply talented cooks who followed the recommended food lists and cookery guidelines in their preparations.

As mentioned in my preface, there are times where you may find a minor "bending of the rules," so to speak, in some recipes. This became necessary in order to hold a recipe together and/or make it more palatable. This, however, is kept at a minimum, and does not disturb the overall principles of healthy eating.

Keep in mind, these recipes are designed for the average person with psoriasis or eczema. If, in addition, there is an underlying condition such as diabetes, hypoglycemia, heart disease or whatever, you must alter your daily menu to fit your particular needs. It is advised that you do so with the approval of your medical practitioner or nutritionist.

Fish

Fish is the most highly recommended meat protein in this regimen. Evidence continues to mount in the scientific community that Omega-3 fatty acids, found in fish, are essential to human health. These fatty acids  change the chemistry of the blood which prevents cholesterol and other blood fats from building up on the inner walls of the arteries. Studies conducted at the Oregon Health Sciences University, Albany Medical College, the State University of New York and the National Institutes of Health at Massachusetts General Hospital all conclude that Omega-3 fish oils lower the cholesterol of the blood, making it less likely to coagulate, thus rendering it less likely to form clots which can lead to sudden cardiac death.

There are however, many other beneficial functions of Omega-3 fish oils. It should be of primary interest to the psoriatic and/or eczema patient that it is a powerful agent in the rebuilding of the inner lining of the intestinal wall—the basic cause of the disease upon which this author's research is based. The following are the suggestions I make to my patients:

Basic Guidelines

- Fish (free-swimming, finfish) should be consumed about 4 times a week. Shellfish is to be avoided because of its high purine content.

- Fish should be fresh or frozen, but fresh is preferred.

- Fish may be prepared by steaming, poaching, baking, microwaving. In short, any way but frying! Use olive oil generously, lemon juice, onions and mild spice in preparing fish. Avoid paprika.

- Fish is high in protein, vitamins and minerals, and is easily digested.

- Fish has been cited as being beneficial also in cases of arthritis, for women of childbearing age, and in boosting the immune system.

- The lack of fish oils is now being linked as having a possible relationship to mental depression. Studies about this connection are under way by Joseph Hibbeln, M.D., a psychiatrist at the National Institutes of Health.

- In short, EAT MORE FISH!

A partial list of fish to enjoy

- Atlantic Cod*
- Atlantic Salmon*
- Blackfish (Tautog)
- Flounder*
- Grey Sea Trout
- Halibut*
- Mackerel*
- Monkfish
- Pollock
- Red Snapper
- Skate
- Sole (Dover and Grey)
- Swordfish
- Tuna* (especially white albacore)
- Atlantic Croaker
- Black Sea Bass
- Bluefish*
- Freshwater Catfish
- Haddock
- Herring*
- Mahi-mahi
- Ono
- Rainbow Trout
- Shark
- Sockeye Salmon*
- Striped Bass*
- Tilefish
- Whiting

---

* indicates richest sources of Omega-3

Special Note about eating fish **raw:** According to Food and Drug Administration statistics, raw or undercooked seafood accounts for 85 percent of all seafood illnesses. Cross-contamination also causes problems, so beware of raw seafood or their juices coming into contact with cooked foods of any kind.

The most important factor to consider in the case of sushi is whether or not the fish came from known polluted waters. It is the bacteria count and fishworms, not to mention pollution due to environmental pollutants, that is the major concern. Fish harvested from clean waters is obviously the most desirable.

For safety that doesn't compromise taste, fish should be cooked at 450 degrees giving it about 10 minutes for every inch of thickness. (Source: *Tufts University Diet & Nutrition Letter*, April 1992)

Poultry (Fowl)

- Chicken
- Cornish Hens
- Turkey
- Wild Game

Basic Guidelines

- Skinless, white meat preferred; dark meat is permitted on occasion (dark meat contains much more fat, cholesterol and salt than white meat). Poultry may be cooked with skin on, but do not eat the skin.

- May be prepared by baking, broiling, steaming, electric rotisserie, quick sautéing. Prepare almost any way except fried. Completely avoid fast food chains where deep frying is the predominant method of cooking!

- No more than 4-6 ounces per day is permitted, two or three times per week. More is permitted in cases where heavy physical labor is demanded in your daily schedule.

- Cooked chicken or turkey may be shredded, diced, or cut in strips, and added to salads, soups, and broths.

- Strips of raw chicken may be sautéed with permitted raw vegetables.

- No duck, goose or other fatty fowl.

Lamb

- Lamb is the only red meat permitted on this regimen. It is the most easily digested of all the red meats.

- All visible fat should be removed before cooking.

- Lamb should be cooked well done by broiling, baking, roasting, or grilling. It may be made into lamb patties or lamb-burgers, but never fried.

- No more than 4-6 ounces per day is permitted, served once or twice per week.

Soups and Salads

Soups and Salads

Soups

⌐☐   Indicates recipe created by Monique Hill

Apple-Butternut Squash Soup

Serves 8

Ingredients:

1 pound butternut squash
3 medium tart apples
1 medium onion
1 stalk celery
¼ teaspoon rosemary, dried
¼ teaspoon marjoram, dried
3 cans 14½ oz. chicken broth (low fat, low salt)
1 cup water
1 teaspoon sea salt
¼ teaspoon black pepper
3 tablespoons parsley, for garnish

Directions:

1. *Cut squash in half, seed, peel and dice. Do the same for the apples. Peel and roughly chop celery and onions.*

2. *Place squash, apples, onions, celery, dried herbs, chicken broth, water, salt and pepper in a large stock pot and over high heat bring ingredients to a boil. Lower heat and simmer for 45 minutes.*

3. *With a slotted spoon, remove squash and apples and place in a blender or food processor and purée ingredients until smooth. Add back to the stock and stir. Garnish with parsley.*

Note: This soup may be frozen.

Barley Soup

Serves 6 to 8

Ingredients:

1 cup barley
10-12 cups water
1 medium onion, chopped
2 cups chopped carrots
2 cups chopped celery
2 cups chopped boiled chicken breast
2 tablespoons vegetable or chicken base
"Better than Bouillon" -or- 2 low sodium
chicken bouillon cubes

Directions:

1. *Boil water. When water comes to a boil, add barley. Cook until barley is half done, then add onions and celery. Return to boil.*

2. *Add cooked chicken and "Better than Bouillon" (or chicken bouillon cubes), continue to boil until the barley is totally done. If necessary, add more water. Add carrots and cook until tender. Add ground black pepper if desired.*

Borscht

(Polish Beet Soup)

Serves 4 to 6

Ingredients:

3 medium beets
6 cups fat-free, low sodium chicken broth
2 cups water
¼ cup plus 2 tablespoons fresh lemon juice
3 large mushrooms, cut into small sticks
Pinch sea salt

Directions:

1. Wash and put beets in a pot, add water to cover. Bring to a boil then reduce heat and simmer about 25 minutes or until beets are tender. Rinse in cold water and peel beets. Grate beets using the shredding disk of a food processor or a hand grater.

2. Put broth, water, mushrooms, lemon juice and grated beets in a soup pot and cook for 35 minutes. Season to taste with a little salt or more lemon juice. Serve hot or cold.

Helpful Hint

When buying beets look for uniform color and firm texture. The peak time for beets is in the months of June, July and August. Available in smaller quantities the rest of the year.

Cabbage Soup

Serves 4 to 6

Ingredients:

1 pound lamb shank, trimmed of fat
   (or leftover leg of lamb bone)
8 cups water
¼ teaspoon thyme
1 bay leaf
2 cups onions, chopped
4 cups cabbage, chopped
¼ teaspoon thyme
Salt and black pepper

Directions:

1. *Remove as much fat as possible from the shank. Put meat in soup pot. Add water, thyme, bay leaf and a little salt and black pepper. Bring to a boil, reduce the heat and simmer for about 1½ hour.*

2. *Add onions, cabbage and thyme and cook for one hour or until meat is tender. Season with salt and pepper.*

3. *Remove the shank, cut meat into small cubes, and put back into the soup; or serve as a meal with vegetable and a salad.*

Note: Will keep in refrigerator 2 to 3 days, and may be frozen.

Carrot Soup

Serves 6

Ingredients:

4 tablespoons unsalted butter
5 large carrots, peeled and halved
2 celery stalks, with leaves, halved
1 large onion
2 tablespoons light brown sugar
¾ tablespoon ground ginger
¾ tablespoon fresh nutmeg (if dry, use less)
7 cups chicken stock
⅓ cup cooked dried beets
Fresh chopped chives for garnish

Directions:

1. *Preheat oven to 350.°*

2. *Place carrots, celery and onions in shallow Pyrex dish. Dot with butter, sprinkle with brown sugar, ginger and nutmeg. Pour two cups of chicken stock over the vegetables. Cover tightly with aluminum foil and bake for two hours.*

3. *Remove dish from oven and transfer contents to a large heavy pot. Add 4 cups of chicken stock and bring to a boil. Reduce heat to medium and cook for ten minutes, partially uncovered.*

4. *Transfer to blender or food processor. Purée vegetables along with cooked beets until smooth. [For a short-cut you can add chopped fresh beets to the casserole that you are baking for two hours.]*

5. *Return to pot, season with salt and pepper. Serve warm, not hot, garnished with chives.*

Chicken and Zucchini Soup

Serves 4 to 6

This is a full-flavored soup, yet it is amazingly light. The lemon gives it a nice zing.

Ingredients:

⅓ cup brown rice
¾ cup water, with a pinch of salt added
2 cups celery, sliced
2 cups leeks, white part only,
    cleaned well and chopped
8 cups water
2 chicken bouillon cubes
3 cloves garlic, thinly sliced
1 chicken breast, skinless, boneless (about ¼ lb)
    and chopped into ½ inch pieces
Black pepper to taste
¼ cup fresh lemon juice
2 cups zucchini, chopped into ½ inch pieces
2-3 tablespoons cilantro*
    or parsley for garnish (optional)

Directions continued on the following page

Chicken and Zucchini Soup Directions:

1. Put rice into a small pan with ¾ cup water. Bring to a boil, reduce heat and simmer about 25 minutes or until water is absorbed. [You may add more water and continue simmering if rice is not cooked enough.]

2. Combine 8 cups water, chicken, bouillon cubes, celery, leeks, garlic, lemon juice and black pepper. Bring to a boil, reduce heat and simmer for 45 minutes.

3. Add zucchini and simmer another 10 to 15 minutes. Add rice, and cook a few more minutes. Adjust seasoning. Garnish with cilantro or parsley.

Helpful Hint

Cilantro is preferred for this recipe, but parsley may be used. This soup will keep in refrigerator for 2 to 3 days and may be frozen.

Chicken Broth

Ingredients:

5-6 pounds chicken necks, backs, wings, etc.
24 cups (or 6 quarts) water
4 carrots
3 large onions
4 stalks celery
2 leeks, washed carefully
3 bay leaves
½ teaspoon thyme

Directions:

1. Place chicken in stock pot, cover with water. Bring to a boil. Using a ladle skim off the fat that rises to the surface. Repeat until broth is quite clear.

2. Coarsely slice the vegetables, and add to the stock pot with the remaining ingredients. Simmer for 3 hours.

3. Strain the broth and allow it to cool uncovered before refrigerating.

4. Remove fat from the surface before using.

Note: Broth may be frozen in small containers.

Chicken Macaroni Soup

Serves 6 to 8

Ingredients:

2 cups Jerusalem Artichoke macaroni pasta
1 cup diced chicken breast
1 cup diced carrots
½ cup finely diced onions
1 teaspoon crushed black pepper
2 tablespoons low sodium soy sauce
½ teaspoon garlic powder
½ teaspoon Italian seasoning
¼ cup fresh parsley
2 teaspoons Superior Touch vegetable base
   or bouillon
8-10 cups of water

Directions:

1. Sauté chicken and onions in ¼ cup of water. When done, add at least 8 cups of water.

2. When water is boiling, add the pasta and carrots. Cook until pasta is al dente.

3. Stir in vegetable base or bouillon, soy sauce and all other seasonings. Add more water if necessary. Garnish with parsley.

Chicken Stock

Ingredients:

4 pounds chicken, cut into pieces
6 cups cold water
1 carrot, sliced
2 stalks celery, sliced
1 onion, sliced
½ bay leaf
¼ teaspoon peppercorns
Salt and Black Pepper to taste

Directions:

1. Wash chicken thoroughly. Place meat (except for breast meat) into kettle. Add water and all remaining ingredients.

2. Gradually bring to a boil. Add breast meat, cover and cook slowly until meat is tender. Skim off fat as it rises to the surface. Cool and remove all fat.

3. Return to boiling, then strain broth to be used for stock in other recipes. [You may use the meat and vegetables in this recipe for other cooking purposes.]

Cool Cucumber Soup

Serves 2 to 4

This is the ideal refresher for those extremely hot summer days.

Ingredients:

1 tablespoon butter
1 tablespoon safflower oil
½ cup onions, chopped
4 cups cucumber, seeded and diced
1½ cups watercress leaves
1 cup white turnip, diced
½ teaspoon dill
5 cups fat-free, low sodium chicken broth
¼ teaspoon sea salt
¼ teaspoon black pepper
½ cup low fat plain yogurt
Chives or parsley for garnish

Directions:

1. *Melt butter and oil in soup pot. Add onions and cook covered over low heat for 5 minutes. Do not let them brown.*

Directions continued on the following page

Cool Cucumber Soup Directions continued:

2. Add remaining ingredients, except for the yogurt and garnish. Bring to a boil and simmer for about 15 minutes or until turnip and cucumber are tender.

3. Purée in an electric blender, add yogurt and blend thoroughly. Season with pepper and salt and more dill, if desired. Chill in refrigerator. [This soup is also delicious served hot, without the yogurt.]

Helpful Hint

Brush cucumbers with a potato brush and water, dry with a towel. Cut cucumber in half, lengthwise, and remove seeds using a teaspoon. Do not remove the skin of the cucumber.

Creamy Artichoke Soup

Serves 4 to 6

You will be surprised at the delicate flavor of this soup. So quick and easy to prepare!

Ingredients:

1½ cups celery, chopped
1 medium onion, chopped
1½ cups leeks, thoroughly cleaned & chopped
1 cup white turnip, chopped
6 cups fat-free, low sodium chicken broth
14½ oz. water-packed artichoke hearts
   (drained and quartered)
1 tablespoon lemon juice
Black pepper to taste

Directions:

1. *Simmer celery, onion, leeks and turnip in chicken broth for 30 minutes. Add artichoke hearts and simmer for 15 minutes.*

2. *Put everything into blender and purée.*

3. *Return mixture to pot and heat to serving temperature. Add lemon juice and black pepper to taste.*

   Note: Soup will keep in refrigerator for 2 to 3 days and may be frozen.

Creamy Carrot Soup

Serves 2 to 4

Ingredients:

1 tablespoon safflower oil
1 teaspoon butter
1 cup onions, chopped
1 pound carrots, sliced
2 white turnips, diced
4 cups fat-free, low sodium chicken broth
Pinch sea salt
Black pepper to taste
2 tablespoons chopped parsley for garnish

Directions:

1. Melt butter in a soup pot with oil. Add onions, cover and cook over very low heat for 5 minutes, stirring occasionally.

2. Add broth, carrots and turnips. Bring to a boil and simmer for about 20 minutes, or until vegetables are completely tender.

3. Purée in a blender and return to the pot. Add seasoning to taste and garnish with parsley.

   Note: Carrots are one of the best sources of Vitamin A. They also contain a small amount of other vitamins and minerals. Look for firm, brightly-colored carrots.

Creamy Celery Soup

Serves 4 to 6

Ingredients:

1 tablespoon corn oil
1 tablespoon butter
2 cups onions, chopped
6 cups celery, chopped (if fresh, include leaves)
6 cups fat-free, low sodium chicken broth
3 cups water
2 cups white turnip, chopped
1 tablespoon parsley, freshly chopped
Sea salt and black pepper to taste

Directions:

1. Melt butter with oil, add onions and celery. Cook covered over low heat for 5 minutes. Do not let it brown.

2. Add chicken broth, water, turnip and parsley. Bring to a boil and simmer for 45 minutes or until celery is very tender.

3. Blend soup in blender until very smooth. (Because celery is a "stringy" vegetable, it is better processed in a blender than in a food processor.)

4. Return soup to pot, bring to a boil, correct seasoning. Garnish with parsley.

Easy Turkey Vegetable Soup

Serves 4 to 6

Ingredients:

8 cups de-greased turkey broth
3 cups frozen mixed vegetables, defrosted
2 tablespoons fresh minced parsley
½ teaspoon dried basil leaves
½ teaspoon garlic flakes
Pinch of sea salt & pepper to taste
Leftover cooked diced turkey (if available)

Directions:

1. Bring turkey broth to a boil, add vegetables and seasoning, add turkey pieces, if available, lower heat and simmer until vegetables are tender.

2. Correct seasoning and serve. Garnish with fresh parsley.

Eight-Vegetable Soup

Serves 6 to 8

Ingredients:

1½ tablespoons butter
2 carrots, chopped
1 white turnip, chopped
2 leeks, washed well and chopped
¼ head Savoy cabbage, shredded
½ cup water
2 quarts fat free, low sodium chicken broth
½ cup peas, frozen
½ cup celery, chopped
½ cup green beans, chopped
1 Boston lettuce
¼ teaspoon thyme (to taste)
¼ cup fresh parsley, chopped
Salt and black pepper to taste

Directions:

1. *With metal blade in place, put carrot in bowl of processor and process, turning on and off until chopped into ¼ inch pieces. Remove and reserve. Repeat process with turnip.*

2. *Remove metal blade and insert slicer. Slice leeks and shred cabbage (with same slicer) using light pressure.*

Directions continued on the following page

Eight-Vegetable Soup Directions continued:

3. In a soup pot, melt butter. Add carrots, turnip, leeks, cabbage and water. Cover and cook over low heat for approximately five minutes. Add chicken broth and bring to a boil.

4. With metal blade in place, add beans and celery, turning on and off until coarsely chopped, then add to soup along with peas and thyme. Simmer for 20 minutes or until vegetables are tender.

5. With the slicer in place, shred lettuce using light pressure, and add to the soup. Add parsley and bring to a boil. Taste and correct seasoning with salt and black pepper.

Helpful Hint

Swanson chicken broth, 100% fat free and low sodium may be used. Although this recipe is written for use with a food processor, you may prefer to chop all the vegetables by hand.

French Fish Soup

Ingredients:

2 large fillets of white flesh fish (cod,
    flounder, etc.)
1 large fillet of salmon
1 large leek, thinly sliced
4 cups low fat, low sodium fish bouillon
    -or- Fish Stock
2 small packages saffron
2 cloves garlic, minced
2 stalks celery, thinly sliced
3 large carrots, thinly sliced
¼ cup fennel, thinly sliced (optional)
1 cup parsnips, thinly sliced
1 tablespoon olive oil
Pinch salt and pepper

Directions:

1. *In a large saucepan, heat olive oil over medium heat. Add garlic and leek. Sauté until tender.*

2. *Add 2 cups bouillon (or stock), fish, all the vegetables, and one package saffron. Cook over medium heat for 5 minutes.*

3. *Add the rest of the bouillon (or stock), saffron, salt and pepper. Cook for another 7-10 minutes until fish is done. Serve in large soup bowls with dark bread.*

Green Soup Suzy

Serves 4 to 6

Ingredients:

2 tablespoons butter or olive oil
3 leeks (using 3" of green part as well)
3 celery stalks
2 onions, medium
10 cups water
1 white turnip, coarsely chopped
4 tablespoons parsley
1 tablespoon salt
1 Boston lettuce, shredded
½ pound fresh or frozen spinach leaves
   (defrosted)
½ cup evaporated skim milk

Directions:

1. Coarsely chop the leeks, celery and onions. Melt butter and add chopped vegetables. Stir and cook covered on low heat for 10 minutes.

2. Add water, parsley, salt and pepper to taste. Bring to a boil and simmer 20 minutes. Add the turnip and continue cooking for 30 minutes.

3. Add the shredded lettuce and simmer 5 minutes, add spinach and simmer 5 minutes more.

4. Put through a food mill or purée in the electric blender.

5. Transfer back to soup kettle, add milk and season.

Holiday Soup

Serves 4

This is a festive soup with a delicate cranberry and orange flavor. We hope it will become part of your family's tradition.

Ingredients:

¾ cup dried cranberries

½ cup warm water

1¾ cups shredded beets (1 large or 2 small)

2 cups water

½ teaspoon orange rind (zest)

¼ teaspoon fructose

¼ cup plus 2 tablespoons orange juice

½ cup chicken broth

⅓ cup low fat yogurt

A few whole cranberries for garnish

Directions:

1. *Put cranberries in a bowl, add warm water and let stand while preparing the beets. Peel and grate the beets using the shredding disk of a food processor or a hand grater.*

2. *Place beets, cranberry and water mixture, orange juice, orange rind, fructose and water in a stock pot and simmer for about 20 minutes, or until the beets are tender.*

Directions continued on the following page

Holiday Soup Directions continued:

3. Purée in a blender and return to the pot. Add chicken broth and simmer for a few minutes. [Add a pinch of cinnamon, if desired.]

4. Serve with a dollop of yogurt floating on each serving, and decorate with a few cranberries on top of the yogurt.

Helpful Hint

Zest refers to the colored portion of the citrus peel. The white portion is bitter. You can use a gadget called a zester. A vegetable peeler will also work to remove strips which you then chop with a knife. It is very important to use fresh orange zest, the store bought dry rind is tasteless. This soup will keep one day in the refrigerator. Its flavor will change if kept longer.

Hearty Spinach Soup with Lamb Meatballs

Serves 8

Ingredients:

For lamb meatballs:
¾ pound ground lamb, lean
2 cloves garlic, minced
3 tablespoons fresh parsley, chopped
1 tablespoon Parmesan cheese
5 fat-free crackers, crushed
1 large whole egg
1 large egg white

For soup:
2 quarts Chicken Stock
2 pounds spinach, washed and chopped

Directions:

1. *In a large bowl, combine ground lamb, garlic, parsley, Parmesan cheese, crushed crackers, egg and egg white until well blended.*

2. *Using a teaspoon, scoop a heaping amount of the lamb mixture and shape into small meatballs, about ½ inch in diameter. Place a wire rack on a baking sheet. Place meatballs on the broil rack and broil for 3 to 5 minutes. Drain on paper towel to remove excess oil.*

3. *In a large stock pot, bring chicken stock to a simmer. Drop the lamb meatballs carefully into the stock and add the spinach. Simmer soup for 10 minutes and serve.*

   Note: You may add ½ cup of cooked rice, preferably brown, and/or ¼ cup cooked wild rice. Also, ½ cup shredded cooked chicken may be added.

Lean and Delicious Garden Soup

Serves 4 to 6

This soup is always welcome in spring. It has such a delicate taste, and is filled with the sweet flavor of fresh peas. Enjoy!

Ingredients:

8 cups leeks, sliced thick
2 tablespoons safflower oil
1 tablespoon fresh lemon juice
1 cup fresh spinach leaves, washed
1 cup green peas, frozen (rinsed in cold water)
1 cup Boston lettuce, shredded
4½ cups water
1 cube chicken bouillon
Sea salt and black pepper
Parsley to garnish

Directions:

1. *Clean leeks well by cutting in half lengthwise and running under cold water until all the dirt is washed away. Pat dry and slice.*

2. *Heat oil in soup kettle, add leeks and a little salt, pepper and lemon juice. Cover and cook on low heat for 10 to 15 minutes. Do not let leeks brown; check and stir from time to time.*

Directions continued on the following page

Lean and Delicious Garden Soup Directions continued:

3. *Add spinach, peas and lettuce. Stir together, then add water and bouillon cube.*

4. *Bring to a boil, reduce heat, cover and simmer 5 to 10 minutes until vegetables are tender but still bright in color.*

5. *Purée in blender and return to the pot. Heat to serving temperature. Adjust seasoning. Garnish with parsley, if you wish.*

Note: Will keep in refrigerator for 2 to 3 days.

Doctor: *"Mr. Schwartz, I'm sorry to say, you have only six months to live."*

Mr. Schwartz: *"But doctor, then I won't be able to pay your bill."*

Doctor: *"In that case, I'll give you another six months."*

Mari-Bob's
Pea Soup

Serves 4 to 6

Ingredients:

Package of Manischewitz Split Pea Soup*
1 onion (Spanish, large)
6 cups of water
Low fat turkey kielbasa (1 large link)
5 leaves fresh basil
1 teaspoon oregano
1 tablespoon olive oil
1 cup chopped carrots
1 cup chopped celery
Salt and pepper to taste

Directions:

1. Peel and chop onion and sauté in olive oil until golden color.

2. Add 6 cups of water in a large covered soup pot (Dutch Oven or Crock Pot preferred).

3. Leave Kielbasa whole while simmering then cut into ½ inch rounds and put back in soup pot. Add beans, 1 cup chopped carrots, 1 cup chopped celery and simmer the entire contents for 1½ hours.

4. Salt and pepper to taste.

Helpful Hint

If you are using dried beans, rinse and drain them first, then leave them in water overnight. (Read package instructions.)

Nanette's Chicken Stock

Ingredients:

4 quarts bottled spring water
3 pounds whole chicken
2 stalks celery
1 large carrot, halved
1 large onion, halved
5 sprigs parsley
Few dry bay leaves
½ teaspoon thyme

Directions:

1. Rinse the chicken under cold water. Remove skin from chicken if you prefer. In a 6-quart stock pot, add water, chicken, celery, carrot, onion, parsley, bay leaves and thyme. Bring to a boil over high heat. Then, reduce heat to low and simmer for 1½ to 2 hours.

2. Remove chicken and discard the vegetables. Pour the stock through a strainer into a large container. Discard any debris.

3. De-bone chicken and use as desired. Skim off any remaining fat from the stock.

4. Use immediately or cool completely before refrigerating or freezing. Makes about 4 quarts.

Onion Soup

Serves 6

This soup, served for lunch with a mixed green salad and some fruit for dessert, is light and delightful.

Ingredients:

7 cups onions, sliced (4 to 5 large onions)
3 tablespoon safflower oil
1 tablespoon butter
3 cloves garlic, minced
5 cups low sodium, low fat beef broth
1 cup water
¼ teaspoon fructose
6 slices Italian whole wheat bread
Pinch thyme leaves
Sea salt and pepper to taste
¾ cup low fat Swiss cheese, grated

Directions:

1. *Brown the onions with oil and butter in a stock pot, over medium heat, for 15 minutes, stirring often. Add garlic and fructose and continue cooking for 20 to 25 minutes. Onions should be dark, but not black.*

2. *Add broth and water, bring to a boil and simmer for 40 minutes. Season with sea salt and pepper.*

Directions continued on the following page

Onion Soup Directions continued:

3. *Preheat oven to 350 degrees. Then place bread slices on a baking sheet and bake until crusty and golden, about 12 to 15 minutes.*

4. *Ladle the hot soup in oven-proof soup bowls. Top with a slice of oven-dried bread and lavish with Swiss cheese. Broil 6 inches from heat until cheese is bubbling, about 3 to 5 minutes.*

Note: This soup can also be eaten without the bread. Serve very hot with floating croutons. Pass the cheese around separately.

Quick Carrot Soup

Serves 4 to 6

*This light and healthy soup has a beautiful
color and a wonderful fresh carrot taste. Resist
the temptation to add more broth or anything
else. Just enjoy!*

Ingredients:

1 pound frozen baby carrots
2 large leeks (white part only), thoroughly
    cleaned and sliced thin
4 cups fat-free, low sodium chicken broth
Parsley for garnish (optional)

Directions:

1. *Place leek slices in a soup pot, add chicken broth, cover and
simmer for 5 minutes. Add carrots and simmer covered for
15 minutes or until completely tender.*

2. *Purée in a blender and return to the pot. Garnish with parsley, if desired.*

Sweet Potato Soup

Serves 6 to 8

This nutritious soup is quickly made and has a smooth and satisfying texture. You will love it, even if you don't usually like sweet potatoes.

Ingredients:

4 cups sweet potatoes, cut into chunks
1½ cups carrots, cut into chunks
3 cups leeks, sliced thick and thoroughly cleaned
2 cups celery, cut into large slices
8 cups water
½ teaspoon dry tarragon leaves (not powdered)
Pinch sea salt

Directions:

1. *Place sweet potatoes, leeks, carrots, celery and water into a soup pot. Add a pinch of salt. Bring to a boil, reduce heat and simmer for 40 minutes.*

2. *Purée mixture in a blender and return to the pot. Heat and correct seasoning with a little more salt or tarragon.*

Note: There is really no difference between the sweet potatoes and the yams that are available in most American supermarkets. Therefore they are interchangeable in recipes. Select smooth plump potatoes that are clean, dry and uniform in shape and color. Sweet potatoes are an excellent source of Vitamin A!

Ten-Minute Vegetable Soup

Serves 4 to 6

This is a quick and easy flavorful soup with lots of vitamins and minerals.

Ingredients:

2 cups celery
1 cup onions
1 cup yellow turnips
1 cup carrots
1 cup leeks, well washed
1 cup zucchini
½ cup fresh parsley
1 tablespoon safflower oil
6 cups fat-free, low sodium chicken broth
1 cup water
½ teaspoon dried thyme
2 tablespoons cornmeal (optional)
Sea salt and black pepper to taste

Directions:

1. *Cut all the above vegetables into about 1" pieces and mix into a large bowl. Put about 1½ cups of this vegetable mixture into food processor and process on/off 10 times. Vegetables should be in about ¼" pieces. Put into a bowl and continue to process the rest of the vegetables the same way.*

Directions continued on the following page

Ten-Minute Vegetable Soup
Directions continued:

2. Put oil in a soup pot, add vegetables, broth, water and thyme. Bring to a boil. Reduce heat and simmer for 7 to 8 minutes.

3. Taste and season. Add cornmeal and simmer a few more minutes. Garnish with fresh parsley.

Helpful Hint

Clean leeks by trimming off root end of green stalk, cutting in half lengthwise and running under cold water until sand and grit is washed away.

Tofu and Spinach Soup

Serves 6

Ingredients:

1 package tofu (firm or extra firm)
2-3 cups fresh spinach cut into strips
   (or use frozen chopped spinach)
1-1½ teaspoons Superior Touch "Better than
   Bouillon" (vegetable or chicken base) -or-
   1-1½ cubes chicken or vegetable bouillon
½ cup chopped onions
8 cups water

Directions:

1. *Boil water. When water comes to a boil, add onions. Cook until onions are done, then add "Better than Bouillon" (or bouillon cubes) and return to boil.*

2. *Add tofu and spinach, let it boil again. Add ground black pepper if desired.*

Turkey Barley Soup

Serves 6 to 8

Ingredients:

12 cups Turkey Stock
3 carrots, diced
3 celery stalks, diced
1 small onion, diced
1 bay leaf
2 tablespoons olive oil
Salt and pepper to taste
⅓ cup raw barley
4 ounces DeBolo's Garlic and Parsley spaghetti, broken into small pieces
Leftover turkey meat

Directions:

1. *In a large pot, sauté onions in oil until clear, then add carrots and celery and sauté about three minutes.*

2. *Add turkey stock and bay leaf and bring to a boil. Reduce to simmer and cook for 20 minutes.*

3. *Add barley and simmer uncovered for 30 more minutes. During last five minutes, add the spaghetti. This will thicken the soup nicely.*

4. *Add the leftover turkey meat, salt and pepper. Remove bay leaf and serve.*

Turkey Stock

Ingredients:

1 turkey carcass and any leftover turkey parts
10 to 12 cups water
2 celery stalks with leaves, cut up
2 onions quartered
1 bay leaf
2 medium carrots, coarsely chopped
5 or 6 parsley sprigs
½ teaspoon thyme
Sea salt and pepper to taste

Directions:

1. Break carcass and place in a stock pot. Add water and bring to a boil. Add remaining ingredients, lower heat and simmer for 2 hours.

2. Strain the stock, cool and refrigerate as quickly as possible. When carcass is cold enough to handle, pick off the meat from the bones, cut up for soup and refrigerate.

3. Before using stock, remove any fat from the surface. Freeze if not using within a day or two.

Turkey Stock

(from the Thanksgiving Turkey)

Ingredients:

1 turkey carcass (bones)
1 onion - quartered
2 carrots, peeled and cut in thirds
2-3 celery stalks, cut in thirds
1 leek, cut in thirds
1 bay leaf

Directions:

1. *Remove any extra meat from turkey carcass and reserve for soup. Place turkey bones in large stock pot, cutting carcass if necessary. Add all other ingredients.*

2. *Cover completely with water and bring to a boil. Then simmer, uncovered, for 5 hours.*

3. *Pour cooked stock through a strainer to render a clear broth. Refrigerate covered overnight. The following day, skim the congealed fat off the top. You now have a clear, fat-free stock which is great as a soup base, or which can be frozen and added to the gravy dripping for your next turkey.*

Vegetable Broth

Serves 6 to 8

Ingredients:

7 cups water
2 carrots
2 large celery stalks
2 large onions
1 leek, cleaned thoroughly
1 clove garlic, unpeeled
1 teaspoon salt
1/4 teaspoon black pepper
2 teaspoons thyme
2 bay leaves
1/4 bunch parsley, washed well

Directions:

1. Slice vegetables, put in soup pot, add water and remaining ingredients.

2. Bring to a boil, simmer for 1 hour over low heat with cover slightly ajar.

3. Strain and discard vegetables. Use for stock in the making of soup.

Note: To make sauce, bring broth back to a boil and cook uncovered until reduced to the desired strength of flavor. (Should be half the original quantity.) Broth freezes very well.

Salads

Arugula, Radicchio & Endive Salad

Serves 4 to 6

Ingredients:

1 package arugula
1 head radicchio
2 Belgian endives
1 Boston lettuce

Dressing:

¼ cup fresh lime juice
1 tablespoon honey
1 teaspoon Dijon mustard
1 small garlic clove, finely chopped
⅔ cup safflower oil
Sea salt and black pepper to taste

Directions:

1. *Rinse and dry arugula, removing heavy stems.*

2. *Wash and dry Boston lettuce and tear into bite-size pieces.*

3. *Rinse radicchio, remove the core, separate the leaves, break into bite-size pieces.*

4. *Remove the core from the endives and slice them vertically about 1" wide.*

5. *Combine all the greens in a salad bowl.*

6. *Place lime juice, honey, mustard and garlic in a small bowl, gradually whisk in the oil, add salt & pepper to taste.*

7. *Pour dressing over mixed greens, toss and serve.*

Arugula with Mushroom Salad

Serves 4

Ingredients:

2 bunches of fresh arugula
2 cups sliced fresh mushrooms
1 cup finely sliced onions
2 tablespoons minced garlic
3 tablespoons olive oil
4 tablespoons apple cider vinegar
½ teaspoon Italian seasoning
Sea salt and black pepper to taste

Directions:

1. Wash arugula 3 times with cold running water. Then soak it with cold spring water and 2 tablespoons cider vinegar for 10-20 minutes. Drain, set aside.

2. Heat 1 tablespoon olive oil over medium heat. Add garlic, then onions, then mushrooms. Stir continuously until all liquid from the mushrooms disappears. Set aside.

3. Toss arugula with Italian seasoning, black pepper and salt. Add 2 tablespoons olive oil and 2 tablespoons apple cider vinegar.

4. When everything is tossed well, add the mushrooms. Serve and enjoy.

Beet Root Salad

Serves 4

Ingredients:

6 pieces round beet root (medium size)
2 cups diced cooked turkey breast
1 cup finely diced celery
¼ cup minced onions
1 tablespoon crushed black pepper
½ teaspoon Italian seasoning
½ teaspoon garlic salt
4 tablespoons olive oil
¼ cup chopped parsley, for garnish

Directions:

1. Boil beets until al dente. Allow to cool, then dice into small cubes.

2. Toss beets, turkey, celery and onions. Add all the other seasonings.

3. Add olive oil and toss well. Garnish with parsley.

Brown Rice Salad

Serves 4 to 6

Ingredients:

1 cup cooked brown rice
1 cup celery, chopped
¼ cup scallions, sliced
¼ cup green olives
1 cup cooked carrots, diced
1 cup cucumbers, peeled, seeded and diced

Dressing:

⅓ cup safflower oil
1 teaspoon sea salt
¼ cup fresh parsley, chopped
¼ teaspoon sugar
3 tablespoons fresh lemon juice
    or 2 tablespoons apple cider vinegar

Directions:

1. *In a large bowl, mix the rice and vegetables.*

2. *Put all the dressing ingredients in a jar and shake well. Pour over salad and mix thoroughly. Refrigerate.*

3. *Before serving, adjust seasoning with ground black pepper and sprinkle over one to two tablespoons of fresh lemon juice. Mix and serve.*

Bulgur Salad

Serves 4

This dish is a variation of tabbouleh. *There are no tomatoes - but you won't miss them! Kalamata olives or Greek olives are preferred, but any variety of black olive can be used.*

Ingredients:

1 cup bottled spring water, boiled
½ cup bulgur wheat
1 medium onion, finely chopped
1 medium carrot, finely chopped
1 medium cucumber, peeled, seeded and diced
½ cup pine nuts
4 large olives, pitted and chopped
½ cup fresh parsley, minced
¼ cup fresh mint, minced
1 medium lemon, juiced
1 tablespoon olive oil
Sea salt and black pepper to taste

Directions:

1. *Place bulgur in a medium bowl. Add boiling water and cover. Let stand 8 minutes or until the water has been absorbed.*

2. *Fluff with a fork and allow to cool. Once cooled, mix in onions, carrots, cucumber, pine nuts, olives, parsley and mint.*

3. *In a small bowl, combine lemon juice and oil. Blend into the bulgur mixture. Season with salt and ground black pepper.*

4. *Allow to chill for at least 2 hours. Serve over lettuce leaves.*

Cabbage Salad

Serves 4 to 6

Ingredients:

1 medium head cabbage, chopped as
   for cole slaw
8 tablespoons slivered almonds
2 tablespoons sesame seeds
8 green onions, chopped
2 packages Top Ramen dry noodles,
   Oriental flavor
2 cooked chicken breasts, cubed (optional)

For dressing:

½ cup apple cider vinegar
½ cup canola oil
⅓ cup water
2 teaspoons salt
2 tablespoons sugar
1 teaspoon Accent

Directions:

1. *Brown almonds and sesame seeds in a pan with a little canola oil. Set aside to cool.*

2. *Mix cabbage and onions in a mixing bowl. Add cooled almonds and sesame seeds.*

3. *Mix dressing ingredients. (You may substitute the Top Ramen flavor packet for the salt, pepper and Accent.)*

4. *When ready to serve, break the Top Ramen dry noodles over the cabbage mixture. Add dressing and toss. Mix in cubed chicken unless a meatless salad is desired.*

Carrot and Celery Salad

Serves 4 to 6

Ingredients:

2 cups shredded carrots
2 cups celery, sliced paper thin
½ cup plain yogurt
2 tablespoons low fat mayonnaise
¼ teaspoon caraway seeds
Sea salt to taste
Black pepper to taste

Directions:

1. *Shred carrots using a food processor or shredder.*

2. *In a bowl, whisk together yogurt, mayonnaise, caraway seeds, salt and pepper. Stir in carrots and celery. Adjust seasoning and serve.*

Carrot and Currant Salad

Serves 4 to 6

Ingredients:

1½ pound carrots, scraped and grated
½ cup dried currants
3 tablespoons fresh lemon juice
4 tablespoons canola or safflower oil
¼ cup fresh mint, chopped
2 tablespoons fresh lemon juice
Black pepper to taste

Directions:

1. Toss carrots in a mixing bowl together with remaining ingredients.

2. Cover and refrigerate for at least 30 minutes to marinate.

Charlton Tuna Salad

Ingredients:

1 can (6 oz.) tuna in water, drained and flaked
½ cup low fat or nonfat plain yogurt
1 teaspoon dried dill weed
1 teaspoon dried mint
¼ teaspoon black pepper
4 lettuce leaves
¼ pound white seedless grapes,
   divided for garnish
2 slices lemon, for garnish

Directions:

1. *In a medium bowl, mix together tuna, yogurt, and herbs. Cover and chill for 1 hour.*

2. *To serve, place on lettuce leaves and garnish with grapes and lemon. Serve with a whole grain roll.*

Chinese Broccoli Salad

Serves 2 to 4

Ingredients:

2 thin slices fresh ginger
2 teaspoons minced fresh ginger
3 cloves garlic—minced
1 teaspoon baking soda
1 pound broccoli florets
3 tablespoons peanut oil
Sea salt and pepper to taste

Directions:

1. *In a large sauce pan, add 8 cups of water, ginger slices, 2 cloves of garlic and baking soda. Bring to a boil and add the broccoli and cook until it turns bright green, about 2 minutes. Drain and rinse under cold running water. Drain well and set aside.*

2. *Mince the remaining clove of garlic. Heat a wok or large skillet over high heat for about 45 to 50 seconds. Add the oil and swirl it around to coat the sides of the wok. Add a pinch of salt, minced ginger and garlic. Stir fry about 30 seconds. Do not let the garlic burn. Add the broccoli and stir fry until crisp and tender, about 1½ to 2 minutes. Transfer to a serving dish. Let cool.*

3. *You can prepare this salad ahead of time. Let cool at room temperature, then refrigerate.*

Helpful Hint

Adding baking soda into the water keeps the broccoli's beautiful green color. Do not overcook the broccoli.

Cold Tuna & Pasta Salad

Serves 4

Ingredients:

1 box, 8 oz. Jerusalem artichoke pasta,
   any small shape
1 can (6 oz.) tuna in water, drained and flaked
¾ cup low fat mayonnaise, or to taste
1 medium red onion, finely chopped
1 stalk celery, finely chopped
Sea salt and black pepper to taste

Directions:

1. *Cook pasta per package directions. Strain and rinse under cold water to stop the cooking. Place in a large bowl.*

2. *Gently blend in flaked tuna, mayonnaise, red onion, celery, sea salt and black pepper. Refrigerate 1 hour.*

3. *Serve on shredded lettuce or on whole wheat bread or pita.*

  Note: For variety, any other permitted vegetable, such as diced carrots and chopped broccoli can be added.

Cold Tuna-Noodle Salad

Serves 4-6

Ingredients:

1 box DeBoles Jerusalem Artichoke Pasta
(any type)
2 tablespoons olive oil
1 can white albacore tuna in water, drained
2 tablespoons low cholesterol mayonnaise
1 medium red onion, diced
2 hard-boiled eggs, cooled and coarsely
chopped
Salt and pepper to taste (optional)
Any permitted vegetable (carrots, broccoli,
celery, etc.) may be diced and added

Directions:

1. Cook pasta as per package directions. Drain pasta and mix
in 2 tablespoons of olive oil. Cool.

2. Add remaining ingredients and mix well. Serve chilled. (You
could also serve it warm - it's delicious either way!)

Cole Slaw

Serves 4 to 6

Ingredients:

1 cabbage (about 2 pounds)
1 carrot, cut into 1" pieces or shredded
¼ cup fresh parsley
½ small onion
½ cup low fat mayonnaise (see Page 191)
½ cup low fat yogurt
Pinch of fructose
2 tablespoons apple cider vinegar
Sea salt and pepper to taste

Directions:

1. *Using a food processor with metal blade in place, add parsley, onion and carrot. Process turning machine on and off until finely minced. Empty into large mixing bowl.*

2. *Insert slicing disk. Cut cabbage into wedges to fit tube. Place wedges into tube and process using light pressure, almost letting cabbage go through by itself. Add to vegetables in mixing bowl. Repeat with remaining cabbage.*

3. *Add the rest of the ingredients to vegetables and mix well. Adjust seasoning and refrigerate.*

Note: You can cut all vegetables by hand using a sharp knife.

Colorful Salad

Serves 4

Ingredients:

1 can hearts of palm, drained and
    cut into 3 slices
1 can, 6 oz., artichoke hearts, drained
¾ cup fresh mushrooms, sliced
Black olives to taste
2 cups grated carrots
Fresh lemon vinaigrette to taste (see page 190)
Leaves of one head of Boston lettuce,
    washed & dried
3 to 4 tablespoons fresh parsley
    or 1 tablespoon dried parsley
Sea salt or pepper to taste

Directions:

1.   *Arrange the lettuce leaves on a large serving dish. Arrange the artichoke hearts, hearts of palm, mushrooms and black olives in an attractive manner around the border of the plate.*

2.   *In the center of the plate, put a mound of grated carrots.*

3.   *Just before serving, pour the vinaigrette over the vegetables. Sprinkle with parsley to garnish and serve.*

Note: You can arrange the vegetables on individual plates if used as a first course.

Cool Cucumber Salad

Serves 4 to 6

Ingredients:

2 English cucumbers or
    3 regular seeded cucumbers peeled,
    cut in half and seeded
Sea salt to taste

Directions:

1. Grate the cucumbers coarsely, add salt and put into a strainer to drain over a bowl. Cover well with heavy foil and refrigerate for a few hours. (It is important to cover it well because some of the foods you have in the refrigerator, especially butter, could get that rather strong cucumber flavor into them.)

2. Before serving, adjust seasoning with salt and serve well-drained cucumbers in a small salad bowl.

Helpful Hint

English cucumbers are also called seedless or gourmet cucumbers and are available in most supermarkets.

Cucumber Salad

Serves 4 to 6

This dish is very good served with grilled or poached salmon.

Ingredients:

2 medium English cucumbers,
   cleaned and sliced thinly
1-1½ cups low fat plain yogurt
2-3 tablespoons fresh dill, finely chopped
1 package scallions, sliced
Sea salt to taste

Directions:

1. *Put cucumber slices into colander to drain for 1 hour. After draining, place cucumber into a bowl, add remaining ingredients and refrigerate for a few hours or overnight.*

2. *Before serving, drain the cucumbers, but reserve the liquid. It makes a lovely low calorie salad dressing.*

Easy Pasta
Primavera Salad

Serves 4 to 6

Ingredients:

1 box, 8 oz., elbow or any small shape
    Jerusalem artichoke pasta
1 package, 16 oz., frozen mixed vegetables
½ cup chopped red or Spanish onions
1 small zucchini
1 cup low fat mayonnaise
1 cup fresh or frozen cooked broccoli florets
2 tablespoons fresh parsley
    or 1 tablespoon dried parsley
Sea salt or pepper to taste

Directions:

1. *Cook pasta according to directions on package and rinse with cold water to stop the cooking process.*

2. *Repeat same procedure with the vegetables, except the zucchini. Cut raw zucchini into bite size chunks.*

3. *Put pasta into a large mixing bowl and add remaining ingredients. Mix well, adjusting seasoning before serving with salt, pepper, and a little fresh lemon juice. Garnish with parsley.*

Helpful Hint

You can find Jerusalem artichoke pasta in speciality supermarkets or health food stores. You can also use spinach pasta, but do not use tomato base pasta.

Fennel Salad

Serves 4 to 6

Ingredients:

2 medium fennel bulbs (approx. 1½ pounds)
6 tablespoons fresh lemon juice
½ cup safflower oil
½ teaspoon sugar
3 tablespoons fresh parsley, finely chopped
Sea salt to taste
Black pepper to taste

Directions:

1. Wash and trim the bottoms from the fennel bulbs. Quarter them lengthwise and cut out any hard core. Slice the quarters crosswise into thin slices and transfer to a mixing bowl. This should yield approximately 3 cups.

2. Toss the fennel with the lemon juice, then add remaining ingredients. Mix well.

3. Chill for about 30 minutes. Adjust seasoning and serve.

Fresh Fruit Salad

Serves 8

Ingredients:

3 tablespoons fresh orange juice
1 tablespoon fresh lemon juice
3 tablespoons peach spread
1 tablespoon fructose
1 cup seedless orange sections
1 cup seedless grapes
1 cup hulled strawberries
1 cup blueberries
2 peaches, sliced
1 cup pears, peeled and sliced
2 kiwis, sliced

Directions:

1. *Combine orange and lemon juices, peach spread and fructose in a large mixing bowl.*

2. *Add the fruit and mix well. Chill until ready to serve.*

Note: For the dressing, I use Sorrel Ridge peach spreadable fruit, sweetened with juice, sold in most supermarkets.

Fresh Spinach & Mushroom Salad

Serves 4 to 6

Ingredients:

8 cups fresh spinach, washed, dried and torn
   into bite-size pieces
⅓ cup fresh mushrooms, sliced
3 to 4 tablespoons Vidalia, Spanish or red onions
5 tablespoons (or to taste) lemon vinaigrette

Directions:

1. Cut off the bottoms of mushroom stems, then wipe off the dirt with a damp cloth or paper towel. Do not soak them to wash, they will get soggy.

2. Combine spinach, mushrooms and onions. Add enough dressing to moisten.

3. Toss and serve.

Garbanzo Bean Salad

Serves 4

Ingredients:

1 can garbanzo beans, drained and rinsed
3 teaspoons olive oil
1 large carrot, sliced
1 stalk celery, sliced
1 medium red onion, thinly sliced
1 cup collard greens, shredded
1½ teaspoons cumin
1 medium lemon, juiced
Sea salt to taste
4 large Romaine lettuce leaves

Directions:

1. *In a medium non-stick sauté pan, add 1 teaspoon olive oil. Sauté carrots, celery and red onion 4-6 minutes or until soft. Mix in drained garbanzo beans and sauté for 5 minutes.*

2. *Stir in collard greens and cook until the leaves are wilted and tender. Remove from heat. Mix in cumin, lemon juice, 2 teaspoons olive oil, and sea salt.*

3. *Chill for 2 hours. To serve, spoon over lettuce leaves and serve with whole grain bread.*

Insalata di Roma

Serves 4 to 5

Ingredients:

8-10 ounces baby spinach leaves
1 cup radicchio, cut into bite-size pieces
1 large carrot, julienne style
1 cup fennel leaves, cut into bite-size pieces

Dressing:

3-4 tablespoons extra virgin olive oil
1 lemon, freshly squeezed

Directions:

1. *Toss all vegetables in a large bowl.*

2. *Mix together olive oil and lemon juice, then pour over salad. Toss, serve, enjoy!*

3. *For variation, you may add a bit of chopped parsley and some slivered almonds.*

Jennifer's Tuna Salad

Serves 2

Ingredients:

2 cans Progresso tuna in olive oil
1 bunch Romaine lettuce
4 carrots
2 onions
1 can unsalted black olives, pitted
4 stalks celery
1 splash apple cider vinegar
Salt and black pepper to taste

Directions:

1. *Wash and cut the Romaine lettuce into bite-size pieces. Peel and slice carrots, onions and celery.*

2. *Place sliced vegetables, tuna (including the oil from the can), olives, salt and pepper into a Tupperware container and seal with the lid. Shake the container until mixture is homogenized.*

3. *Remove mixture from container and spread out on a large, shallow dinner plate. Sprinkle vinegar over the salad.*

   Note: You may sprinkle low-salt low-fat grated cheese on top of the salad if you wish.

Jen's Plain and Simple Salad

Serves 1 to 2

Here is a salad that's quick and easy to prepare, yet it's a powerhouse of nutrition!

Ingredients:

> 1-2 carrots, peeled or scraped
> 5-6 leaves of Romaine lettuce
> 1-2 tablespoons extra virgin olive oil
> Juice of one fresh lemon or lime
> Dash Apple Cider Vinegar
> A few parsley sprigs, chopped

Directions:

1. *Wash lettuce in cold water and dry. Cut or break lettuce leaves into 1" pieces.*

2. *Wash, then peel or scrape carrots. Slice into ½ " rounds. Add carrots to lettuce. Add parsley.*

3. *Toss with olive oil, lemon or lime juice, and apple cider vinegar. Serve.*

Lamb Salad

Serves 6

Ingredients:

3 lamb shanks, trimmed of excess fat
1 onion, coarsely chopped
1 carrot, cut into large chunks
¼ teaspoon cinnamon
Pinch of sea salt and pepper to taste

Dressing:

½ red onion, chopped
½ cup olive oil
½ cup apple cider vinegar
Pepper to taste

Directions:

1. *Rinse shanks in cold water, place into a large pot with cold water to just cover the meat. Bring to a boil, skimming often.*

2. *Add onions, carrots, cinnamon, salt & pepper. Cover and simmer for 1½ to 2 hours or until meat is very tender.*

3. *Remove lamb and place in a plate to cool. When cool enough to handle, remove lamb from bones cutting it into strips.*

4. *In a large bowl, combine lamb with red onions. In a small bowl, whisk together, oil, vinegar, salt & pepper and pour over enough of the dressing to coat salad well. Let set for about ½ hour before serving.*

Leftover Lamb Salad

Ingredients:

2-2½ cups leftover lamb, cut into strips
1 6 oz. jar marinated artichoke hearts
½ cup green beans, cut up
¼ cup red onions, chopped
½ cup black olives, halved
1 tablespoon chopped fresh mint
 or ½ tablespoon dried
¼ teaspoon oregano
Pinch of sea salt and pepper to taste

Dressing:

Reserve artichoke marinade
3 tablespoons olive oil
¼ cup fresh lemon juice

Directions:

1. In a large bowl, combine meat strips, vegetables and herbs, set aside.

2. Combine all dressing ingredients and toss with the meat mixture. Chill before serving. Adjust seasoning to taste.

Mandarin Spinach Salad

Serves 2

Ingredients:

3 cups baby spinach (or cut up regular spinach)
1 cup shredded carrots
1 cup thinly sliced red onions
1 cup mandarin oranges (preferably fresh,
    but well drained canned are fine)
½ cup crumbled feta or blue cheese (optional)
Nanette's Salad dressing, 2 oz. (see page 188)

Directions:

1. Combine all ingredients in an attractive salad bowl.

2. Keep well chilled until just before serving.

3. Add salad dressing and toss to serve.

   Note: You may sprinkle low salt, low fat grated cheese
   on top of the salad if you wish.

Marinated Bean Salad

Serves 6 to 8

Ingredients:

1½ cups green beans, cooked,
  cut into one inch pieces
1½ cups yellow wax beans, cooked,
  cut into 1 inch pieces
1½ cups cooked garbanzo beans, canned
1½ cups cooked red kidney beans, canned
1 cup large red onions, chopped
⅔ cup canola or safflower oil
2 tablespoons olive oil
⅔ cup fresh lemon juice
Pinch sea salt
Black pepper to taste

Directions:

1. Combine all the beans in a mixing bowl.

2. Make vinaigrette by mixing all the remaining ingredients. Then pour vinaigrette over the beans.

3. Toss until everything is thoroughly combined. Cover the bowl and refrigerate for a few hours or overnight.

Marinated Mushroom Salad

Serves 4

Ingredients:

4 tablespoons safflower or canola oil
2 garlic cloves, chopped
1 pound mushrooms, sliced
¼ cup finely chopped red onions
1 teaspoon fresh rosemary
 (or ½ teaspoon dried)
2 tablespoons fresh lemon juice
¼ cup imported black olives, chopped (optional)
1 tablespoon olive oil
Sea salt & black pepper to taste

Directions:

1. *Heat safflower oil in a large skillet, add garlic and sauté for a few seconds. Add mushrooms and sauté over high heat until the liquid they give off has almost evaporated, and the mushrooms begin to brown. Add the onions, and sauté another couple of minutes.*

2. *Stir in the rosemary, lemon juice and olives. Remove from heat. Season to taste. Cool to room temperature. Add the olive oil. Mix well and serve.*

Mesclun with Lemon Vinaigrette

Serves 4 to 6

Ingredients: Salad

¾ pound mesclun
⅓ cup chopped red onions
Sea salt and pepper to taste

Ingredients: Lemon Vinaigrette

1 tablespoon Dijon mustard
5 tablespoons fresh lemon juice
Sea salt and ground black pepper to taste
¾ cup safflower oil
1 garlic clove, peeled

Directions:

1. *Place mustard in a bowl and whisk in the lemon juice. Season with salt and pepper and gradually whisk in the oil until mixture thickens. Put in a jar, add the garlic clove and refrigerate. Will keep for a week. Bring back to room temperature before you use it and remove garlic clove.*

2. *To assemble salad, put the greens in a large bowl, add onions. Toss with some of the vinaigrette just before serving.*

Helpful Hint

Mesclun is the name given to a combination of baby salad greens, made up of different textures and flavors. It can be purchased already mixed from speciality supermarkets or green grocers.

Mixed Vegetable Salad

Serves 6

Ingredients:

1½ cup broccoli florets, cooked
1½ cup carrots, cut into bite-size pieces
1½ cup zucchini, cut into bite-size pieces
½ cup chopped red onions
Sea salt and pepper to taste
Low fat mayonnaise
2 or 3 tablespoons fresh lemon juice

Directions:

1. Bring a large quantity of salted water to a vigorous boil, add carrots and cook until tender, but not soft. Remove with a slotted spoon, plunging the carrots into cold water to stop their cooking process. Drain well and cool.

2. Add broccoli florets to the same boiling water and repeat same procedure as above.

3. Put broccoli, carrots and raw zucchini chunks and onions together and toss lightly. Add mayonnaise to taste and correct seasoning.

4. Just before serving, add fresh lemon juice and mix lightly.

Note: Fresh vegetables are preferred, but you can use frozen broccoli and/or carrots, cooked as directed on their packages. But do not use a lemon juice substitute, nothing has true lemon flavor but real lemons.

Oriental Chicken Salad

Serves 6 to 8

Ingredients:

1 pound grilled chicken breast, in chunks
2½ cups broccoli florets, steamed crisp
1 cup fresh mushrooms, sliced
1 cup snow pea pods, cleaned
½ cup scallions, chopped

Dressing:

¼ cup olive oil
2 teaspoons sesame oil
1 tablespoon fresh lemon juice
1 tablespoon fresh dill, chopped
3-4 garlic cloves, minced
½ teaspoon salt
½ teaspoon pepper

Directions:

1. *For dressing: mix all ingredients in a bowl until well blended. Set aside.*

2. *In a large bowl, mix together steamed broccoli, sliced mushrooms, snow pea pods and chopped scallions. Add dressing, then chill for a couple of hours.*

3. *Just before eating, add grilled chicken chunks, toss and serve.*

Pasta Salad with Chicken and Garlic

Serves 4

Ingredients:

15-20 cloves garlic, peeled
¾ cup extra virgin olive oil
5-10 fresh rosemary sprigs
¼ cup basil
½ pound cooked pasta
2 cups cooked chicken breast, cut in strips
3-4 scallions, finely chopped
½ cup grated Parmesan
Sea salt and black pepper to taste
Romaine Lettuce

Directions:

1. *In a saucepan, heat 1 tablespoon olive oil, add garlic and half of the rosemary. Sauté for 5-10 minutes, then cook covered over medium heat for another 10 minutes until garlic is tender. Remove rosemary and discard.*

2. *Purée garlic with remainder of olive oil and rest of rosemary.*

3. *Toss pasta, chicken, scallions, Parmesan and spices with the garlic purée. Refrigerate several hours or overnight. Serve on a bed of romaine lettuce.*

Pasta Salad with Olives & Artichokes

Serves 4 to 6

Ingredients: Salad

1 box, 8 oz., pasta shells Jerusalem
   artichoke pasta
2 6 oz., jars marinated artichokes, reserve liquid
¾ cup black small olives
¾ cup low fat mozzarella cheese
   cut into ½" pieces
1 package fresh arugula
Sea salt and pepper to taste

Ingredients: Dressing

Mix together:
½ cup of the reserved artichoke marinade
3 tablespoons lemon juice
½ tablespoon oregano

Directions:

1. Cook pasta according to directions on package and rinse with cold water to stop the cooking process. Drain well.

2. Drain artichokes and reserve liquid.

Directions continued on the following page

Pasta Salad with Olives & Artichokes
Directions continued:

3.   Wash and dry arugula by putting the leaves in between paper towels to dry. Remove any heavy stems. Tear leaves into bite-size pieces.

4.   Put pasta into a large mixing bowl and add artichokes, olives, cheese, arugula, salt and pepper. Mix together. Add dressing. Toss well. Taste and adjust seasoning by adding more oregano, lemon juice and artichoke marinade, if there is any left. Refrigerate for a few hours.

Helpful Hint

You can find Jerusalem artichoke pasta in specialty super markets or health food stores. You can also use spinach pasta, but do not use tomato base pasta.

Pineapple & Sweet Potato Salad

Serves 6 to 8

This is a wonderful salad or side dish during the holidays or any time. It has a very refreshing, pleasing flavor.

Ingredients: Salad

3 pounds sweet potatoes,
   peeled and cut into large chunks
4 stalks celery, sliced thin
¾ cup sliced almonds, toasted (optional)
1 cup raisins
1 can (20 oz.) crushed pineapple in
   unsweetened juice well drained, reserve juice

Ingredients: Dressing

⅔ cup low fat mayonnaise
1 tablespoon lemon juice
1½ cup, well drained, low fat yogurt
Grated rind of 1 orange
4 tablespoons chopped crystallized ginger
2 tablespoons orange juice
2 tablespoons of the reserved pineapple juice
   or to taste

Directions continued on the following page

Pineapple & Sweet Potato Salad Directions:

1. Place yogurt in a colander lined with a cheese cloth over a bowl and leave to drain in the refrigerator for a few hours.

2. Cook potatoes in salted boiling water for about 10 minutes, until they are just tender. DO NOT OVERCOOK. Put in a large bowl of cold water to stop the cooking process, drain and cool in the refrigerator for a few hours, if possible.

3. Stir together the dressing ingredients.

4. Mix cooled sweet potatoes lightly with celery, almonds, raisins and pineapple. Add the dressing and toss carefully so you don't mash the potatoes.

Helpful Hint

You can purchase crystallized ginger in a Chinese supply store or specialty supermarkets. For this recipe you can chop the ginger finer if you like.

Princess Salad
(Green Beans & Lettuce)

Serves 4 to 6

Ingredients:

½ pound string beans, cut into 1½" length
2 heads Boston lettuce
3 tablespoons scallions, finely sliced,
   including 1" of the green tops
1 tablespoons red onion, finely chopped
¼ teaspoon dried tarragon
½ cup safflower oil
4 tablespoons fresh lemon juice
Sea salt, to taste
Ground black pepper, to taste

Directions:

1. *Drop string beans into enough boiling salted water to cover. Boil until tender but still crisp, about 5-6 minutes. Drain in sieve and run cold water over them to cool. Spread on paper towel to dry. Refrigerate until ready to serve.*

2. *Combine lemon juice, tarragon, salt & pepper. Mix well with whisk. Whisking constantly, pour the oil in a slow stream until the dressing is smooth.*

3. *Shred the lettuce and put into a salad bowl, then add the beans, scallions, and red onions. Pour dressing over to taste and toss well. Serve at once.*

Red Onion &
Cucumber Salad

Serves 4

Ingredients:

1 English cucumber* peeled and diced
¼ cup red onions, chopped
3 tablespoons lemon juice
1 tablespoon olive oil
Pinch dry tarragon or dill
Sea salt and black pepper - to taste
Boston lettuce leaves - to garnish plate

Directions:

1. Combine cucumbers with onions.

2. Mix lemon juice, oil, tarragon or dill, salt and pepper.

3. Pour over cucumber mixture and mix well. Chill.

4. Just before serving, line salad plate with lettuce leaves. Top with cucumber salad and serve.

*Helpful Hint

English cucumbers are also called seedless or gourmet cucumbers and are available in most supermarkets.

Romaine Anchovies Salad

Serves 2

Ingredients:

2-3 hearts of Romaine lettuce, broken
Cold natural spring water
2 tablespoons apple cider vinegar
½ tablespoon Italian seasoning
1 teaspoon black pepper
1 teaspoon garlic salt
1 teaspoon onion powder
1 teaspoon minced garlic
2 tablespoons onions, finely chopped
3-4 tablespoons extra virgin olive oil
2-3 tablespoons lemon juice
10 unsalted fillets of anchovies

Directions:

1. *Wash lettuce 3 times, then soak it for 10-20 minutes with cold natural spring water and 2 tablespoons apple cider vinegar. Drain water out.*

2. *Toss salad with Italian seasoning, black pepper, garlic salt and onion powder.*

3. *Add garlic and onions, pour in olive oil and lemon juice.*

4. *Toss well, then add the anchovies.*

Romaine & Endive Salad with Scallion Dressing

Serves 4 to 6

Ingredients:

6 cups sliced Romaine, washed
2 Belgium endives, trimmed and sliced
3 tablespoon fresh lemon juice
⅓ cup safflower oil
¼ cup sliced scallions,
    including some of the green part
Sea salt and black pepper to taste

Directions:

1. Wash greens well. After washing, if you want crisp, cold salad leaves, arrange them in a single layer on a clean, damp kitchen towel. Gently roll up the towel and refrigerate for at least one hour.

2. In a blender or food processor, purée the scallions with the lemon juice, oil, salt and pepper until the dressing is emulsified.

3. Pour dressing over the greens, tossing them well.

Romaine Salad with Creamy Lime Dressing

Serves 6

Ingredients:

3 heads of Romaine, using inner pale green
   leaves, washed, spun dry
1 large clove of garlic, minced and mashed
   with ½ teaspoon sea salt
½ teaspoon Dijon mustard
1½ tablespoons fresh lime juice
2 tablespoons low fat mayonnaise
⅓ cup safflower oil
1-2 tablespoons water
Sea salt and pepper to taste

Directions:

1. *Tear Romaine into bite size pieces. You should have about 10 cups. Set aside.*

2. *In a blender or small food processor, blend the garlic, the remaining ingredients, except oil and water. With the motor running, add the oil in a steady stream. Blend until mixture is emulsified. Add enough of the water to thin the dressing to the desired consistency.*

3. *Toss the Romaine with the dressing in a large bowl and serve.*

Helpful Hint

Note: You can use a whisk to do the dressing, whisking all the ingredients except the oil. Then add the oil gradually, whisking constantly.

Salmon Pasta Salad

Serves 4 to 6

Ingredients:

2 salmon steaks
2 cups cooked Jerusalem Artichoke macaroni
4 carrots, diced into ¼" cubes
4 celery stalks, diced into ¼" cubes
1 small onion, chopped
2-3 tablespoons extra virgin olive oil
1 tablespoon lemon juice
1 teaspoon apple cider vinegar
1½ teaspoon crushed black pepper
1½ teaspoon Italian seasoning
1½ teaspoon garlic powder
1½ teaspoon onion powder

Directions:

1. Boil macaroni until al dente, drain and set aside.

2. Sprinkle salmon with ½ teaspoon each of crushed black pepper, Italian seasoning, garlic powder and onion powder. Broil for 20 minutes until done, flake it and set it aside.

3. Mix carrots, celery, onions with ½ teaspoon each of crushed black pepper, Italian seasoning, garlic powder and onion powder. Broil for 10 minutes. Watch closely–they have to be crunchy!

4. Mix and toss the pasta and vegetables with ½ teaspoon each of crushed black pepper, Italian seasoning, garlic powder and onion powder. Toss in olive oil, lemon juice and apple cider vinegar. Lastly mix in the flaked salmon.

Sliced Chicken and Romaine Salad

Serves 4 to 6

Ingredients:

2 whole skinless, boneless chicken breast halves
4 cups no fat, low sodium, chicken broth
5 to 6 cups Romaine lettuce,
   torn into bite-size pieces
1 small cucumber, cut into bite-size pieces
¼ cup chopped celery
¼ cup chopped red onions
¼ cup black or green olives
½ teaspoon dried mint leaves

Dressing:

½ cup fresh lemon juice
1 tablespoon canola oil
½ teaspoon French's mustard
Dash of sea salt & pepper

Directions:

1. *In a deep skillet, bring broth to a boil, add chicken and simmer, turning once, until cooked through. Let cool in cooking liquid.*

2. *Combine dressing ingredients in a covered jar and shake well. Transfer chicken onto a cutting board and cut into ½" pieces.*

3. *Place lettuce together with remaining salad ingredients in a large salad bowl, add chicken and mix. Spoon enough dressing over all to coat salad and toss again.*

String Bean Salad

Serves 4 to 6

Ingredients:

1 pound green beans
½ medium red onion, finely chopped
1 small garlic clove, minced
5 tablespoons safflower oil
3 tablespoons fresh lemon juice
Sea salt to taste
Ground black pepper
Pinch of dry tarragon
1 tablespoon low fat parmesan cheese
    to garnish (optional)

Directions:

1. Wash the beans, snip off the ends.

2. Drop them into boiling salted water and cook until just tender. Drain and pour cold water over them to stop cooking.

3. Mix the rest of the ingredients (except the cheese) and pour over the beans. Toss until everything is thoroughly combined. Chill and serve.

4. If using the cheese, sprinkle over salad before serving.

Sweet Potato Salad

Serves 4 to 6

Ingredients:

2 sweet potatoes
½ cup fresh orange juice
3 teaspoons fresh lemon juice
2 tablespoons honey
1½ tablespoons crystallized chopped ginger
2 tablespoons sliced almonds

Directions:

1. Peel sweet potatoes and cut in half. Steam or boil until tender but firm. Rinse with cold water to stop the cooking process. Let cool, then slice and set on a serving plate.

2. Put the orange and lemon juices and the honey in a small pan, bring to a boil. Remove from heat and cool, slightly. Pour over sliced sweet potatoes.

3. Chop ginger a little finer than it is and sprinkle over potatoes. Cover and refrigerate. Before serving, sprinkle sliced almonds over the potatoes.

Helpful Hint

You can purchase crystallized ginger in a Chinese supply store or specialty supermarkets.

Toasted Bagel Salad

Serves 2

Ingredients:

2 oatmeal, rye or whole wheat bagels
4 cups Romaine lettuce, shredded
6 pieces deli-sliced oven roasted turkey breast,
   shredded
2 tablespoons extra virgin olive oil
½ teaspoon Italian seasoning
½ teaspoon crushed black pepper
½ teaspoon garlic powder
½ teaspoon onion powder
1 tablespoon fresh parsley, chopped
1 tablespoon onions, finely chopped
1 tablespoon lemon juice

Directions:

1. Toss lettuce, turkey, all the seasonings, parsley and onions. Add olive oil and lemon juice.

2. Slice bagels in half, scrape out all the soft inside part. Toast, then place salad in hollowed bagels. Serve.

Tofu, Spinach and Tuna Salad

Serves 4

Ingredients:

2 bags (or 2 bunches) fresh spinach, washed
1 package Silken Tofu cut into medium cubes
Homemade Fresh Tuna, drained and flaked
  (see recipe on page 220)
2-3 tablespoons extra virgin olive oil
1 teaspoon lemon-pepper powder
1 teaspoon Italian seasoning

Directions:

1. Boil water in a saucepan. When water is boiling, place spinach in a steamer basket over boiling water. (The spinach should be above the level of the water.) Steam spinach for 2-3 minutes. Drain and set aside.

2. Steam tofu for 2-3 minutes the same way you steamed the spinach. Drain and set aside.

3. Toss the spinach and the tuna (using the entire Homemade Fresh Tuna recipe) with the olive oil, lemon-pepper powder and the Italian seasoning.

4. Place tofu in a serving bowl and pour tuna-spinach mixture over it. Serve.

Turkey Salad with Peach Yogurt Dressing

Serves 4

Ingredients:

3 cups cut up, cooked turkey breast
¾ cup seedless grapes
½ cup chopped red onion
1 red apple, cored and diced, but not peeled

Dressing:

1 cup no fat plain yogurt
2 tablespoons peach spread
1½ tablespoons low sodium soy sauce
2 tablespoons orange juice

Directions:

1. Combine all salad ingredients in a large bowl.

2. In a small bowl, place 2 tablespoons of yogurt and the peach spread and mix well with a fork. Add remaining yogurt, orange juice, soy sauce and mix with a fork to blend well.

3. Add dressing to salad and toss.

   Note: For the dressing, I use Sorrel Ridge peach spreadable fruit, sweetened with juice, sold in most supermarkets.

Vegetarian Wild Rice Salad

Serves 6

Ingredients:

⅔ cup wild rice, raw
¼ pound fresh sliced mushrooms
¼ cup parsley, chopped
¼ cup scallions, chopped
¼ teaspoon dried rosemary
1 tablespoon apple cider vinegar
2 tablespoons olive oil
4 ounces solid tofu, cut in bite-size
    pieces (optional)

Directions:

1. Cook rice according to package directions. Cool.

2. In a large bowl, gently toss all remaining ingredients. Mix in with cooked, cooled rice. Chill and serve.

Warm Burmese-Style Vegetable Salad

Serves 2

This exotic vegetable dish has a flavor typical of Burmese dishes. The vegetables in this recipe are filled with valuable vitamins and minerals.

Ingredients:

1 large carrot, sliced
½ pound butternut squash, peeled and diced
½ cup bottled spring water
½ cup broccoli florets
2 stalks celery, sliced
4 cups kale, shredded
1 teaspoon olive oil
1 medium onion, chopped
2 cloves garlic, minced
½ teaspoon turmeric
1 medium lemon, juiced
1 tablespoon sesame seeds, toasted

Directions:

1. *Boil water in a large saucepan with a tight-fitting lid. Add carrots and squash. Cover and steam for 12 minutes.*

2. *Add broccoli and celery. Steam covered another 4 minutes or until all the vegetables are tender. Add kale and steam covered until wilted and tender. Place in a large glass bowl, set aside.*

3. *In a medium non-stick sauté pan, heat olive oil and sauté onions and garlic until soft, about 2-4 minutes. Add the mixed vegetables to the pan and mix in turmeric and lemon juice.*

4. *Before serving, sprinkle with sesame seeds and gently toss. Serve with brown rice.*

Yogurt & Cucumber Salad

Serves 4 to 6

This makes a delicious sauce over grilled salmon or any fish.

Ingredients:

2½ cups low fat yogurt
2 long, seedless English cucumbers
[or 3 regular seeded cucumbers] peeled,
halved lengthwise and thinly sliced
2 cloves garlic, crushed
2-3 teaspoon dried mint
Sea salt to taste
Mint sprigs to garnish (optional)

Directions:

1. *Drain yogurt in a sieve lined with cheese cloth, over a bowl to collect liquid, for one hour. Discard liquid.*

2. *Place cucumber slices in a bowl and salt them. Let stand for one hour. Then drain well in a colander.*

3. *Mix cucumber with drained yogurt, add garlic and mint. Add salt to taste. Garnish with mint leaves.*

Helpful Hint

English cucumbers are also called seedless or gourmet cucumbers and are available in most supermarkets.

Dressings, Sauces, Spreads

⌐   Indicates recipe created by Monique Hill

Apple "Ciderette" Dressing

Serves: 4 to 6

Ingredients:

¼ cup apple cider vinegar
2½ tablespoons olive oil
2½ teaspoons dried mixed herbs (mild)
2 large garlic cloves, minced
¼ teaspoon sea salt
Dash black pepper

Directions:

In a glass bottle with a tight-fitting lid, add all ingredients together and shake well. (Shake well before each use.)

Very Easy and Tasty Dressing

Makes 1 cup

Ingredients:

½ cup lemon juice
¼ cup honey
4 tablespoons safflower oil

Directions:

Stir everything together thoroughly with a whisk or fork in order to mix the honey well into the other ingredients.

Cucumber Dill Dressing

Serves 8

Ingredients:

1 medium cucumber, peeled, seeded and
   chopped
1 cup plain lowfat yogurt
1 tablespoon olive oil
1 teaspoon fresh lemon juice
¼ teaspoon sea salt
1 large garlic clove, minced
1 tablespoon fresh dill (or 1½ teaspoons dry dill)

Directions:

Place all ingredients in a blender and pulse until smooth. Refrigerate for 2 hours before serving. Use as a dressing for salads, or try it with any fish, especially salmon!

Nanette's Salad Dressing

Makes 8 ounces

Ingredients:

4 oz. olive oil
4 oz. lemon juice or apple cider vinegar
1- 2 cloves garlic, finely chopped
½ teaspoon oregano
Salt and pepper to taste

Directions:

Place olive oil and lemon juice (or apple cider vinegar) in an eight ounce jar with a lid. Add all ingredients. Shake before each use.

Peach Yogurt Dressing

Serves 4

Ingredients:

1 cup no fat plain yogurt
2 tablespoons peach spread
1½ tablespoons low sodium soy sauce
2 tablespoons orange juice

Directions

In a small bowl, place 2 tablespoons of yogurt and the peach spread and mix well with a fork. Add remaining yogurt, orange juice, soy sauce and mix with a fork to blend well.

Note: For this recipe you may use Sorrel Ridge peach spreadable fruit, sweetened with juice, which is sold in most supermarkets.

Pineapple-Lemon-Mint Dressing

Makes 1 cup

Ingredients:

¾ cup vegetable or salad oil
¼ cup unsweetened pineapple juice
½ teaspoon lemon peel
2 tablespoons lemon juice
1 teaspoon dried mint, crumbled
¼ teaspoon salt

Directions:

Combine all ingredients in a large screw-top jar. Cover and shake thoroughly. Refrigerate until ready to use.

Yogurt Honey Dressing

Makes 1 cup

Ingredients:

1 cup low fat yogurt
1 tablespoon lemon juice
2 teaspoons honey

Directions:

Stir everything together thoroughly with a whisk or fork in order to mix the honey well into the other ingredients.

Helpful Hint

This is a lovely dressing to use with fruit. It could also be served as a cream with fresh fruit for dessert.

Lemon Vinaigrette I

Ingredients:

6 tablespoons fresh lemon juice
3 tablespoons safflower oil
1/4 teaspoon sea salt
1/3 teaspoon black pepper
1 clove garlic, peeled and cut in half

Directions:

Combine ingredients in a covered jar, shake well, and refrigerate. Take out of refrigerator 10-15 minutes before using and remove garlic. [This will keep in the refrigerator for five or six days.]

Lemon Vinaigrette II

Ingredients:

1 tablespoon Dijon mustard
5 tablespoons fresh lemon juice
Sea salt and ground black pepper to taste
¾ cup safflower oil
1 garlic clove, peeled

Directions:

Place mustard in a bowl and whisk in the lemon juice. Season with salt and pepper and gradually whisk in the oil until mixture thickens. Put in a jar, add the garlic clove and refrigerate. Serve at room temperature, removing garlic clove before use. Will keep in refrigerator for a week.

Low Fat Mayonnaise

Ingredients:

1 cup Hellman's low fat mayonnaise dressing
2 tablespoons fresh lemon juice
1 teaspoon Dijon mustard
1 clove garlic, crushed (optional)
2 tablespoons fresh parsley, chopped
½ teaspoon dry tarragon leaves
1 tablespoon fresh or frozen chives

Directions:

Mix all ingredients well and refrigerate. Serve. For variation add: 1 tablespoon capers, 1 teaspoon green relish, 1 tablespoon shallots, chopped fine. Mix with mayonnaise above and serve with any kind of poached or grilled fish.

Lime Dill Sauce

Ingredients:

¼ cup fresh dill, chopped
3 tablespoons scallions, chopped
3 tablespoons fresh lime juice
1 tablespoon hot honey mustard
½ teaspoon salt
¼ teaspoon freshly ground pepper
2-4 tablespoons olive oil

Directions:

In a blender or food processor, combine dill, scallions, lime juice, mustard, salt, pepper and oil. For a chunkier sauce, process liquid ingredients first, then add chopped scallions and dill.

Tartare Sauce

Ingredients:

1 cup fat-free mayonnaise
2 tablespoons fresh or frozen sliced chives
1 tablespoon fresh chopped parsley
1 tablespoon capers
3 tablespoons fresh lemon juice
¼ teaspoon tarragon
1 hard-boiled egg, finely chopped
1 teaspoon Dijon mustard
1 teaspoon minced shallots -or- red onions

Directions:

Combine all ingredients and refrigerate.

Pesto Sauce

Makes about 1½ cups

Ingredients:

2 cups packed fresh basil leaves, washed and
well drained
¾ cup freshly grated low-fat Parmesan cheese
½ cup olive oil
2 garlic cloves
A few parsley sprigs (optional)
Roasted pignoli or almonds (optional)

Directions:

*Put basil (and parsley, if using) in a blender, add cheese, oil
and garlic. Blend until a coarse purée is formed. Use at once,
or cover and refrigerate up to a week. You may freeze it in
small portions. The surface will darken when exposed to air,
so stir the pesto before using.*

Helpful Hint

*Pesto sauce is not only delicious on pasta, but
also over fish dishes such as swordfish, halibut, salmon, etc.*

Vegetable Dip

Ingredients:

2 cups low fat cottage cheese
¼ cup low fat yogurt
¼ cup carrots, finely minced
¼ cup scallions, thinly sliced
5 radishes, finely minced
1 clove garlic, finely minced (use garlic press)
2 tablespoons parsley, minced

Directions:

Process cottage cheese and yogurt in a food processor or beat until smooth. Add the remaining ingredients. Refrigerate until ready to use.

Chick Pea Dip or Spread

Ingredients:

1 can chick peas
Juice of one lemon
½ teaspoon salt
1 scallion, chopped
16 oz. lowfat cottage cheese

Directions:

Drain and wash chick peas, then purée in blender or food processor. Add remaining ingredients and purée until smooth. Refrigerate several hours before using.

Tofu Spread

Ingredients:

8 ounces tofu, pressed and mashed
1 clove garlic, minced
⅓ cup celery, chopped
½ cup alfalfa sprouts
3 tablespoons fresh dill, minced
3 tablespoons fresh parsley, minced
1 teaspoon any dried herb
Few drops olive oil
Juice of ½ a lemon or lime
1 teaspoon wheat-free, low sodium tamari
   (optional)
¼ cup sesame seeds (optional)

Directions:

Combine all ingredients in a bowl. Chill for a few hours to improve flavor. Serve on rice cakes, or in a pita bread sandwich.

Fish, Fowl, Lamb

Fish, Fowl, Lamb

Fish

⌐⊐   Indicates recipe created by Monique Hill

Angel Hair Pasta with Homemade Fresh Tuna

Serves 6

Ingredients:

1 box Jerusalem Artichoke angel hair pasta
2 tablespoons garlic, minced
4 tablespoons onions, finely chopped
4 tablespoons parsley, finely chopped
½ teaspoon Italian seasoning
½ teaspoon lemon-pepper powder
½ teaspoon garlic powder
½ teaspoon onion powder
Homemade Fresh Tuna, drained and flaked
(see recipe on page 220)

Directions:

1. Boil pasta for two or more minutes until al dente, drain and set aside.

2. Place olive oil in skillet on medium heat, add garlic and onions, sauté until golden brown.

3. Mix the entire amount of Homemade Fresh Tuna recipe with the parsley, and all other seasonings.

4. Remove from heat and toss the cooked pasta into the mixture.

Baked Fish à la Dee

Serves 4

This preparation is ideal for many different types of fish.

Ingredients:

1¾ pounds fish
4 tablespoons olive oil
2 carrots, shredded
½ yellow onion, chopped
2 celery stalks, diced
1 tablespoon basil, dry
3-4 parsley sprigs, chopped
4 cloves garlic, chopped
2 lemons, squeezed for juice
½ cup dry white wine (you may add ½ cup
    water with wine for more sauce)
Salt and black pepper to taste

Directions:

1. *Wash fish, pat dry with paper towel and cut into 4 equal portions. Using a pastry brush, coat shallow roasting pan or oven wear dish with olive oil. Place fish in pan and coat lightly with olive oil, using pastry brush. Pour juice of two lemons over the fish. Then, sprinkle fish with the chopped garlic. Add salt and pepper and set preparation aside.*

Directions continued on the following page

Baked Fish à la Dee Directions continued:

2. In a teflon pan, add remaining oil, garlic and basil and sauté for 3-4 minutes with celery, carrots and onions. Add wine, cook for 1½ min. (to burn off alcohol). Remove from heat.

3. Spoon vegetables and liquid on top of fish and place slice of lemon on each portion. Place preparation in a preheated 350° oven for 25 minutes or until fish is tender.

Helpful Hint

Add the following to make it better:

Flounder: Sliced zucchini rounds and bread crumbs

Sole: Asparagus tips with chopped hard-boiled eggs

Scrod: Cut string beans and one slice lowfat cheese

Salmon: * Fresh dill (instead of the basil); bake on a bed of fresh spinach (cooked)

Haddock: Petite peas

Red Snapper: Garnish with warm, bite-sized, small prunes

Mahi-Mahi: * Seedless grapes and sliced almonds

Tuna: * Bake on top of boiled sliced sweet potatoes

Swordfish: * Yellow squash

Grouper: Fresh pineapple chunks or canned pineapple chunks in their own juice

*May be necessary to cook longer than time called for in key recipe.

Baked Flounder

Ingredients:

1½ pounds flounder fillets
1 teaspoon dried tarragon
3 tablespoons minced fresh parsley
1 teaspoon dried garlic flakes
3 tablespoons fresh lemon juice
Pepper to taste
1 tablespoon olive oil

Directions:

1. Preheat oven to 400.°

2. Rub the inside of a 2-quart rectangular baking dish with the oil. Place the fish fillets in dish, turning under the thin edges to make an even thickness. Sprinkle with herbs and pepper.

3. Bake until fish flakes easily with a fork, about 6-10 minutes. With a spatula, transfer fish fillets to serving platter and drizzle with lemon juice.

Baked Fish Steaks

Serves 4

Ingredients:

4 fish steaks (salmon, halibut, etc.)
¼ cup unbleached flour
1 egg white
¼ cup whole wheat bread crumbs
¼ teaspoon Italian seasoning
½ teaspoon basil

Directions:

1. Preheat oven to 400.°

2. Beat egg white until frothy. Mix bread crumbs with herbs. Dip only one side of each steak into flour (shaking off any excess), then dip into egg white, and then into bread crumb mixture.

3. Place steaks into an oiled shallow baking pan, coating side up. Bake for 10-15 minutes or until cooked through.

4. Serve with tartar sauce.

Baked Flounder Fillets with Vegetables

Serves 4

Ingredients:

4 fillets of flounder, about ¾ pound each
2 tablespoons olive oil
1 small fennel bulb, cut into fine 2" long strips
2 leeks, white part only, cleaned
   and cut into fine 2" long strips
1 carrot, cut into fine 2" long strips
1 zucchini, cut into fine 2" long strips
1 garlic clove, finely minced
¼ teaspoon tarragon
Dash sea salt and pepper to taste
4 tablespoons fresh lemon juice

Directions:

1. Preheat oven to 400.°

2. Cut 4 large sheets of heavy duty aluminum foil large enough to accommodate the fish.

3. Heat olive oil in a large skillet and sauté the vegetables and garlic for 5 minutes, stirring often. Add tarragon and cook a few minutes more to soften vegetables. Season with pepper.

4. Spread vegetables evenly over the 4 fish fillets. Sprinkle 1 tablespoon lemon juice over each fish. Enclose fish in the foil and crimp the edges together well. Place the foil package of fish on a baking sheet and bake for 20 minutes or until fish is cooked through.

Baked Flounder Florentine

Serves 4 to 6

Ingredients:

2 pounds flounder fillet (small ones if possible)
2 10 oz. packages frozen chopped spinach
1 teaspoon onion, finely chopped
Pinch of sea salt and pepper

Sauce:

2 tablespoons butter
2 tablespoons corn oil
¼ cup unbleached, all-purpose flour
2 cups lowfat milk
3 tablespoons grated lowfat Swiss cheese
3 tablespoons grated lowfat Parmesan cheese

Directions:

1. Preheat oven to 400°

2. Cook spinach per package directions. Drain well, add onions, salt and pepper. Mix well.

3. Oil a shallow Pyrex dish (about 12 x 7 x 1½). Wash and dry the fillets well with paper towel. Lay half of the flounder fillets into the dish, sprinkle with a little salt and pepper. Cover with the spinach mixture and place remaining fillets on top of the spinach.

4. To make the sauce: Melt butter and oil, add flour and stir for a few minutes on low heat, add milk all at once, whisking constantly over medium heat until sauce comes to a boil.

5. Cook sauce for 2-3 minutes stirring constantly. Fold in Swiss cheese. Pour over fish. Sprinkle with Parmesan.

6. Bake for 20-25 minutes. Let rest 5 minutes before serving.

Baked Haddock Fillets

Serves 4

Ingredients:

4 pieces of haddock fillet, about 6 oz. each
¼ cup dry white wine
   or 2 tablespoons lemon juice
½ teaspoon butter
1 large shallot, minced
   or 1 tablespoon red onions, minced
1 cup water
2 tablespoons fresh parsley, chopped
½ teaspoon Italian seasoning
⅛ teaspoon lemon pepper

Directions:

1. Preheat oven to 400.°

2. Place haddock pieces into a shallow baking dish just large enough to hold fillets in one layer. Add wine, shallots, water and butter. Sprinkle herbs over fish and liquid.

3. Bake for 10-15 minutes depending upon thickness of fillets, or until cooked through. Serve fish with some of its tasty cooking liquid.

Baked Rainbow Trout

Serves 2

Ingredients:

2 whole rainbow trout, gutted, heads on
1 cup chopped onions
1 cup chopped parsley
1 teaspoon crushed black pepper
1 teaspoon garlic powder
1 teaspoon Italian seasoning
1 teaspoon garlic powder
2 tablespoons extra virgin olive oil
Dash of salt

Directions:

1. Thoroughly wash trout, then stuff with parsley and onions.

2. Sprinkle all the spices all over the fish on both sides.

3. Bake trout in the oven in a covered dish at 375° for 30 to 45 minutes, until done.

4. Remove baked trout to a serving dish and pour olive oil over both sides.

Baked Salmon Steak

Serves 2

Ingredients:

2 salmon steaks
1 tablespoon garlic powder
1 tablespoon onion powder
1 tablespoon crushed black pepper
1 tablespoon Italian seasoning
2 tablespoons extra virgin olive oil

Directions:

1. *Preheat oven to 375.°*

2. *Wash salmon well and drain. Sprinkle both sides with all the spices. Place in covered baking dish and bake 20-30 minutes, until done.*

3. *Drizzle olive oil over each steak before serving.*

Broiled Bluefish Fillets

Serves 4

Ingredients:

2 pounds bluefish fillets
2 tablespoons olive oil
4 tablespoons fresh lemon juice
Pepper to taste
3 tablespoons fresh parsley

Directions:

1. Spray the rack of a broiler pan with nonstick spray coating. Brush fish with olive oil and place on rack, skin side down. Broil slowly on one side only until cooked through, about 12-15 minutes.

2. To serve, drizzle with lemon juice and garnish with parsley.

Broiled Flounder Fillets

Serves 4

Ingredients:

6 flounder fillets
White pepper to taste
1 tablespoon corn oil
2 tablespoons lowfat mayonnaise
1 tablespoon Dijon mustard
1 teaspoon fresh lemon juice
¼ teaspoon dried parsley flakes
4 lemon wedges

Directions:

1. Preheat broiler to "High."

2. Place washed and dried fillets on a flat surface. Sprinkle with pepper and brush with oil.

3. Blend mayonnaise, mustard, juice and parsley. Brush evenly over fish.

4. Place under the broiler, about 3-4 inches from the source of heat. Broil 4-5 minutes or until golden brown and fish is just cooked through. Serve with lemon wedges.

Broiled Halibut or Salmon Steaks with Dill Sauce

Serves 4

Ingredients:

4 halibut or salmon steaks
Olive oil

Sauce:

2 teaspoons olive oil
2 tablespoons red onions, finely chopped
1 garlic clove, minced
1 cup fat-free, low sodium chicken broth
½ cup nonfat yogurt
2 tablespoons unbleached flour
1 tablespoon fresh parsley, minced
1 teaspoon dried dill
Lemon wedges

Directions:

1. *In a small bowl, mix together yogurt and flour, add broth and mix well.*

2. *In a small saucepan cook together onions and garlic in olive oil, on low heat until tender (about 3 minutes), stirring often. Add the yogurt mixture all at once, whisking constantly over medium heat until thickened. Stir in parsley and dill.*

3. *Spray the unheated rack of a broiler pan with non-stick spray coating. Place steaks on rack. Lightly brush with oil. Broil 4" from heat about 4-6 minutes on each side, or until cooked through.*

4. *Serve with sauce and lemon wedges.*

Broiled Salmon Fillet with Cucumber Sauce

Serves 4

Ingredients:

4 salmon fillets, about 6 oz. each
Balsamic vinegar

Sauce:

1 cup nonfat yogurt
1½ tablespoons green onions,
   including tops, sliced
½ cup cucumbers, seeded and grated
1 tablespoon fresh lemon juice
·¼ teaspoon dill
Pinch sea salt

Directions:

1. Whisk sauce ingredients together in a small bowl. Refrigerate. (Could be made a few hours earlier.)

2. Line a jelly roll pan with heavy foil. Rinse salmon and pat dry. Place on foil-lined pan and rub thoroughly with balsamic vinegar. Broil 4" from heat for 5-6 minutes on each side, or until cooked through.

3. Serve with cucumber sauce.

Broiled Shark Steaks with Orange Sauce

Serves 4

Ingredients:

1½ pounds shark steaks, ¾" thick

Marinade:

⅓ cup orange juice
3 tablespoons olive oil
1 teaspoon dried basil
1 teaspoon apple cider vinegar
2 garlic cloves, minced

Directions:

1. *In a small bowl, combine all marinade ingredients.*

2. *Cut shark into serving pieces, place in a shallow dish and pour marinade over. Cover with plastic wrap and refrigerate for about 1 hour.*

3. *Spray the unheated rack of a broiler pan with nonstick spray coating. Drain fish and place on rack. Broil 4" from the heat for 5 minutes. Turn over, brush with marinade and cook for another 5-6 minutes or until fish flakes easily.*

Court Bouillon

Ingredients:

4 cups water
1 carrot, sliced
1 small onion, sliced
10-12 fresh parsley sprigs, with stems
1 bay leaf
¼ teaspoon thyme
¼ cup fresh lemon juice
White pepper to taste
Pinch sea salt

Directions:

1. Combine all the ingredients in a pan, cover and bring to a boil.

2. Simmer uncovered for 30 minutes and strain. Allow bouillon to cool, then refrigerate. Use for poaching fish.

Fish Stock

Fish Stock is used as the base for sauce or soup

Ingredients:

1 cup sliced onion
1 teaspoon butter
1 ½ pounds fish bones
4 cups water
½ cup dry white wine
2 tablespoons fresh lemon juice
1 celery stalk, cut up
10-12 fresh parsley sprigs with stems
White pepper to taste
Pinch sea salt

Directions:

1. *Melt butter in a kettle, add onions and cook on low heat covered, for 3-4 minutes.*

2. *Add remaining ingredients. Bring slowly to a boil, skimming occasionally. Simmer uncovered 20 minutes.*

3. *Strain through a fine sieve into a bowl. Stock can be made 2 days ahead. Cool uncovered before chilling covered. (It can be frozen for up to 3 months.)*

   Note: Search for a fresh fish store or the fresh fish department of your supermarket to find the fish bones. You can, however, make a "fast" fish stock by using Knorr fish bouillon cubes using 1 cube in 2 cups boiling water.

Grilled Swordfish with Vegetables

Serves 4

Ingredients:

4 swordfish steaks, about 6 oz. each
2 small zucchinis, halved lengthwise
2 small yellow squash, halved lengthwise
4 slices red onion, ½" thick
Lemon pepper to taste

Marinade:

⅓ cup olive oil
2 garlic cloves, crushed
3 tablespoons fresh lemon juice
1 teaspoon thyme
1 tablespoon dried rosemary, crumbled

Directions:

1. *Combine marinade ingredients. Place fish and vegetables in a large baking dish, and brush them with marinade, turning to coat them well. Marinate in the refrigerator for 1-2 hours.*

2. *Prepare barbecue (medium-high heat). Season fish and vegetables with lemon pepper and brush with marinade.*

3. *Grill fish and vegetables together for about 4 minutes on each side. Fish should be cooked through and vegetables just tender.*

Grilled Swordfish Steaks

Ingredients:

4 swordfish steaks

Marinade:

2 tablespoons red onions, diced
2 tablespoons fresh lemon juice
1 garlic clove, crushed
1 tablespoon olive oil
Pepper to taste

Sauce:

2 garlic cloves, minced or pressed
1 tablespoon capers
3 tablespoons fresh lemon juice
3 tablespoons olive oil
1 tablespoon chives, fresh or frozen
1 tablespoon fresh parsley, chopped

Directions:

1. *Mix marinade ingredients and marinate the swordfish for a few hours, turning occasionally.*

2. *Mix together all the sauce ingredients.*

3. *Wipe onions and garlic off steaks and grill or broil for about 4-5 minutes on each side or until fish is fairly firm and springy to the touch.*

4. *Pour sauce over the fish and serve.*

Grilled Whole Fish

Serves 4

Ingredients:

1 whole fish of any kind (3-4 pounds), cleaned
4 lemon slices
2 tablespoons olive oil
1 tablespoon fresh lemon juice
¼ teaspoon dill weed
Pepper to taste

Directions:

1. Place lemon slices inside fish and season the inside with pepper.

2. Grease long-handled wire mesh grids and place fish inside.

3. Mix remaining ingredients and brush all over fish. Grill over hot coals 10-12 minutes on each side, turning only once and basting with more oil if necessary.

Halibut Fillets with Zucchini

Serves 6

Ingredients:

6 individual servings of halibut fillets
4 small zucchinis, unpeeled, washed and sliced
Sea salt and pepper
2 teaspoons olive oil
3 tablespoons minced red onions
⅓ cup fish stock
⅔ cup water
2 tablespoons dry white wine
1 teaspoon tarragon or oregano
1 tablespoon parsley flakes

Directions:

1. Preheat oven to 400.°

2. Butter a roasting or gratin pan large enough to hold fish in a single layer.

3. Bring 3 quarts of water to a boil, add zucchini slices, and, as soon as water comes to a boil again, remove the slices. Place zucchini in a colander under running cold water and drain.

4. Place fillets in the pan, season with a pinch of salt and pepper. Cover the fillets with overlapping zucchini slices and drizzle with oil.

5. In a small saucepan, add onions, fish stock, water, wine and herbs. Bring to a simmer and pour around the fish. Cover with foil and transfer to hot oven. Cook for 12-15 minutes. Do not overcook. Fish should be firm to the touch. Serve spooning sauce over fish.

Homemade Fresh Tuna in Olive Oil

Ingredients:

2 tuna steaks
2 cups extra virgin olive oil
2 bay leaves
10 whole black peppercorns
¼ teaspoon salt
4 round slices lemon
Sterilized glass jar with lid

Directions:

1. Boil water. Add tuna steaks and lemon slices to boiling water. Boil for 10-20 minutes until done. Remove tuna from water and cut into large cubes.

2. Place tuna in sterilized glass jar and pour olive oil until the tuna is submerged. Drop in bay leaves, peppercorns and salt.

3. Set aside to cool, then store in refrigerator for a day, a week or up to a month until needed. When needed, remove from refrigerator an hour before use.

Lemon-Dill
Salmon Fillet

Serves 4

Ingredients:

1 pound salmon fillet
2 tablespoons dry white wine
2 tablespoons shallots, minced
Dash salt and pepper

Sauce Ingredients:

1/4 cup skim milk
1/4 cup lowfat mayonnaise
1 tablespoon lemon juice (fresh)
1 teaspoon grated lemon rind
2 teaspoons Grey Poupon mustard
2 tablespoons fresh dill, chopped

Directions:

1. Preheat oven to 425.º

2. Spray cooking oil in a Pyrex dish, then add salmon, with skin side down. Add wine (or water if you prefer), shallots, salt and pepper over fish. Bake in preheated oven, covered with foil, for about 18-20 minutes.

3. While salmon bakes, prepare the sauce. Whisk milk into mayonnaise, then cook for about 2 minutes in a small saucepan over medium heat, whisking constantly. Do not let it boil.

4. Take sauce off stove and gently stir in remaining ingredients. When salmon is ready, remove it to a serving dish, then pour the sauce into the juices in the baking dish. Stir together thoroughly, then pour finished sauce over salmon and serve. Sprinkle with a bit of fresh chopped dill for garnish if desired.

Lime and Dill Salmon

Serves 4

Ingredients:

4 salmon fillets
1 scallion, chopped, for garnish
1 lime, cut into 4 wedges, for garnish

Sauce:

¼ cup fresh dill, chopped
3 tablespoons scallions, chopped
3 tablespoons fresh lime juice
1 tablespoon honey mustard
3 tablespoons olive oil
Salt and pepper to taste

Directions:

1. *Preheat oven to 375.°*

2. *Rinse fillets and pat dry. Arrange in a single layer in a greased baking dish.*

3. *Place all sauce ingredients in a blender and mix. (If you prefer a chunkier sauce, process all the liquid ingredients first, then briefly process the dill and scallions).*

4. *Cover fish with sauce and bake uncovered 15-25 minutes.*

5. *To serve, garnish each fillet with some of the scallion tops and a lime wedge.*

Linda's Fish or Chicken in Parchment or Brown Bag

Serves 2

Ingredients:

1 pound fish fillet of your choice
1 leek, sliced
1 carrot, sliced
1 stalk celery, sliced
½ teaspoon garlic powder
1 tablespoon parsley, chopped
¼ cup fish or vegetable broth
Salt and pepper to taste

Directions:

1. *Preheat oven to 350.°*

2. *Place fish on flat parchment or in open bag. Arrange vegetables around fish. Sprinkle with salt, pepper and garlic powder. Drizzle fish or vegetable broth over all.*

3. *Seal package and place in preheated oven for 10-15 minutes.*

4. *Remove from parchment or bag and serve fish and vegetables on the same plate.*

   Note: If using a pound of boneless chicken breast instead of fish, replace the fish or vegetable broth with chicken broth, and bake 20-25 minutes.

Linda's Microwave-Poached Salmon

Serves 4

Ingredients:

2 pounds salmon fillet
¾ teaspoon garlic powder
1 tablespoon fresh or dried rosemary
¾ cup white wine
Freshly ground black pepper to taste

Directions:

1. *Place washed salmon in Pyrex baking dish skin side down.*

2. *Sprinkle garlic powder, pepper and rosemary over the top.*

3. *Pour white wine into the dish around (not over) the fish.*

4. *Seal with plastic wrap. Cook in microwave oven at least 12 minutes, or until done, depending on the thickness of the salmon.*

Mackerel à L'Orange

Serves 4

Ingredients:

8 mackerel fillets
½ cup orange juice
4 tablespoons olive oil
3 teaspoons chopped parsley
4 oranges, thinly sliced
Salt and pepper to taste

Directions:

1. Mix orange juice, olive oil, parsley, salt and pepper in a shallow dish. Marinate fillets in this mixture for one hour in the refrigerator.

2. Preheat broiler to 350.° Broil fillets in a shallow pan about 6" from heat source. Baste with marinade during cooking process. Broil for 8-10 minutes. Fillets should be slightly browned on top.

3. Serve fillets with orange slices arranged over the top and sprinkled with a little fresh chopped parsley.

Recipe by the "New Jersey Fish & Seafood Cookbook" published by the New Jersey Department of Agriculture.

Marinade for Fish

This marinade is ideal for all types of fish.

Makes 1¼ cups

Ingredients:

1 cup dry white wine
2 tablespoons safflower oil
1 medium lemon, juiced
1 tablespoon parsley, minced

Directions:

1.   *In a medium bowl, whisk together all ingredients.*

2.   *In a shallow dish, marinate fish for 15 to 20 minutes.*

3.   *Bake, broil or grill desired fish.*

Mr. Wok's
Mango Salmon

Serves 2

Ingredients:

12-16 ounces salmon fillet, about 6 slices
2 medium size fresh mangoes
5-6 fresh asparagus stalks, cut in 2" lengths
8-10 snow peas or sugar pea pods
2 carrots, sliced
1 cup spinach, chopped

Ingredients for stir-fry:

2 tablespoons apple cider vinegar
2 tablespoons Chinese rice wine -or- dry sherry
2 tablespoons sugar -or- 1 tablespoon honey
2 teaspoons cornstarch

Directions:

1. Grill or boil the salmon until done. Meanwhile, peel the mangoes and slice them into 2-3" pieces. Set aside.

2. With a little water in the wok, steam the spinach and the other vegetables for 1 or 2 minutes. Remove vegetables and wipe wok dry.

3. Sauté all the vegetables in the hot wok with the vinegar, wine, and sugar. Add the mango, then add the cornstarch. Stir-fry 1-2 minutes.

4. Serve the stir-fried vegetables and mango on top of the cooked salmon.

Mr. Wok's
Steamed Fish

Serves 2

Ingredients:

1½-2 pounds of fish (sea bass, red snapper
    or flounder)
4 scallions, sliced lengthwise and cut into
    2" lengths

For Steaming:

2 teaspoons Chinese rice wine -or- dry sherry
3 slices ginger (about the size of a quarter)

For Dipping Sauce:

¼ teaspoon finely minced fresh ginger
1 tablespoon apple cider vinegar
1 tablespoon soy sauce
¼ teaspoon sesame oil

Directions:

1. *Place rice wine or sherry and ginger into the water in the steaming vessel, and bring it to a gushing boil over high heat.*

2. *Add the scallion topped with the fish to the steaming basket. Cover the steamer and steam the fish over high heat for 15 minutes. Remove from steamer.*

3. *Mix together sauce ingredients and serve on the side.*

Poached Orange Roughy with Spinach

Serves 4

Ingredients:

1½ pounds orange roughy
2 packages frozen spinach leaves
¾ cup water
¼ cup dry white wine
⅛ teaspoon thyme
½ teaspoon parsley flakes
2 tablespoons chopped red onions
Pepper to taste

Directions:

1. Cook spinach according to package directions and set aside.

2. Cut fish into serving portions and set aside.

3. Combine remaining ingredients in a nonstick skillet and bring to a boil. Add fish and return to boiling. Reduce heat, cover and simmer gently for about 6 minutes.

4. When ready to serve, put some spinach on each serving plate. Remove fish with a slotted spatula and place on spinach. Spoon some of the cooking juices on fish and spinach.

   Note: You may substitute white fish or sea bass fillets for the orange roughy in this recipe.

Salmon Burgers

*Make sure the salmon fillet is free of bones.
Canned salmon can be used, but fresh is best!
Cooked, leftover burgers are as good as the
day you made them!*

Serves 4 to 6

Ingredients:

1 pound salmon fillet, cooked, cooled and flaked
10 - 12 fat free crackers, finely crushed
¼ cup celery, finely chopped
¼ cup red onion, sliced very thin
1 tablespoon lemon juice
1 tablespoon fresh basil, finely chopped
1 tablespoon fresh parsley, finely chopped
1 small garlic clove, minced
1 large whole egg
1 large egg white
1 teaspoon sea salt
½ teaspoon black pepper

Directions:

1. *Preheat oven to 350.° Lightly coat a baking sheet and a shallow baking pan with vegetable oil. Set aside.*

2. *Rinse and remove skin from fresh salmon, pat dry. Place fillets in baking pan with a sprinkle of lemon juice. Bake for 12 to 15 minutes or until the fillet flakes apart when cut with a fork. Dry well before using in the recipe.*

3. *The cooked salmon must be completely cool and free of excess liquid. In a medium-sized bowl, add flaked salmon, celery, red onion, crushed crackers, lemon juice, basil, parsley and garlic.*

Directions continued on the following page

Salmon Burgers continued:

4. In a small bowl, beat whole egg and egg white. Add to the salmon mixture and blend well. Add sea salt and pepper.

5. Form salmon mixture into patties about ½ inch thick. (Add cracker crumbs if the mixture is too moist.) Place on prepared baking sheet. Be sure there is enough room between the patties.

6. Bake for 8 minutes. Turn and bake an additional 6 minutes, or until firm. To broil, preheat broiler. Place patties on a pre-pared baking sheet and broil about 5 to 7 minutes on each side, or until salmon burgers are firm.

Spaghetti with Asparagus and Tuna

Serves 4

Ingredients:

1 package Jerusalem artichoke spaghetti
1 bunch asparagus, diced
6 cloves finely minced garlic
¼ cup finely minced onion
1 small can (2 oz.) light tuna in water, drained
½ tablespoon black pepper
¼ teaspoon lemon salt
2 tablespoons light soy sauce
3 tablespoons olive oil

Directions:

1. Boil pasta until al dente. Drain and set aside.

2. Heat oil on medium, sauté onion. Add garlic and sauté a bit longer, then add asparagus.

3. When asparagus is cooked, turn heat to low, add pasta, tuna, and remaining seasonings, toss well and serve.

Steamed Fish
and Vegetables

Serves 4

Ingredients:

Any white fillet of fish (fluke, flounder,
   halibut, sole)
2 tablespoons olive oil
Juice of one lemon
½ cup sliced carrots
½ cup broccoli florets
½ cup string beans
2 cloves garlic, finely diced
½ cup diced red onion
2-4 bay leaves
Sweet basil, oregano and garlic powder to taste

Directions:

1. *Preheat oven to 350.°*

2. *Place fish in a Pyrex dish with a tight-fitting lid. Cover with olive oil and lemon juice.*

3. *Mix together vegetables, onion, garlic and bay leaf and pour over fish.*

4. *Sprinkle with basil, oregano and garlic powder.*

5. *Cover dish tightly and bake for 20-25 minutes, depending on thickness of fish. Remove bay leaves before serving.*

Swordfish Kabob

Serves 4

Ingredients:

1½ pounds swordfish, cut into 1" cubes
2 zucchini, cut into 1" cubes

Marinade:

3 tablespoons lemon juice
2 tablespoons olive oil
1 tablespoon low sodium soy sauce
2 small garlic cloves, minced

Directions:

1. Combine all marinade ingredients. Place fish and vegetable cubes into a large bowl. Pour marinade and toss well. Refrigerate 2-4 hours.

2. On 8 long metal skewers, alternately thread fish and zucchini cubes, leaving about ¼" between each piece.

3. Grill on a greased grill rack set about 6" over coals for 8-10 minutes, or until fish turns opaque, turning kabob over and brushing with marinade halfway through grilling time.

Swordfish Stir-fry

Serves 4

Ingredients:

2 pounds swordfish steak, cut into ½" chunks
4 cups broccoli
4 cups snow pea pods
2 tablespoons olive oil
Salt and pepper to taste
½ cup salt-free, sodium free chicken broth
1 tablespoon cornstarch

Directions:

1. *Heat wok, then add olive oil. (You can do this in a deep frying pan if a wok is not available.)*

2. *Add snow peas, broccoli, salt and pepper. Toss until almost cooked.*

3. *Add swordfish chunks, chicken broth and cornstarch, and cook, stirring continuously, until fish is done. Serve over brown rice.*

Chicken

⌐⌐   Indicates recipe created by Monique Hill

Almond Chicken

Serves 2

Ingredients:

2 skinless, boneless chicken breasts, sliced
⅔ cup finely ground raw almonds
⅓ cup grated Parmesan cheese
1 cup lowfat plain yogurt
½ cup parsley flakes
Dash ground black pepper (optional)

Directions:

1. *Preheat oven to 375.°*

2. *Thoroughly mix ground almonds, Parmesan cheese and parsley flakes, then spread out on a sheet of wax paper.*

3. *Whip yogurt with a fork, then marinate chicken in the yogurt for a 10-15 minutes.*

4. *Remove chicken from marinade, then coat liberally with the almond mixture.*

5. *Spray a light coating of vegetable oil on a baking dish, then place the coated chicken in the dish. Bake for 35-45 minutes.*

Baked Chicken with Herbs

Serves 6

Ingredients:

3 tablespoons whole wheat flour
3 tablespoons chopped almonds
½ teaspoon dried sage
1 teaspoon dried rosemary
1 teaspoon sea salt
2 large egg whites
4 pounds skinless chicken,
   cut into serving pieces
1 can evaporated skim milk
1¼ cups bottled water
1 medium onion, chopped

Directions:

1. Preheat oven to 350.°

2. In a large shallow dish, mix together flour, nuts, sage, rosemary and sea salt. Set aside.

3. In a shallow dish, beat egg whites with 1 tablespoon of water. Dip chicken pieces one by one into egg whites, then dredge them in the flour mixture. Arrange in a large glass baking dish.

4. Pour the milk and arrange the onions around the chicken.

5. Bake for 1½ hours or until the juices run clear and the meat is tender. The chicken should be lightly browned.

Barbecue Chicken

Serves 6

Ingredients:

2 broiler chickens, quartered

For Sauce:

1 cup water
1 cup apple cider vinegar
½ cup canola oil
Salt to taste

Directions:

1. *Prepare fire using a gas grill with bed of lava rocks. (Avoid charcoal grills.)*

2. *Brush chicken with sauce and place on grill, skin side up. (Most grilling should be done with bone side down to avoid blistering of the skin.)*

3. *The hotter the fire, the more frequently you will need to turn the chicken. Baste with the sauce several times. Poultry is done when the drumstick easily twists out of the thigh joint.*

Barbecue Chicken with Apple Cider Vinegar

Serves 4

Ingredients:

1 whole chicken (about 3 pounds)
½ cup water
½ cup apple cider vinegar
2 tablespoons canola oil
1 large garlic clove, minced
1 tablespoon mixed herbs

Directions:

1. Wash chicken and cut into serving pieces; remove skin. Arrange in a shallow dish.

2. In a blender or food processor, mix the water, vinegar, oil, garlic and herbs.

3. Pour mixture over chicken and marinate in refrigerator for 45 minutes. Meanwhile, preheat the grill to "high."

4. Reduce heat to medium. Arrange chicken pieces on the grill. Baste with marinade every few minutes. Cook chicken for 13-15 minutes on each side. [After final basting, discard any leftover marinade.] Fully cooked chicken will no longer be pink inside and the juices will run clear.

Broiled Chicken with Mushroom Sauce

Serves 4

Ingredients:

3 skinless, boneless chicken breasts, halved
4 tablespoons olive oil
Pinch tarragon

Sauce:

1½ tablespoons fresh
   or frozen mushrooms, sliced
1½ tablespoons olive oil
2 tablespoons shallots, chopped
½ teaspoon tarragon
1 cup no fat, low sodium chicken broth
¼ teaspoon Kitchen Bouquet sauce
1 teaspoon arrowroot or cornstarch

Directions:

1. *Heat oil and shallots in a saucepan over low heat for 3 to 4 minutes to soften shallots–do not let them brown, they will taste bitter.*

2. *Add mushrooms and ½ teaspoon tarragon, sauté for a few minutes. Reserve 2 tablespoons of broth to mix with the arrowroot, and add remaining broth and Kitchen Bouquet to mushrooms. Cook over medium-high heat until mushrooms are tender. Add arrowroot or cornstarch and broth mixture to the saucepan, stirring constantly until thickened.*

3. *Preheat broiler. Mix olive oil and tarragon, brush over chicken. Broil 4 inches from heat for about 4 minutes on each side, or until chicken is golden and cooked through.*

4. *Warm up sauce and serve over chicken.*

Chicken Adobo

Ingredients:

1 1½-2 pound skinless chicken,
   cut into serving pieces
½ cup apple cider vinegar
½ head of garlic, crushed
10 pieces whole black peppercorn
2 bay leaves
4 tablespoons low sodium soy sauce
1 pinch salt
2 cups water

Directions:

1. *In a saucepan, combine vinegar, garlic, peppercorns, bay leaves, salt and soy sauce.*

2. *Add chicken and let it marinate for 30 minutes.*

3. *Add water to pot and simmer uncovered, until chicken is tender.*

4. *Strain sauce and set aside.*

5. *Broil chicken for at least 10-20 minutes until crispy. Check it every 5 minutes, turning it each time, so that chicken doesn't burn. Serve with reserved sauce.*

Chicken Breasts with Artichokes

Serves 4

Ingredients:

2 whole chicken breasts, skinned,
   boned and halved
¾ cup sliced carrots, about ½" thick
¾ cup frozen pearl onions, defrosted
1 6 oz. jar marinated artichoke hearts
1 garlic clove, chopped
¾ cup nonfat, low sodium chicken broth
¼ teaspoon Italian seasoning
Parsley flakes to garnish

Directions:

1.   *Preheat oven to 375.°*

2.   *Parboil carrots and onions in boiling water for 5 minutes. Drain the artichoke hearts, reserving the marinade.*

3.   *Place chicken in a single layer in a shallow baking dish. Heat broth with artichoke marinade, pour over chicken, add carrots, onions, garlic, artichokes and Italian seasoning.*

4.   *Bake for 25-30 minutes or until cooked through but still moist. Remove from heat and sprinkle with parsley.*

    Note: This dish would be good served with brown rice and broccoli.

Chicken Breast in Cucumber Sauce

Serves 6

Ingredients:

4 whole chicken breasts, skinned,
   boned and halved
1 cup nonfat, low sodium chicken broth
1-2 carrots, cooked and cut into
   ½" cubes (about ¼ cup)
1 small cucumber, peeled and seeded
1 teaspoon dill weed
¾ cup lowfat cottage cheese
1½ cup nonfat yogurt
½ teaspoon cornstarch or arrowroot

Directions:

1. *Dice cucumber into ½" pieces and parboil for 3 minutes. They should be tender but still crisp. Pour into a bowl of cold water to stop the cooking. Drain well and reserve.*

2. *Place cottage cheese, yogurt, dill and cornstarch (or arrowroot) in food processor, process until very smooth.*

3. *Brown chicken breast in a nonstick frying pan on low heat for about 3 minutes on each side. Add broth and continue cooking on low heat until done, about 10 minutes. Broth should be reduced to about ½ cup.*

Directions continued on the following page

Chicken Breast in Cucumber Sauce
Directions continued:

4. Remove chicken, put on a plate and cover with foil to keep warm. Add yogurt mixture slowly, whisking constantly on low heat until you have a sauce of good consistency.

5. Add carrots, cucumber cubes and chicken to the sauce. Turn chicken over to coat both sides and heat for a few minutes on very low heat. Correct seasoning with dill if needed.

Note: It is good to keep some of the yogurt mixture–if sauce starts to curdle, add a few tablespoons of it back to the sauce.

Smile Oft,

Speak Gently,

Be Kind.

Edgar Cayce #262.109

Chicken Pita Sandwich

Ingredients:

2 slices whole wheat pita bread
1 whole chicken breast, skinless, boneless
3 cups shredded lettuce, Romaine or iceberg
1 tablespoon onion, finely chopped
½ teaspoon black crushed pepper
½ teaspoon lemon powder
½ teaspoon garlic powder
½ teaspoon Italian seasoning
½ teaspoon parsley
2-3 tablespoons extra virgin olive oil
1½ tablespoons lemon juice

Directions:

1. Boil chicken in water with a pinch of salt. When fully cooked, shred it.

2. Toss chicken, lettuce, onions, parsley and all other seasonings. Add olive oil and lemon juice, set aside.

3. Cut pita bread in half and toast, then place salad mixture inside pockets. Have fun.

Couscous with Chicken and Vegetables

Serves 6

Ingredients:

2 cups couscous
4¼ cups water
¾ pound skinless chicken breast,
   roasted and diced
1 medium onion, chopped
1 large garlic clove, minced
1 medium zucchini, diced
1 medium yellow squash, diced
1½ tablespoons fresh parsley, chopped
1 teaspoon dried basil
½ teaspoon dried oregano
Sea salt and pepper, to taste

Directions:

1. *Boil 4 cups water in a saucepan with a tight-fitting lid. Stir in couscous. Remove from heat, cover and set aside for 5 minutes, or until all the water has been absorbed. Fluff with a fork; set aside and keep warm.*

2. *In a large saucepan with a tight-fitting lid, heat ¼ cup water over medium heat. Stir in onions and garlic. Cover and "sweat" the vegetables for 2-3 minutes or until soft. Stir in the zucchini and squash and "sweat" covered for 3-5 minutes more or until soft.*

3. *Mix in the roasted chicken, basil, parsley and oregano. Cook for 3 minutes or until heated through. Season with sea salt and pepper.*

4. *To serve, place the couscous in a large serving platter. Spoon the chicken and vegetable mixture over the couscous.*

Easy Oven-Baked Chicken with Vegetables

Serves 4

Ingredients:

1 5-pound oven-roaster chicken
2 cups nonfat, low sodium chicken broth
3 large carrots, cut into 2" pieces
3 large parsnips, cut into 2" pieces
1 large sweet potato, cut into 2" pieces
1 cup broccoli florets, divided
1 cup cauliflower florets, divided
1 yellow squash, cut into 2" pieces
3-4 garlic cloves, minced
All purpose Herb Seasoning

Directions:

1. *Preheat oven to 450.°*

2. *Place seasoned chicken in the middle of a large baking pan. Mix carrots, parsnips, sweet potato and garlic and arrange around chicken. Season vegetables with herbs; bake covered for 20 minutes. Pour 1 cup of broth over all, then bake for another 20 minutes.*

3. *Add remaining vegetables and bake for 20 minutes. Pour 1 cup of broth over chicken and bake for another 15-20 minutes until chicken and vegetables are browned.*

4. *Let stand for a few minutes to cool off. Either slice the chicken before you serve it, or let your family dig in!*

Golden Grilled Chicken

Serves 4 to 6

Ingredients:

12 chicken legs with thighs
½ cup low sodium soy sauce
¼ cup olive oil
2 garlic cloves, finely chopped
¼ cup dry sherry or rice wine
2 tablespoons fresh ginger, grated
1 tablespoon orange rind, finely shredded

Directions:

1. *Combine all ingredients (except chicken) in a large bowl and mix well. Add chicken and marinate for 2 hours, turning occasionally.*

2. *Remove chicken from marinade and grill over hot coals, turning and basting frequently with marinade until chicken is nicely browned and cooked through. Move around to prevent burning while cooking.*

Grilled Chicken Breast

Serves 4

Ingredients:

2 whole chicken breasts, skinned,
boned and halved
3 tablespoons olive oil
1 tablespoon canola oil
1 teaspoon oregano
Large pinch garlic powder
Pepper to taste

Directions:

1. In a bowl, whisk together all ingredients except chicken. Add chicken and marinate for 1 hour.

2. Grill the chicken on a rack set 5-6 inches over glowing coals for 4-5 minutes on each side, or until cooked through.

Note: Very good served with grilled vegetables and salad. [You could also grill the chicken on a well seasoned ridge pan over moderate high heat for about the same amount of time. Make sure you heat the pan first.]

Grilled Chicken Brochettes

Serves 4

Ingredients:

1½ pounds skinless, boneless chicken breast,
    cut into 1" cubes
2 zucchinis, cut into 1½" pieces
1 large onion, cut into 1½" pieces

Marinade:

¼ cup minced fresh mint leaves
½ teaspoon fructose
1 teaspoon minced garlic
2 teaspoons fresh lemon juice
2 tablespoons olive oil
1 cup plain yogurt
Pepper to taste

Directions:

1. Combine mint, fructose and garlic into a large bowl and mash with a fork. Stir in lemon juice, oil and yogurt, and mix well.

2. Add chicken, zucchini and onion to yogurt mixture and toss to coat thoroughly. Cover bowl with plastic wrap and refrigerate for several hours or overnight.

3. Alternately thread chicken and vegetables onto long metal skewers. Season with pepper.

4. Grill over charcoal for 4 minutes. Brush with any remaining marinade, turn the skewers over and grill about 4 minutes longer, until chicken and vegetables are browned and chicken is cooked through but still moist.

Grilled Chicken with Zucchini

Serves 4

Ingredients:

4 chicken cutlets, cut into ¼" strips
2 zucchinis, sliced
1 medium onion, cut in half and thinly sliced
2 garlic cloves, minced
1 teaspoon Italian seasoning
Pinch salt and pepper
Olive oil

Directions:

1. *Place a chicken cutlet and one fourth of each other ingredient on each of 4 large sheets of heavy duty aluminum foil. Sprinkle each "package" with a few drops of olive oil. Wrap securely and place on grill over hot coals.*

2. *Cook for 20-25 minutes, turning frequently. Make sure chicken is cooked through.*

   Note: You can also use turkey cutlets for this dish. You could also bake it at 400° for 20 minutes.

Grilled Rosemary Chicken

Serves 2

Ingredients:

2 skinless, boneless chicken breasts
2 large garlic cloves, crushed
1 tablespoon olive oil
1 tablespoon fresh rosemary, crushed
1 teaspoon fresh lemon juice
   -or- apple cider vinegar

Directions:

1. Combine garlic, rosemary, olive oil and lemon juice and marinate chicken for at least 15 minutes with this mixture.

2. Preheat broiler or grill to medium high and cook chicken 5-7 minutes on each side, basting frequently with marinade, until thoroughly cooked. Be sure chicken is no longer pink inside.

Honey Chicken

Serves 2

Ingredients:

2 chicken breasts (skinless, boneless)
1 teaspoon lightly seasoned sea salt
⅓ cup honey
Juice of 1 lime

Directions:

1. Preheat oven to 450.°

2. Sprinkle chicken breasts with sea salt and place on a rack in baking pan. Mix freshly squeezed lime juice and honey, baste breasts with half of the mixture, and bake for 15 minutes.

3. Turn meat, baste with remaining honey/lime mixture, bake for another 10 minutes.

Lemon Baked Chicken

Serves 4 to 6

Ingredients:

1 whole chicken, about 2½ pounds
1 large lemon
Fresh minced garlic
Sea salt and pepper to taste

Directions:

1. Preheat oven to 350.°

2. Rub chicken all over with salt, pepper and garlic. Leave the skin on.

3. Prick 25 holes into the large lemon and place it in the cavity of the chicken.

4. Close up the cavity by sewing or with a skewer.

5. Bake for approximately 1½ hours, or until done, basting periodically with pan juices.

Lemon Herb Cornish Hens

Serves 4

Ingredients:

2 medium Cornish game hens
Sea salt and pepper to taste
2 tablespoons canola oil
¼ cup onions, finely chopped
2 large garlic cloves, minced
½ cup fresh lemon juice
2 teaspoons low salt chicken seasoning
2 teaspoons fresh parsley, finely chopped
2 teaspoons dried rosemary, crushed

Directions:

1. Preheat oven to 350.°

2. Wash hens thoroughly and pat dry with paper towel. Split in half lengthwise. Season with salt and pepper. Cover and refrigerate.

3. In a medium size saucepan, heat oil over medium heat. Add onions and garlic, cook for 3-5 minutes or until soft. Add lemon juice, chicken seasoning, parsley and rosemary. Reduce heat to low and simmer for 5 minutes.

4. Place hens skin side up in a roasting pan. Cover with lemon sauce. Place in oven; baste every 15 minutes. The total roasting time is 1¼ hours.

5. Remove hens to a platter and cover with foil to keep warm. Remove fat from lemon sauce and serve with hens.

Note: Cornish hens can also be grilled by roasting over electric or gas grill. Baste frequently and cook for at least 30 minutes, or until the juices run clear and the inside is no longer pink.

Lemon/Lime Broiled Chicken

Serves 2

Ingredients:

2 chicken breast fillets (or turkey)
Juice of freshly squeezed lemon or lime
Lemon peel, freshly grated
6-10 fresh lettuce and/or spinach leaves
Dash Salt
Dash Lemon Pepper
3-4 small cooked beets and/or steamed carrots

Directions:

1. *Remove all visible fat from meat. Brush with lemon juice and sprinkle with lemon pepper.*

2. *Broil about 10 minutes turning often. Cook until meat is no longer pink.*

3. *Arrange fillets on a bed of fresh lettuce and/or spinach leaves.*

4. *For color and nutrition, garnish with diced or sliced beets and/or carrots.*

Mr. Wok's
Sesame Chicken

Serves 2

Ingredients:

2 skinless, boneless chicken breasts, cut into
flat 1-2" pieces
3-4 broccoli florets
3-4 cauliflower florets

Ingredients for stir-fry:

2-3 tablespoons sesame seeds
5 tablespoons apple cider vinegar
1 tablespoon sugar -or- ½ tablespoon honey
1 teaspoon soy sauce
1 teaspoon minced garlic
½ teaspoon minced ginger
1 teaspoon sesame oil
1 teaspoon corn or soybean oil
1 tablespoon cornstarch

Directions:

1. *Heat the wok. Place sugar (or honey), soy sauce, and sesame oil in wok and stir-fry for 1-2 minutes.*

2. *Add the rest of the stir-fry ingredients and stir for 1-2 minutes. Mix the cornstarch with the chicken. Add chicken to wok and stir-fry for 1-2 minutes.*

3. *Boil the broccoli and cauliflower florets for two minutes, place them around the edge of the serving plate, with the prepared sesame chicken in the middle.*

Mr. Wok's Steamed Chicken and Fish With Mixed Vegetables

Serves 2

Ingredients:

6 ounces skinless chicken breast
6 ounces sliced flounder fillet
3-4 stalks fresh asparagus, diced
2-3 carrots, diced
10-12 pieces baby corn
6-8 broccoli florets
4-6 Chinese black mushrooms, sliced

Directions:

1. Heat a cup of water in the wok for 3 minutes.

2. Place chicken, fish and vegetables in the hot water. Stir and broil for several minutes, until ready.

Mung Bean Guisado

Serves 4 to 6

Ingredients:

1 cup mung beans
3 cups water
2 cloves garlic, crushed
1 cup cooked turkey or chicken, sliced into strips
3-4 tablespoons low sodium soy sauce
4 cups water or broth
1 teaspoon black crushed pepper

Directions:

1. Boil mung beans in 3 cups water until soft. Rub cooked beans through a fine sieve, or purée. Set aside.

2. Sauté garlic and onions in 3-4 tablespoons of water. Add the turkey or chicken.

3. Cook for 1 minute. When done, add soy sauce and prepared beans. Add 4 cups water or broth.

4. Season with pepper and add some fresh chopped parsley if desired. Serve hot.

Oven Poached Chicken Breast

Serves 4

Ingredients:

2 whole chicken breasts, skinned,
   boned and halved
1 tablespoon fresh lemon juice
Just enough water to cover chicken
⅛ teaspoon thyme leaves
Dash salt and pepper

Directions:

1.   *Preheat oven to 375.°*

2.   *Place chicken in a single layer in a shallow baking dish, add remaining ingredients. Cover lightly with a piece of aluminum foil.*

3.   *Bake for about 20 minutes or until tender and springy to the touch. Chicken is cooked when juice is clear with no trace of rosy color.*

4.   *Let cool in liquid for about ½ hour.*

     Note: This is very good in sandwiches and salads.

Pan Roasted Chicken Breast with Turnip and Cucumber Sauce

Serves 4

Ingredients:

2 whole chicken breasts, boned,
   skinned and halved
2 tablespoons olive oil
Dash pepper and dill
2 medium white turnips, cut into small chunks
1 large cucumber, peeled, seeded
   and cut into large chunks
2 cups fat free, low sodium chicken broth
Dash salt, pepper and thyme
½ teaspoon dried parsley
¼ teaspoon dill weed
Parsley sprigs to garnish

Directions:

1. *Mix together oil, pepper and dill. Brush over chicken and let rest while making sauce.*

2. *In a saucepan, put together turnip, cucumber, broth, salt, pepper and thyme. Bring to a boil, lower heat and cook until vegetables are very tender.*

Directions continued on the following page

Pan Roasted Chicken Breast with Turnip and Cucumber Sauce Directions continued:

3. Transfer to blender or food processor and purée until very smooth. [Caution! Never fill blender more than half full when puréeing hot foods!] Add more broth if sauce is too thick. Transfer back to saucepan, add parsley and dill.

4. Heat a ridged grill pan or well seasoned cast iron skillet over moderate heat; do not let it get too hot, it will burn the chicken. Cook chicken about 4 minutes on each side, or until springy to the touch and just cooked through.

5. Reheat sauce and pour over chicken.

Poached Chicken Breast with Lemon

Serves 4

Ingredients:

2 whole chicken breasts, skinned,
    boned, and halved
2 teaspoons olive oil
¼ cup fresh lemon juice
1 garlic clove, minced
¼ teaspoon oregano
¼ cup pitted Spanish green olives, cut in half

Directions:

1. Preheat oven to 350.°

2. Place chicken in a single layer in a shallow baking dish.

3. Combine oil, lemon juice, garlic and oregano, pour over chicken and marinate for 30 minutes. Add olives and bake for 30-35 minutes or until firm to the touch. Do not over bake. Baste frequently during baking.

Poached Chicken Legs with Vegetables

Serves 4 to 6

Ingredients:

8 whole chicken legs
1 onion
2 stalks of celery
1 bay leaf
½ teaspoon thyme
1 teaspoon dried parsley
¼ teaspoon celery seeds
Pinch sea salt and pepper
Enough water to cover ingredients by 3"
6 carrots
4 small onions
1 small cabbage
2 white turnips
Green beans (or any vegetable you like)
Parsley sprigs for garnish

Directions:

1. Combine first 9 ingredients into a stock pot, bring to a boil, lower the heat and simmer about 45 minutes or until chicken is tender. Strain broth, correct seasoning, cool and refrigerate.

2. Remove skin from chicken, let cool. Discard remaining vegetables.

3. Shortly before serving, skim fat from broth and bring to a boil. Cut onions and turnips in half and add to the broth together with remaining vegetables. Cook until tender. Add chicken legs to reheat just before serving.

4. Place some vegetables and chicken in a large soup plate and spoon about ½ cup of cooking liquid over it for each serving. Garnish with parsley.

Quick Chicken

Ingredients:

1 broiler or fryer, quartered, skin removed
Fresh lemon juice
Salt and Black Pepper to taste
Water

Directions:

1. Preheat oven to 475.°

2. Brush chicken quarters with lemon juice, salt and pepper. Place bone side up in broiler pan and broil about 5 minutes, or until brown.

3. Turn pieces over, and cover bottom of pan with about ¾" of boiling water. Place in preheated oven. Bake for 25 minutes until tender and brown.

Roasted Chicken

Serves 4

Ingredients:

1 3½-4 pound chicken
2 tablespoons olive oil
2 tablespoons canola oil
¼ teaspoon tarragon
¼ teaspoon thyme
¼ teaspoon dried parsley
½ teaspoon low sodium soy sauce
Pepper to taste
1 teaspoon onion flakes
⅓ cup water

Directions:

1. Preheat oven to 400.°

2. Season chicken with pepper and onion flakes inside the cavity. Mix oils, tarragon, thyme, parsley, soy sauce, and pepper. Brush all over chicken.

3. Place the chicken in a roasting pan on its side, and bake for about 20 minutes. Turn on the other side, baste with some of the oil mixture, and bake for another 20 minutes.

4. Turn oven down to 375.° Place chicken on its back, and baste again. Bake for another 45-50 minutes, or until done, basting frequently. Chicken is done when drumsticks are tender and move easily in the socket or when juice is clear with no trace of rosy color.

5. Set chicken on a carving board and let rest 15 minutes before serving. Add water to the pan to melt the solidified juices to make a natural gravy.

Savory Roasted Cornish Game Hens

From Carol, with Love!

Serves 2 to 4

Ingredients:

2 Cornish game hens
2 tablespoons olive oil
2 tablespoons oregano
1 teaspoon garlic powder
1 teaspoon salt
1 teaspoon pepper

Directions:

1. Preheat oven to 375.°

2. Wash hens thoroughly and pat dry with paper towel.

3. Split hens by cutting down the back bone, leaving breast bone intact. Spread hens to lay flat.

4. Generously brush both sides of hens with olive oil.

5. Mix together all dry ingredients and sprinkle both sides of hens. Place hens, breast side down, in shallow baking pan.

6. Bake 25 minutes in preheated oven, then turn breast side up, and continue baking for 25 minutes, or until skin is brown and crispy. Serve on a bed of wild or brown rice.

Summer Chicken

Serves 6

Ingredients:

3 whole chicken breasts, skinned,
   boned and halved
2 tablespoons orange juice
2 tablespoons low sodium soy sauce
Pinch pepper
Enough water to cover chicken

Sauce:

4 cloves garlic, minced
¾ cup light olive oil
1 teaspoon sesame oil
½ cup low sodium soy sauce
2 tablespoons sesame seeds
4-5 scallions, thinly sliced

Directions:

1. Preheat oven to 375.°

2. Place chicken in a single layer in a shallow baking dish, add orange juice, 2 tablespoons soy sauce, pepper and water. Bake for about 20-25 minutes, or until tender and springy to the touch.

3. In mixing bowl, combine sauce ingredients except sesame seeds and scallions. Set aside.

4. Dry chicken with paper towels. Cut against the grain into ½" wide strips.

5. Arrange layers of chicken strips in a nice oval platter. Pour enough sauce over the chicken to moisten. Sprinkle with sesame seeds and scallions. Serve cold, with remaining sauce on the side.

The Perfect Poached Egg

Serves 1

Ingredients:

2 eggs
2 cups of water

Directions:

1. Bring water to a rapid boil in a small saucepan.

2. Carefully crack open the eggs, taking care not to break the yolk. Drop eggs into boiling water and cover.

3. Poach for 2-4 minutes as desired. Remove with slotted spoon and serve.

Turkey

⌐🗀   Indicates recipe created by Monique Hill

Butternut Squash and Turkey Casserole

Serves: 8

Ingredients:

1 cup chicken stock, fat removed
1 medium onion, finely chopped
1 stalk celery
½ teaspoon dried sage
½ teaspoon dried thyme
½ teaspoon dried rosemary
½ teaspoon sea salt
½ teaspoon pepper
4 cups butternut squash, diced and cooked
2 cups turkey breast, cooked and diced
2 cups dried whole wheat bread cubes
½ cup low fat cheddar cheese, shredded

Directions:

1. Preheat oven to 325.° To make dried cubes, cut day-old thick whole wheat bread into 1" cubes. Spread on a baking sheet and place in the preheated oven with the oven turned off. Let "bake" for 30 minutes. Check for hardness (all moisture must be removed); remove from oven and let cool. Store in an air-tight container for up to 5 days.

2. To steam butternut squash, peel, remove seeds and cut into 1" pieces. Place in steamer basket, cover, steam for 12 to 18 minutes or until tender. Remove excess liquid before using.

3. Preheat oven to 350.° Lightly oil a medium casserole dish. Set aside.

Directions continued on the following page

Butternut Squash and Turkey Casserole Directions *continued:*

4. In a large pot with a tight-fitting lid, heat ¼ cup chicken stock over low heat. Stir in onions and celery and cover. Cook ("sweat") for 3-5 minutes, or until soft.

5. Add sage, thyme, rosemary, remaining chicken stock, salt and pepper. Gently mix in butternut squash, turkey and bread cubes.

6. Place in casserole and bake for 12 minutes. Sprinkle cheddar cheese and return to oven for 3 minutes, or until cheese is completely melted.

Grilled Turkey Cutlets with Vegetables

Serves 4

Ingredients:

4 turkey cutlets (about ¼" thick)
⅓ cup olive oil
2 tablespoons mixed herbs (thyme, oregano, rosemary, etc.)
2 packages frozen mixed vegetables, green beans, or broccoli
2 teaspoons corn oil
1 large garlic clove, finely minced
1 teaspoon fresh lemon juice

Directions:

1.   *Combine olive oil and herbs in a large bowl, add cutlets and marinate for one hour.*

2.   *Remove wrapper from frozen vegetables. Mix corn oil, garlic and lemon juice and sprinkle on each frozen block. Wrap in aluminum foil. Grill on hot coals for 15-20 minutes, turning frequently.*

3.   *Grill cutlets on a rack set 5-6 inches over hot coals for about 5-6 minutes on each side or until cooked through.*

Note: Turkey cutlets can be bought prepackaged or you can buy a small boneless turkey breast, pull back the skin and slice off the meat into cutlets. It will be easier to slice if you freeze the meat for half an hour before cutting.

Poached Turkey Breast

Serves 6 to 8

Ingredients:

1 turkey breast (bone in), about 5 pounds
2 cups nonfat, low sodium chicken broth
1 onion, quartered
1 carrot, chopped
2 celery stalks, chopped
1 bay leaf
¼ teaspoon thyme
1 tablespoon dried parsley
Pepper to taste

Directions:

1. Wash turkey breast and place in heavy casserole. Add chicken broth and bring to a boil. Lower heat, skim off particles which rise to the surface.

2. Add remaining ingredients and simmer covered for 1½ hours or until cooked through. Thermometer inserted in thickest part of breast should register 180.° Let stand uncovered for 30 minutes.

3. Place vegetables and broth into a blender or use a hand blender and blend to make a sauce. Correct seasoning.

4. To use for salad or sandwiches, cool turkey and refrigerate.

Roast Turkey

Serves 6 to 8

Ingredients:

1 8-10 pound turkey
1 onion, quartered
¼ teaspoon sage
½ teaspoon garlic flakes
Pepper

Basting Mixture:

¼ cup olive oil
¼ cup fresh lemon juice
¼ cup low sodium soy sauce
¼ cup white wine

Directions:

1. *Preheat oven to 450.°*

2. *Wash turkey and dry with paper towels. Season inside with garlic flakes, sage and pepper, then add onion inside cavity. Tie legs and wings to body.*

3. *Mix together oil, lemon juice, soy sauce and wine and brush some of it over turkey. Place the bird on a rack in a large roasting pan and put in the oven.*

4. *Reduce heat to 350° allowing about 20 minutes to the pound, basting frequently with the basting mixture.*

5. *Insert instant thermometer in the inner part of the thigh without touching the bone. When temperature reaches 180° and the thigh juices run clear, remove from oven and let rest for 20 minutes before carving.*

   Note: If turkey is browning too fast, place a loose aluminum foil tent over it.

Roast Turkey Breast

Serves 8 to 10

Ingredients:

1 6-7 pound turkey breast
½ teaspoon poultry seasoning
¼ teaspoon dry thyme
2 tablespoons olive oil
Pinch sea salt and pepper

Directions:

1. Preheat oven to 325.º

2. Mix all ingredients together except turkey. Brush this mixture all over turkey breast.

3. Place turkey breast skin side up on a rack in a shallow roasting pan. Roast for about 2-2½ hours. Thermometer inserted in thickest part of breast should register 180.º Let stand 20 minutes before serving.

4. Serve with Turkey Gravy.

Tasty Turkey Burgers

Ingredients:

1 large garlic clove, minced
1 teaspoon fresh ginger, finely chopped
   (or ¼ teaspoon dried ginger)
¼ cup fresh coriander, chopped
⅓ cup fresh mint, chopped
   (or 2 tablespoons dried mint)
¼ cup fresh basil, chopped
   (or 2 tablespoons dried basil)
2 tablespoons fresh lime juice
1 teaspoon fructose
1½ pounds ground turkey
3 tablespoons whole wheat bread crumbs
Pepper to taste

Directions:

1. *Into a food processor with the motor running, drop the garlic and ginger through the feeding tube and process for a few seconds. Add the herbs, lime juice, fructose and process a few seconds to mince and blend well. Do not over process. If you are using dried herbs, chop and mix by hand. (Using fresh herbs is what makes this recipe so very tasty!)*

2. *In a bowl, combine turkey, herb mixture, bread crumbs and pepper and then form the mixture into four 1" thick patties.*

3. *Grill on an oiled rack 5-6 inches over coals for 8-9 minutes on each side or until cooked through.*

4. *Serve with a cucumber salad and enjoy!*

Turkey Breast with Lemon and Herbs

Serves 4 to 6

Ingredients:

1 boneless turkey breast (about 4 pounds)
1 cup low sodium chicken broth
3 tablespoons fresh lemon juice
1 teaspoon dried tarragon, crushed
⅛ teaspoon garlic powder
1 teaspoon olive oil or safflower oil
Freshly ground black pepper to taste

Directions:

1. *Preheat oven to 325.°*

2. *Remove webbing or string, trim all fat, then re-tie the turkey breast and place it on a rack in a small roasting pan.*

3. *Stir together the chicken broth, lemon juice, tarragon, oil, and garlic powder. Brush the turkey with this basting liquid and sprinkle lightly with black pepper.*

4. *Place in oven and roast for 2 hours, or until the internal temperature reaches 175° on a meat thermometer. Brush with the basting liquid every 15-20 minutes. When cooked, remove the string and serve thinly sliced.*

Turkey Gravy

Ingredients:

Roast turkey pan containing drippings
4 cups fat free chicken or turkey broth
¼ teaspoon celery seeds
¼ teaspoon marjoram
Pinch thyme
½ teaspoon parsley flakes
½ teaspoon Kitchen Bouquet
2-3 tablespoons cornstarch
    or arrowroot diluted in ¼ cup broth
Pinch salt and pepper

Directions:

1. *Remove excess fat from roasting pan. Add stock, stirring to loosen brown particles from bottom of pan. Add celery seeds, marjoram, thyme, parsley, Kitchen Bouquet, salt and pepper. Bring to a boil, lower heat and simmer for 5 minutes.*

2. *Add cornstarch or arrowroot mixture and cook, stirring constantly until thickened. Taste and adjust seasoning.*

Turkey and Mushroom Loaf

Serves 6 to 8

Ingredients:

1 10 oz. package fresh mushrooms, sliced
2 tablespoons safflower oil
½ cup finely chopped onions
1 garlic clove, chopped
½ teaspoon thyme
2 pounds ground turkey
¾ cup fresh whole wheat bread crumbs (3 slices)
⅓ cup skim milk
2 eggs
Pinch sea salt and pepper
3 tablespoons fresh parsley, finely chopped
¼ teaspoon Lea & Perrins Worcestershire sauce
2 bay leaves

Directions:

1. *Preheat oven to 350.°*

2. *Process bread in food processor to make bread crumbs. Heat oil in a heavy skillet, add onions and garlic and sauté about 3 minutes. Add mushrooms and thyme and cook until mushrooms are tender, stirring often. Let cool in a large mixing bowl.*

3. *When cool, add turkey, bread crumbs, milk, eggs, salt, pepper, Worcestershire sauce and parsley. Work the mixture with your hands until thoroughly blended. (You may want to wear disposable rubber gloves to mix this.) Pack the mixture into a 9" x 5" x 3" loaf pan. Place the bay leaves on top.*

4. *Bake 1¼ hours. Let stand 15 minutes before serving.*

Turkey-Spinach Pie

Serves 4

Ingredients:

2 pounds ground turkey
1 package frozen spinach, defrosted and drained
1 medium onion, finely chopped
2 eggs
¾ cup crushed saltines
½ teaspoon sage
Sea salt and black pepper to taste

Directions:

1. Preheat oven to 350.°

2. Place all ingredients in a large bowl and mix thoroughly.

3. Spray pie dish (glass preferred) with Pam. Press prepared mixture into pie plate. Bake for one hour until done.

Note: The mixture can also be shaped into meatloaf and baked.

Turkey Stew
with Mushrooms

Serves 4

Ingredients:

2 tablespoons canola oil
2 pounds turkey breast, cut into 1½" cubes
6 cups water
¾ cup carrots, cut into 1" pieces
⅓ cup celery, sliced
½ pound mushrooms, sliced
20-25 frozen pearl onions, defrosted
½ teaspoon tarragon
½ teaspoon Kitchen Bouquet
4 tablespoons arrowroot
Chopped fresh parsley for garnish
Pinch sea salt and pepper

Directions:

1. *Heat oil and brown pieces of turkey in a casserole (a few pieces at a time, not to crowd the pan). Place browned pieces into a dish. Deglaze pan with water stirring constantly. Add meat, salt and pepper and simmer covered 20 minutes.*

2. *Add carrots, celery, mushrooms, onions, tarragon and Kitchen Bouquet and bring to a boil. Lower heat and simmer covered until meat is tender and cooked through, about 30 minutes.*

3. *Reduce heat to a gentle simmer, mix arrowroot with a little water, and slowly add to the stew, stirring constantly for a few seconds, just enough to thicken sauce. Correct seasoning, garnish with parsley and serve.*

Turkey and Spinach Loaf

Ingredients:

1 10 oz. package frozen chopped spinach
1½ pounds ground turkey
½ cup fresh whole wheat bread crumbs (2 slices)
½ teaspoon pepper
Pinch sea salt
½ cup celery, coarsely chopped
¼ teaspoon oregano
½ cup fresh parsley
¼ cup skim milk
1 clove garlic, finely minced
2 tablespoons olive oil
½ cup onions, finely chopped
2 eggs
2 bay leaves

Directions:

1. *Preheat oven to 350.°*

2. *Cook spinach according to package directions. Transfer to a colander, pour cold water over to cool. Drain and press with your hands to extract the moisture.*

Directions continued on the following page

Turkey and Spinach Loaf Directions continued:

3. Put bread broken into pieces in food processor and process to make bread crumbs. Remove, add celery and parsley to food processor bowl and process until very finely chopped.

4. Put meat in a large mixing bowl, add spinach, bread crumbs, milk, parsley mixture, garlic and eggs.

5. Heat oil, add onions and cook until wilted, then add to the meat mixture. Blend thoroughly with your hands, wearing disposable rubber gloves if preferred. Place in a loaf pan, put the bay leaves on top. Bake for 1¼ hours. Let stand 20 minutes before serving.

Turkey-Yogurt Burgers

Serves 4

Ingredients:

1 pound lean, ground turkey
3 tablespoons plain, lowfat yogurt
⅓ cup skim milk
¼ teaspoon black pepper
⅛ teaspoon ground nutmeg
1 cup whole-grain bread crumbs*

Directions:

1. *In medium bowl, mix turkey, yogurt, milk, pepper, nutmeg and half of the bread crumbs.*

2. *Form meat mixture into four patties. Coat both sides of the burgers with remaining bread crumbs.*

3. *Set on a rack and refrigerate, uncovered, for 20 minutes.*

4. *Broil or grill for 5 minutes on each side.*

  * *For whole grain bread crumbs: Place 3 slices of whole grain bread in a toaster oven turned to low heat. Leave them for about 20 minutes until the bread dries. Cool and crumble with your hands.*

Lamb

⌐📖   Indicates recipe created by Monique Hill

Apple Cider Lamb Stew

Serves 8

Ingredients:

3½ pounds boned leg of lamb
4 cups apple cider
½ cup whole wheat flour
3 tablespoons olive oil
1 small onion, finely chopped
3 garlic cloves, minced
1¼ cups nonfat, low sodium chicken broth
½ cup dry white wine (optional)
½ teaspoon black pepper
½ teaspoon sea salt
4 lemon rind strips (about 1"x3")
3 bay leaves
1 cinnamon stick
3 cups parsnips, cut into 1" pieces
1¼ cups sliced carrots
1½ cups sliced green zucchini
1¼ cups broccoli florets, divided

Directions:

1. Trim fat from lamb, cut into 2" cubes. Combine lamb and 3 cups cider in a large zip-top plastic bag. Seal, shake, and marinate in refrigerator for at least 8 hours, or preferably overnight.

2. Drain lamb, discarding marinade. Pat lamb dry with paper towels. Place flour in a large, dry, zip-top plastic bag. Place

Directions continued on the following page

Apple Cider Lamb Stew continued

half of the lamb in the bag, seal, and shake to coat. Heat 1 tablespoon oil in a Dutch oven over medium heat; add floured lamb and cook for about 5 minutes until browned. Remove from pan. Repeat this procedure with the rest of the lamb.

3. Heat 1 tablespoon olive oil, add onion and garlic; sauté 5-6 minutes. Return lamb to pan; add 1 cup cider, broth, and next six ingredients, through cinnamon. Bring to a boil, cover, reduce heat and simmer 1½ hours or until lamb is tender.

4. Add parsnips and carrots; bring to a boil. Cover, reduce heat, and simmer 15 minutes. Stir in zucchini and broccoli; cook 5 minutes.

5. Remove lemon rind, bay leaves, and cinnamon stick before serving.

French Lamb Stew

Serves 6

Ingredients:

4 tablespoons corn oil
2½-3 pounds boneless leg of lamb,
    trimmed of all fat, cut into cubes
1 large onion, diced
¼ cup unbleached all-purpose flour
4 cups water
1 cup fat-free, low sodium chicken broth
3 garlic cloves, finely chopped
1 bay leaf
½ teaspoon thyme
½ teaspoon Kitchen Bouquet
Pinch sea salt and pepper to taste
4 carrots, cut into 1" pieces
18-20 frozen pearl onions
3 small white turnips, peeled and quartered
12-15 snow peas (optional)

Directions:

1. *Heat oil in a large, heavy casserole, add lamb cubes and brown well on all sides, turning the pieces only after they have been browned. Do this in batches not to crowd the pan, or the meat will steam instead of brown. Remove browned meat and set in a platter as you go along.*

Directions continued on the following page

French Lamb Stew Directions continued:

2. When all the meat is browned and out of the pan, add onions and stir well to loosen any particles that have adhered to the pan from browning the meat. Cook for a few minutes.

3. Sprinkle flour and stir over low heat for a few minutes. Add water and broth, whisking constantly to thicken the sauce.

4. Add meat, garlic, bay leaf, thyme and Kitchen Bouquet, stir well. Simmer for about 1½-2 hours, or until meat is very tender.

5. Separately boil vegetables until tender but still crisp. Add to the stew and cook about 10 minutes more. Skim any fat remaining on the sauce and serve.

Gravy for Lamb

Serves 4 to 6

Ingredients:

1 tablespoon corn oil
1 tablespoon butter
1 small onion, minced
3-4 mushrooms, finely chopped
2 tablespoons minced parsley
½ carrot, grated
Pinch thyme and rosemary
1 bay leaf
1½ tablespoons unbleached flour
1 cup fat-free, low sodium chicken broth
Pepper to taste

Directions:

1. Pour all ingredients into saucepan except broth. Cook on low heat for about 10 minutes stirring constantly.

2. Add chicken broth whisking constantly and simmer for 2-3 minutes or until thickened.

3. Strain and season to taste.

Garlic Broiled Lamb Chops

Serves 4

Ingredients:

4 loin lamb chops (¾" thick)
1 tablespoon olive oil
1 teaspoon garlic powder
½ teaspoon mild herbs, dried
¼ cup vegetable bouillon

Directions:

1. Preheat broiler to 500.°

2. In a medium saucepan, mix olive oil, garlic powder, mild herbs and bouillon. Cook over low heat, stirring occasionally, for 3-4 minutes.

3. Brush lamb chops with half of the mixture, then place in broiler. Broil 3-4 inches from heat for 5-6 minutes.

4. Turn chops, brush with remaining oil/garlic mixture, then broil 5-6 minutes until well done.

Greek-style Herbed Roast Leg of Lamb

Serves 10

Ingredients:

1 leg of lamb (about 6 pounds)
1 teaspoon garlic powder or fresh garlic cloves
1½ teaspoons salt
½ teaspoon ground black pepper
3 teaspoons oregano
½ cup olive oil
2 tablespoons fresh lemon juice

Directions:

1. *Preheat oven to 325.°*

2. *Trim all visible fat, wash lamb, then pat dry with paper towel.*

3. *With a sharp knife make 5 or 6 slits, ½" wide and 2 inches deep, over the top of the roast. Fill each slit with a little garlic powder or minced fresh garlic.*

4. *Mix together 1 teaspoon oregano, 1 teaspoon salt, ¼ teaspoon black pepper and ¼ teaspoon garlic powder. Rub this mixture all over outside of lamb.*

5. *Combine remaining salt, black pepper, oregano, oil and lemon juice. Heat this mixture, then brush all over lamb.*

6. *Put meat on a rack and place rack in a large, shallow baking pan. Cook uncovered for 3 to 3½ hours, basting several times with hot herbed oil and lemon juice.*

7. *Remove lamb from roasting pan and place on a serving platter. [The psoriatic should not use the pan drippings as a gravy.]*

Grilled Lamb Burgers

Serves 4

Ingredients:

1 pound ground lamb
¼ cup minced onion
1 garlic clove, finely chopped
Dash of oregano

Directions:

1. Mix all ingredients very well, then form into 4 patties.

2. Grill on both sides until they are well done.

   Note: Outdoor grills should not be started using liquid or spray starter fluid. They should be started by an automatic igniter within the unit, by an electric starter or by lighting kindling.

Ground Lamb on Skewers

Serves 4 to 6

Ingredients:

1½ pound boneless leg of lamb
1 large onion, chopped
½ teaspoon allspice powder
Dash sea salt and pepper to taste
2 tablespoons olive oil

Directions:

1. Remove fat and sinew from meat, cut into 1" cubes. Place half of meat in food processor and process, turning on and off rapidly until meat is chopped to desired texture, about 10 seconds. Do not process until smooth. Repeat with remaining meat. (Or, pass the lamb cubes through a meat grinder twice. Or, ask the butcher to grind the meat for you. Sometimes you can find ground lamb in the supermarket.)

2. Mix in onions, allspice, salt and pepper, carefully and thoroughly working the meat into a smooth texture.

3. Divide the mixture into 12 equal portions and shape around moistened sword-like skewers. (The skewers should be flat and wide, not thin or round.) Press the meat on the skewers into a thin flat sausage shape, about 5" long. Moisten your hands frequently with cold water as you go along. (You could also shape the meat into patties and cook them as you would a hamburger.)

4. Cook over hot coals, turning skewers frequently to brown evenly. Cook about 8-10 minutes, brushing with the olive oil occasionally. Slide meat off skewers to serve.

Irish Lamb Stew

Ingredients:

3 pounds chuck lamb, cubed
6 medium rutabagas (yellow turnips),
  peeled and sliced
3 large Spanish onions, sliced
1 pound carrots, thickly sliced
2 tablespoons fresh parsley, chopped
1 tablespoon fresh thyme, chopped
2-3 cups water
Salt and pepper to taste

Directions:

1. *Place alternating layers of turnips, onions, carrots, and meat in a stewing pot. Add the herbs, salt and pepper as you go along.*

2. *Add water, cover and bring to a boil on top of stove. Let simmer for about 2 hours. Add water if needed. Stir gently so it won't stick to the bottom of the pot. The gravy should be fairly thick.*

Lamb Burgers in Pita Bread

Serves 4

Ingredients:

1½ pounds ground lamb, trimmed of all fat
2 tablespoons onions, finely chopped
1 garlic clove, very finely chopped
¼ teaspoon oregano
Pinch sea salt and pepper
4 individual size pita breads
Yogurt Sauce:
1 cup nonfat yogurt
1 clove garlic, minced and mashed to a paste
2 tablespoons fresh mint, chopped
¼ cup red onion, chopped

Directions:

1. Put yogurt in a sieve lined with paper towels or cheesecloth set over a bowl and let drain for 30 minutes. Transfer yogurt to a small bowl, add garlic, mint and red onions and stir to mix. Refrigerate.

2. Combine lamb with onions, garlic, oregano, salt and pepper. Form into four patties. Grill on an oiled rack set 5-6 inches over hot coals for about 6-7 minutes on each side, or until lamb is well done.

3. Serve burgers into the pita bread with some of the yogurt sauce.

   Note: You can ask the butcher to grind the lamb for you, or you can use leg of lamb cut into 1" cubes and processed in the food processor for about ten seconds using on and off method, or pass the lamb through a meat grinder twice.

Lamb and Barley Stew

Serve with crusty whole grain bread.

Serves 4

Ingredients:

1 pound boneless lamb shoulder, trimmed
    and cut into 2" cubes
2 tablespoons all-purpose flour
1 tablespoon olive oil
1 large onion, chopped
1 large garlic clove, minced
1 large carrot, sliced
2 large parsnips, sliced
½ cup barley
3 cups chicken stock, fat removed
1 whole bay leaf
1 teaspoon sea salt
½ teaspoon black pepper
¼ teaspoon dried thyme
¼ teaspoon dried rosemary
1 package frozen string beans, thawed

Directions:

1. *Preheat oven to 350.°*

2. *Dredge lamb in flour. In a 5-quart Dutch oven; heat oil over medium heat. Add lamb and sauté until brown, about 5 minutes. With a slotted spoon, remove and set aside.*

3. *Lower heat and add onions, garlic, carrots, parsnips and ½ cup chicken stock. Cook for 6 minutes.*

Directions continued on the following page

Lamb and Barley Stew *continued*

4. Return lamb to Dutch oven and add barley, remaining chicken stock, bay leaf, sea salt, pepper, thyme and rosemary. Bring to a boil.

5. Cover and transfer into oven. Bake for 40 minutes. Add string beans and bake for an additional 10 minutes, or until lamb is tender. Remove bay leaf before serving.

A patient suffering from allergies visited a medical doctor who specialized in that field. As a routine question, the M.D. asked him if he had been to any other doctors before coming to him.

"Yes, my chiropractor," replied the patient.

"And what ridiculous advice did he give you?" asked the allergist.

"He told me to come and see you!" said the patient.

Lamb with Cabbage

Serves 6

Ingredients:

1 tablespoon olive oil
3 pounds boned leg of lamb,
  trimmed of all fat, cut into 1" cubes
1 cabbage (about 2 pounds), quartered,
  cored, and sliced
1 large onion, sliced
2 bay leaves
¼ teaspoon allspice
1 teaspoon fructose
2 cups boiling water
2 whole carrots
Pinch salt and pepper

Directions:

1. Preheat oven to 350.°

2. Mix cabbage and onions together. Oil a heavy casserole, make a layer of cabbage mixture, season with a piece of bay leaf, sprinkle with some allspice and fructose. Make a layer of lamb pieces and season the same way. Repeat the cabbage and lamb layers.

3. Add hot water, place carrots on top. Season with salt and pepper

4. Cook covered for 2-2½ hours, until the meat is tender and well cooked. Check after one hour of cooking and add more water if necessary.

Lamb and Celery Stew

Ingredients:

1 pound lamb meat, cut in 1" cubes
4 tablespoons olive oil
1 large onion, finely chopped
Sea salt and pepper to taste
½ teaspoon cinnamon
¼ teaspoon nutmeg
2 cups water
4 cups celery, diced
1 cup fresh parsley, chopped
3 tablespoons lemon juice

Directions:

1. *In a large saucepan, sauté onions in 2 tablespoons olive oil. Add meat and seasonings, and stir until meat is browned on all sides. Add water, cover, cook on medium heat for about 30-40 minutes or until meat is tender.*

2. *In a medium saucepan over medium heat, sauté celery and parsley for about 10 minutes.*

3. *Add vegetables and lemon juice to the meat, simmer for another 15 minutes. Serve over rice.*

Lamb Patties
or Meatballs

Serves 2 to 4

Ingredients:

1 pound fresh ground lamb
1 medium onion, finely chopped
½ teaspoon garlic powder
⅛ teaspoon ground coriander
1 teaspoon parsley flakes

Directions:

1. Mix all ingredients thoroughly, preferably by hand.

2. Shape into 4 patties or 16 meatballs. Broil 10-12 minutes, turning once, until done.

Lamb Pot Roast

Serves 6

Ingredients:

5-6 pounds boneless leg of lamb,
   tied with a string
3 tablespoons olive oil
4 cups no-fat, low sodium chicken broth
1 cup dry red wine
2 cups carrot chunks
2 cups diced yellow turnips
1½ cups frozen pearl onions
1 cup sliced celery
1 teaspoon thyme
1 bay leaf
Pinch sea salt and pepper to taste

Directions:

1. Preheat oven to 350.°

2. Heat oil in dutch oven or heavy casserole pan and brown meat slowly on all sides. Add broth, wine, thyme, bay leaf, salt and pepper. Cover tightly and cook for 2 hours turning meat once or twice during cooking.

3. Add remaining ingredients, adding some water or broth if necessary. Liquid in casserole should just cover vegetables. Cook for 1 hour or until meat is very tender and vegetables are cooked through.

4. Transfer meat to a deep serving platter. Arrange vegetables around it. Spoon a little sauce over all. Serve remaining sauce in a gravy boat.

Marinated Broiled Leg of Lamb

Serves 6 to 8

Ingredients:

1 6-7 pound leg of lamb
⅓ cup olive oil
3 tablespoons fresh lemon juice
3 large garlic cloves, crushed
1 tablespoon rosemary or oregano
2 tablespoons low sodium soy sauce
Pepper to taste

Directions:

1. Have the butcher butterfly a leg of lamb for broiling with all the excess fat and gristle removed.

2. Place lamb in a shallow baking dish. Combine remaining ingredients and pour over lamb. Cover and refrigerate for 5-6 hours, turning the meat frequently.

3. Drain lamb, reserving the marinade. Grill over hot coals for about 15 minutes on each side or to desired doneness, basting frequently with the marinade.

4. Cut into thin slices and serve.

Marinated Lamb Kabobs

Serves 4

Ingredients:

1 ½ pounds boneless leg of lamb,
   trimmed of all fat
1 cup no-fat plain yogurt
2 garlic cloves, crushed
¼ teaspoon rosemary
Dash sea salt and pepper to taste
1 red onion

Directions:

1. Cut lamb into 1" cubes. In a large bowl, combine remaining ingredients, except onion. Add meat cubes, stir to coat, cover and refrigerate for several hours, or preferably overnight.

2. Cut onion into 1½" pieces. Alternately thread pieces of onion and marinated lamb cubes onto 5 or 6 skewers, leaving a little space between cubes for even cooking. Brush off excess marinade.

3. Grill over hot coals turning frequently during cooking until meat is well done. Serve with grilled vegetables and salad.

Mr. Wok's
Hunan Lamb

Serves 2

Ingredients:

12-14 ounces boneless leg of lamb, thinly sliced
8-10 medium whole scallions, cut into 1-2
  inch lengths
8-10 baby corn
6-8 broccoli florets

Ingredients for stir-frying:

½ teaspoon soybean oil -or- olive oil
2 teaspoon soy sauce
½ teaspoon sugar
1 teaspoon fresh ginger, minced
2 scallions, minced
1-2 cloves garlic, minced

Directions:

1. *Steam the scallions, corn, and broccoli over boiling water for about 1 minute. Set aside.*

2. *In the wok, heat the oil. Add the minced garlic and ginger, then add the lamb slices. Stir-fry for about a minute. Add the steamed vegetables and stir-fry for another minute.*

3. *Add the minced scallions, sugar and soy sauce and stir-fry for about half a minute. Serve.*

Roast Leg of Lamb with Artichokes

Serves 6 to 8

Ingredients:

1 leg of lamb, 5-6 pounds, trimmed of fat
2 garlic cloves, sliced
2 tablespoons olive oil
1 teaspoon oregano
½ teaspoon thyme
¼ cup lemon juice
3 cups boiling water
2 packages frozen artichokes,
   rinsed and defrosted
Pinch sea salt and pepper to taste

Directions:

1. Preheat oven to 400.°

2. Make small slits into the leg of lamb and insert garlic slices.

3. Mix oil with thyme, oregano, salt and pepper and rub all over roast. Place in a roasting pan, cook in the oven for 30 minutes.

4. Reduce heat to 350° and continue baking for 1½ hours. Add water and lemon juice, basting the roast with juices. Add artichokes, bake for another ½ hour or until lamb is done and artichokes are tender.

5. Let the lamb rest for 10 minutes before serving.

Roast Leg of Lamb

Serves 6 to 8

Ingredients:

1 leg of lamb, 6-7 pounds, trimmed of fat
2 garlic cloves, sliced
3 tablespoons olive oil
2 teaspoons rosemary
Dash sea salt and pepper to taste
¾ cup no fat, low sodium chicken broth

Directions:

1. Preheat oven to 400.°

2. Make small slits into the leg of lamb and insert the garlic slices. Mix oil with rosemary, salt and pepper and rub all over the surface. Place in a roasting pan and place in oven. Reduce temperature to 375.°

3. Roast for about 1½-2 hours. Instant meat thermometer inserted into thickest part of the meat should register 145° for medium and 155° for well done. Let stand 10 minutes before serving.

4. Add broth to the pan stirring to melt the solidified juices, boil for a few minutes to make a natural gravy.

Rosemary Lamb Roast

Ingredients:

Lamb (cut and amount of your choice)
Garlic cloves, whole and minced
Rosemary, dried or fresh
Poupon Mustard
White wine
Salt and pepper

Directions:

1. Preheat oven to 450.°

2. Cut away all visible fat, then place lamb in roasting pan. With a sharp knife-point, make slits all over the top of the lamb. Insert a peeled garlic clove into each slit.

3. Combine minced garlic, rosemary, mustard, wine, salt and pepper in a mixing bowl. Use a wire whisk to blend it to the consistency of a paste. Spread this mixture over the entire surface of the lamb.

4. Place in oven and cook until the covering of the lamb turns golden brown. Lower heat to 375° and continue to cook until done to your preference.

Helpful Hint

(Note: Size of lamb cut does not matter, it is the manner of preparation that counts. Adjust the amount of ingredients to the size of the cut you have.)

Vegetarian Dishes

Vegetarian Dishes

Vegetarian Dishes

Please refer to 'Side Dishes' for further recipes that may be
used in a vegetarian diet.

⌐⌐   Indicates recipe created by Monique Hill

Brown Rice with Carrots and Leeks

Serves 4 to 6

Ingredients:

4 leeks, rinsed well
2 cups boiling water
2 tablespoons canola oil
2 cups carrots, sliced
1 cup brown rice
2 cups fat-free, low sodium chicken broth
Salt and pepper to taste

Directions:

1. Split leek and cut into 1" pieces, then place in a large bowl and cover completely with boiling water. Let stand for 5 minutes.

2. Heat oil in a medium sized sauce pan. Add carrots, cover and cook slowly for 10 minutes or until soft, but firm.

3. Drain and dry leek and add to carrots. Cover and cook for 2 minutes.

4. Add rice and chicken broth. Cover and bring to a boil. Lower heat and simmer for 40 minutes.

Brown Rice with Lentils

Serves 4 to 6

Ingredients:

2 cups brown rice
½ cup brown lentils
1 large onion, chopped
3 tablespoons safflower oil
4 cups boiling water
Sea salt to taste

Directions:

1. In a heavy, deep pan, heat oil, add onions and sauté until transparent and lightly flecked with brown. Add rice and lentils and stir over medium heat for 3 minutes.

2. Add boiling water slowly and salt to taste. Return to a boil, stirring occasionally. Reduce heat to low, cover and simmer gently for 45 minutes or until liquid is absorbed.

3. Remove from heat and let stand for 10-15 minutes before serving.

Brown Rice, Mushroom and Green Pea Medley with Tofu

Serves 2

Ingredients:

½ cup brown rice
1¼ cup bottled spring water
4 large mushrooms (white or shiitake), sliced
2 tablespoons low sodium soy sauce or tamari
2 tablespoons rice wine
1 teaspoon honey
1 cup tofu, cubed
½ cup green peas, fresh or frozen
1 scallion, sliced (including green part),
   for garnish

Directions

1. Bring rice and water to a boil in a medium size saucepan with a tight-fitting lid. Lower heat and cover. Simmer until all water is absorbed, about 40 minutes.

2. In a small saucepan over medium heat, add mushrooms, soy sauce or tamari, rice wine and honey. Bring to a boil and reduce heat to low. Simmer until the mushrooms are limp. Add peas and tofu and heat for a few minutes.

3. Gently stir mushroom mixture into cooked rice. Serve with sliced scallions.

Brown Rice with Zucchini

Serves 4 to 6

Ingredients:

1 small onion, chopped fine
1 tablespoon olive oil
2 garlic cloves, minced
1 cup brown rice
2 cups fat-free, low sodium chicken broth
1 medium zucchini, diced into ¼" pieces

Directions:

1. *Preheat oven to 350.°*

2. *In a 2-quart, flameproof casserole or sauce pan heat olive oil and add onion and garlic. Reduce heat to low and cook covered, stirring occasionally, about 3-4 minutes. Increase heat and add rice. Cook rice, stirring 3 minutes. Add broth slowly and bring to a boil.*

3. *Bake rice, covered in the middle of the oven about 20 minutes or until liquid is absorbed. Stir in zucchini and let stand covered for 5 minutes before serving.*

Carrot Broth with Kombu

Serves 4

This broth has an Asian flavor and is a light, healthy mixture. Kombu, also called kelp, is found in health food stores and Asian markets. It contains a considerable amount of sodium, so no other salt should be necessary in this recipe.

Ingredients:

5 cups bottled spring water
1 1" piece kombu seaweed, soaked in hot water
   10 minutes, drained
1 teaspoon canola oil
1 medium onion, chopped
1 clove garlic, minced
3 large carrots, sliced
1½ teaspoons grated fresh ginger
Low sodium soy sauce -or- tamari, to taste
6 fresh cilantro sprigs, for garnish

Directions:

1. *In a large saucepan, bring water to a boil. Add softened kombu, cover, simmer 5 minutes.*

2. *Meanwhile, in a medium saucepan, heat oil over medium heat. Stir in onions, garlic, carrots and ginger. Cook until soft, about 5-8 minutes.*

3. *Add the vegetables to the kombu water. Simmer 15 minutes or until the carrots are tender.*

4. *Purée mixture in a blender or food processor until smooth. Add soy sauce or tamari. Serve garnished with cilantro.*

Carrot Caraway Pockets

Serves 2

Ingredients:

¾ cup spelt flour*
1 teaspoon caraway seeds
¼ cup bottled spring water, lukewarm
1 teaspoon olive oil
1 large carrot, grated
1 small onion, chopped
2 tablespoons fresh parsley, minced
2 ounces low fat cheddar cheese
    (or cheddar-style soy cheese), shredded

Directions:

1. In a large bowl, mix together flour and caraway seeds. Add water and mix to form a ball. Knead for 5 minutes. Cover and let rest for 5 minutes.

2. Meanwhile, in a medium non-stick sauté pan, heat oil over medium heat. Add carrots and onion. Sauté for 4 minutes or until the vegetables are soft. Add parsley and transfer to a medium bowl. Cool completely.

3. On a surface dusted with spelt flour, divide the dough into 4 equal pieces. Roll out each piece to about ⅛" thickness.

4. Place one-fourth of the carrot mixture on the center of each piece of dough; top with cheese. Brush water around the edges of each piece, then fold in half to make a pocket; press edges firmly to seal tight.

5. Lightly oil a large non-stick skillet. Over high heat, cook each pocket until crisp, about 2 minutes on each side. Move the pockets around gently while cooking to avoid over-browning. Serve immediately.

* Spelt flour can be purchased in health food stores.

Ceylon-Style Lentils

Serves 2

Dabl *is the name given to lentil dishes that come from southern Asia. This recipe is from Sri Lanka. Red lentils can be found in health food stores and in specialty food stores.*

Ingredients:

1 cup red lentils
2 cups bottled spring water
2 teaspoons olive oil
1 clove garlic, minced
1 medium onion, chopped
1 bay leaf
1 teaspoon fresh ginger, grated
¼ teaspoon turmeric
¼ teaspoon ground cinnamon
½ cup plain soy beverage
1 tablespoon almond butter
¼ teaspoon sea salt
1 tablespoon lemon juice

Directions:

1. *Sort, wash and drain the lentils. Place lentils and water in a medium saucepan. Bring to a boil over high heat. Reduce heat, cover and simmer for 5 minutes. Set aside.*

Directions continued on the following page

Ceylon-Style Lentil Directions:

2. In a large saucepan, heat oil over medium heat. Add garlic, onions and bay leaf. Sauté until onions are soft and lightly brown.

3. Stir in ginger, turmeric and cinnamon. Gently stir in lentils, cover and simmer 15-20 minutes or until lentils are soft.

4. In a small bowl, stir together plain soy beverage, almond butter and sea salt. Add this to the lentil mixture and cook 5 minutes. Stir in lemon juice and simmer for an additional 5 minutes. Serve with whole-grain bread.

Cumin Rice

Serves 4

Ingredients:

1 cup brown rice
2 cups bottled spring water
1 teaspoon cumin seeds
1 pinch turmeric
Sea salt and black pepper, to taste
1 tablespoon fresh cilantro or parsley, minced

Directions:

1. *In a medium saucepan, add rice, water, cumin and turmeric. Bring to a boil, reduce heat to low, and cover. Simmer for about 20 minutes.*

2. *Add sea salt and ground pepper. Cover and simmer for 20 minutes more, or until tender.*

3. *Transfer to a large bowl and toss with cilantro or parsley.*

Crêpes with Spinach and Fresh Goat Cheese

Serves 6 to 8

Ingredients for Crêpes:

4 cups whole wheat flour
6-8 cups low fat milk
2 eggs
Pinch sea salt

Ingredients for Filling:

2 bags spinach, washed
8 ounces low fat fresh goat cheese
2 cloves garlic, minced
2 teaspoons canola oil
Sea salt and pepper to taste

Directions:

1. Preheat oven to 200.° In a large bowl, whip together flour, eggs, salt, and 4 cups of the milk, until the mix is smooth. Gradually add more milk and whip thoroughly until the mix is a good consistency.

2. Use a paper towel to rub the inside of a large skillet with a bit of canola oil. Heat skillet over medium heat. Pour a small amount of the mix into the middle of the skillet. Holding the handle of the skillet, move it around until the mixture spreads out in a thin layer. Cook for 1-2 minutes, then turn crêpe over and cook for another minute until the crêpe is light brown. Repeat until the batter is gone, placing crêpes stacked in warm oven as you go along.

Directions continued on the following page

Crêpes with Spinach and Fresh Goat Cheese
Directions:

3. Wash spinach. Heat 1 teaspoon canola oil in large skillet over medium heat. Add garlic and cook until tender. Add spinach to the pan with a bit of water, salt and pepper. Sauté until soft.

4. Remove crêpes from oven. Place some of the spinach mixture in a line along the middle of each crêpe, top it with a tablespoon of the cheese, then roll it up. Place the crêpes back in the oven for a minute so the cheese can melt a bit. Serve immediately.

Note: There are many other options for filling, such as chicken and mushrooms, asparagus and shaved Parmesan cheese, etc. Be creative!

Easy Garlic and Onion Pasta

Serves 4 to 6

Ingredients:

1 8 oz. package Jerusalem artichoke pasta
½ cup onions, chopped
2 cloves garlic, chopped
1 tablespoon olive oil
1 tablespoon soy sauce
1 tablespoon safflower oil

Directions:

1. Bring a large pot of water to a boil.

2. Heat the oil in a skillet, add the onions and sauté gently until almost golden. Add the garlic and sauté 3-4 minutes more.

3. Add pasta to boiling water and cook until al dente. Drain and toss into a warm serving dish with the onion mixture. Add soy sauce and the safflower oil to moisten the pasta.

4. You can adjust seasoning with a little more soy sauce if desired.

Helpful Hint

You can find Jerusalem artichoke pasta in specialty supermarkets or health food stores. You can also use spinach pasta, but do not use tomato based pasta.

Green Vegetable Casserole

Serves 3-4

Ingredients:

2 cups leek, finely chopped
2 cups spinach, finely chopped
1 cup Romaine lettuce, finely chopped
1 cup fresh parsley, finely chopped
1 cup scallions, finely chopped
1½ tablespoons flour
1 teaspoon sea salt
½ teaspoon black pepper
8 eggs
1 tablespoon olive oil

Directions:

1. Preheat oven to 325.°

2. Place all the chopped vegetables together in a large bowl, mix well. Add flour, salt and pepper, and mix well.

3. In another bowl, beat the eggs and add them to the vegetables. Mix well.

4. Rub the inside of a rectangular pyrex dish with olive oil. Pour the egg and vegetable mix into the dish. Bake for an hour, or until the top is crisp and brown. May be served hot or cold. Delicious served with plain yogurt.

Italian-Style Pasta Sauce

Serves 4

This sauce is a great example of improvisation. Since tomatoes are not permitted on the pso-riasis-eczema diet, this is a tasty alternative!

Ingredients:

1 cup bottled spring water
1 large carrot, chopped
1 large beet, peeled and chopped
1 teaspoon olive oil
1 small onion, finely chopped
1 stalk celery, finely chopped
2 cloves garlic, minced
½ teaspoon dried oregano
½ teaspoon dried basil
1 tablespoon fresh parsley, minced
1 bay leaf
Sea salt and black pepper to taste

Directions:

1. *Bring water to a boil in a medium-sized saucepan with a tight-fitting lid. Place carrots and beets in a steam basket. Cover and steam until tender. Reserve the water.*

Directions continued on the following page

Italian-Style Pasta Sauce Directions:

2. *Purée vegetables in a blender or food processor. Add water as needed to make the mixture smooth. Set aside.*

3. *In a large saucepan, heat oil on medium heat. Add onions, celery and garlic. Sauté for 2-3 minutes or until soft. Add oregano, basil and bay leaf. Sauté for 1 minute.*

4. *Mix in vegetable purée, the reserved liquid and ¼ cup of bottled spring water. Cover and reduce heat to low. Simmer 10 minutes.*

5. *Serve over your choice of permitted pasta, garnished with parsley.*

Kasha and Sweet Brown Rice

Serves 4

Ingredients:

½ cup kasha
¼ cup sweet brown rice
¼ cup shelled sunflower seeds
½ teaspoon ground cinnamon
1 teaspoon sweet white miso
2 cups bottled spring water
4 large cabbage leaves
¼ cup raisins, soaked for 5 minutes in boiling
water, then drained

Directions:

1. Preheat oven to 325.°

2. On a 15" x 20" baking sheet spread kasha, rice and sun-flower seeds; roast in pre-heated oven for 8-10 minutes or until lightly brown. Remove and place in a shallow dish to cool.

3. Dissolve miso in one cup spring water. In a medium sauce-pan, add another cup of spring water, stir in miso mixture and cinnamon.

4. Add roasted grains and sunflower seeds, cover and bring to a boil over medium heat. Lower heat and cook for 45 minutes, or until the grains are tender.

Directions continued on the following page

Kasha and Sweet Brown Rice Directions:

5. Meanwhile, steam cabbage leaves in this way: in a medium saucepan with a tight-fitting lid, add 2 inches of bottled spring water and bring to a boil. Add cabbage leaves and steam 8-10 minutes or until tender. Remove from pan and arrange on a serving platter.

6. Spoon grain mixture onto the steamed cabbage leaves. Garnish with raisins.

Helpful Hint

Kasha, *known as buckwheat groats, adds a heartiness to this dish.* Sweet brown rice *is a short-grain rice variety which becomes sticky when cooked.* Sweet white miso *adds sweetness to this hearty grain dish. These three ingredients can be purchased in health food stores.*

Pungent Broccoli with Baby Corn

Serves 4

Ingredients:

1 bunch broccoli, cut into 1" pieces
2 teaspoons cornstarch mixed with 2 teaspoons cold water
2 tablespoons water
2 tablespoons honey
2 tablespoons lemon juice
1 teaspoon finely chopped garlic
1 teaspoon grated lemon peel
1 cup canned baby corn, rinsed and drained
Dash of low-sodium soy sauce, optional

Directions:

1. *Place broccoli in steamer basket and steam over boiling water until crisp-tender, about 3-4 minutes. Set aside.*

2. *Place water, honey, lemon juice, garlic and lemon peel into wok, heat and stir frequently. Add dissolved cornstarch. Cook for one minute until thickened.*

3. *Add broccoli and baby corn, stir together until heated through, about one minute. Add dash of soy sauce if desired.*

Seitan Stew "Vegetarian"

Serves 2

Ingredients:

1 teaspoon olive oil
2 cloves garlic, minced
½ cup seitan, cut into ½" cubes
1 teaspoon whole wheat flour
1 large carrot, sliced
1 cup broccoli florets
1 medium onion, chopped
1 cup bottled spring water
1 1" piece Kombu seaweed (soak in warm water
   10 minutes, drain)
1 tablespoon fresh lemon juice
Sea salt and black pepper to taste

Directions:

1. *Heat oil in a medium-sized pan, sauté garlic for 1 minute. Add seitan and sauté for 2 minutes. Add whole wheat flour and mix well.*

2. *Mix in carrots, broccoli, onions, water and kombu seaweed. Bring to a boil, reduce heat, and simmer 10 minutes.*

3. *Stir in lemon juice, salt and pepper.*

Sesame Noodles with Kale

Serves 4 to 6

Ingredients:

1 large bunch kale, carefully washed
and thinly sliced
2 cups broccoli florets
1 can chick peas, drained
12 ounces udon or soba noodles
2 tablespoons olive oil
2 tablespoons tamari (or to taste)
2 tablespoons sesame seeds

Directions:

1. Bring large pot of water to a boil. Add pasta and cook for 5 minutes less than cooking time on package directions.

2. Add kale, broccoli and chick peas to pot, gently pressing them down to be fully submerged. Continue cooking uncovered for about 3-5 minutes, until vegetables and pasta are tender.

3. Drain pasta and vegetables and return to pot. Add olive oil and tamari and toss with a fork. Add sesame seeds and toss again. Serve hot or at room temperature.

Soba Medley

Soba or buckwheat noodles *are a nutritious Japanese pasta. They can be found in Asian markets and in health food stores.*

Ingredients:

¼ cup bottled spring water
1 teaspoon fresh ginger, grated
1 clove garlic, minced
1 large carrot, diced
1½ cups savoy cabbage, shredded
1 scallion, chopped
½ cup almonds, toasted and chopped
1 package soba or buckwheat noodles
Low sodium soy sauce or tamari, to taste

Directions:

1. *Boil the water in a medium saucepan with a tight-fitting lid. Add ginger and garlic. Cook for 1 minute.*

2. *Stir in carrots, cover and cook over low heat for 5-7 minutes, or until soft. Meanwhile, cook noodles according to package directions.*

3. *Add cabbage to the carrots and cook covered until wilted, about 4-6 minutes. Toss in scallions and almonds.*

4. *Toss vegetables with drained noodles. Serve with low sodium soy sauce or tamari.*

Sri Lankan-Style Turnip Greens and Soba Noodles

Serves 4

Ingredients:

2 teaspoons canola oil
1 medium onion, chopped
¼ teaspoon turmeric
10 medium turnip greens, shredded
1 package soba noodles
½ cup chopped almonds
2 tablespoons lemon juice
Sea salt and pepper to taste

Directions:

1. *In a medium saucepan, heat oil over medium heat. Sauté onion and turmeric for 3 minutes. Add shredded turnip greens. Adjust heat to low, cover and cook turnip greens until wilted, about 5-7 minutes.*

2. *Mix in almonds and cook for 2 minutes. Add lemon juice, sea salt and pepper.*

3. *Cook soba noodles according to package directions.*

4. *To serve, place turnip greens over soba noodles.*

Tacos by Maribel

Serves 4

Ingredients:

1 box (8 pieces) El Paso white corn taco shells
1 medium onion, minced
1 cup minced asparagus
1 cup minced broccoli
1 cup minced cauliflower
¼ cup fresh minced parsley
½ teaspoon garlic powder salt
½ teaspoon Italian seasoning
½ teaspoon ground black pepper
¼ cup extra virgin olive oil
2 cups shredded head of lettuce
2 cups lowfat cottage cheese

Directions:

1. *Mix onions, asparagus, broccoli, cauliflower, parsley, garlic powder, Italian seasoning and black pepper in a Pyrex dish.*

2. *Broil mixture in the oven for 10-20 minutes until done, but vegetables have to be crunchy. When done add olive oil to mixture. Set aside.*

3. *Heat taco shells according to the box directions.*

4. *When tacos are done put 2 tablespoons of vegetable mixture in the bottom of each shell, add the lettuce on top, then top it off with cottage cheese.*

Tempeh & Vegetables

Serves 4

Tempeh is a traditional Indonesian soy food. It is high in protein and useful digestive enzymes. Be sure to purchase tempeh prepared without nightshades. Rice wine, also called mirin, can be found in health food stores and Asian markets.

Ingredients:

1 package plain soy tempeh, cubed
½ cup bottled spring water, boiled
2 large carrots, sliced
2 cups cabbage, shredded
1 medium onion, chopped
2 cloves garlic, minced
2 stalks celery, sliced
1 teaspoon arrowroot
1 tablespoon tamari
1 tablespoon rice wine mirin
1 tablespoon fresh ginger, grated
1 cup Romaine lettuce, finely shredded

Directions:

1. *Place tempeh and water in a medium-sized saucepan. Add carrots, and cook covered for 5 minutes over medium heat. Add cabbage, onions, garlic and celery. Cover and cook for another 2-3 minutes.*

2. *Dissolve arrowroot in tamari and rice wine. Mix in ginger and add this mixture to the tempeh. Over medium heat, cook until thickened, about 3 minutes.*

3. *Add Romaine lettuce and cover for 4 minutes. Serve immediately over brown rice.*

Tofu in Spinach

Serves 4

Ingredients:

4 large pieces tofu
1 bag fresh spinach
½ cup low fat milk
½ cup low fat, low salt chicken broth
1 medium onion, chopped
6-8 cloves of garlic, minced
2-3 tablespoons canola oil
Sea salt to taste

Directions:

1. Thoroughly wash, chop, and drain spinach, discarding large stems.

2. Place oil in large pan, sauté onions until lightly brown. Add garlic and sauté briefly. Add spinach and stir over medium heat until you see it wilting.

3. Add milk and chicken broth, stir. Simmer for 5 minutes. Add tofu, stir, and simmer for another 5-8 minutes. Serve with pita bread.

Vegetable and Tofu Stir-Fry

Serves 6

Ingredients:

1 tablespoon canola oil
1 clove garlic, minced
1 medium onion, chopped
1 teaspoon fresh ginger, grated
1 large carrot, sliced
1 stalk celery, sliced
4 stalks bok choy*
1½ cups broccoli florets
1 pound tofu (firm), diced into ½" pieces
½ cup fresh parsley, minced
2 medium scallions, chopped
2 teaspoons miso (soy bean paste)
1 cup bottled spring water
2 teaspoons cornstarch
Low sodium soy sauce -or- tamari, to taste

To prepare the bok choy, separate the stalk from the leaves and slice diagonally. The stalks will be used in the stir-fry. Shred the leaves and save them for use at the end of the preparation.

Directions:

1. *In a large wok or stock pot, add oil over medium heat. Stir-fry garlic, onions and ginger for 2 minutes or until onions are soft.*

Directions continued on the following page

Vegetable and Tofu Stir-Fry Directions:

2. Add carrots, celery, sliced bok choy stalks and broccoli. Stir-fry for 1 minute. Cover and cook for 6-8 minutes or until the vegetables are soft.

3. Gently toss in tofu, parsley and scallions. In a small bowl, blend together miso, water and cornstarch. Add to the vegetables, taking care not to crush the tofu. The liquid should become thick and translucent; about 2-3 minutes.

4. Place shredded bok choy leaves on top and cover for 4 minutes, or until the leaves are wilted.

Patient: "Doctor, I simply cannot sleep at night."

Doctor: "Have you tried counting sheep?"

Patient: "No Doctor, I'm a strict vegetarian!"

Doctor: "Then try counting carrots."

Vegetable Brown Rice

Ingredients:

1½ cups brown rice (Japanese variety
   preferred—it's crunchier!)
2 cups broccoli, diced into ¼" cubes
2 cups asparagus, diced into ¼" cubes
1 medium onion, chopped
¼ cup extra virgin olive oil
2 tablespoons low sodium soy sauce
1 teaspoon crushed black pepper
1 teaspoon garlic powder
1 teaspoon onion powder

Directions:

1.   Cook brown rice as directed, toss with a fork, set aside.

2.   Mix broccoli, asparagus and onion with ½ teaspoon each of
       black pepper, onion powder and garlic powder. Place in
       Pyrex dish and bake or broil for 5-10 minutes. Watch
       closely—they need to stay crunchy.

3.   Mix vegetables with the cooked rice, add olive oil and soy
       sauce. Sprinkle with the remaining ½ teaspoon each of black
       pepper, onion powder and garlic powder. Toss well and
       serve.

Directions for Sprouting Beans or Seeds

Almost any bean will sprout. Small seeds such as alfalfa and radish are available in health food stores. Beans, such as garbanzo and lentil, are readily available. Whenever possible, purchase organic seeds and beans.

Add a generous amount of sprouts to salads and sandwiches. This will help you get an additional amount of fresh vegetables and fiber into your diet.

Directions:

1. *Place seeds or beans in a medium-sized, wide-mouth glass jar. A quart-size jar works well.*

2. *Add water at a 3:1 ratio, (i.e. three times the amount of water to the amount of beans). Soak for 15-20 minutes. Remember, the larger the bean, the longer it needs to soak. Please refer to chart below.*

3. *Cover mouth of jar with cheesecloth secured with elastic band, drain water.*

4. *Place the jar at an angle or on its side in a dark, warm environment (about 70º). Sprouts will appear in 2-3 days. Rinse and drain sprouting beans DAILY.*

5. *After the 2-3 days, place jar in direct sunlight for one day. Sprouting time is dependent on type of seed or bean used (see chart).*

6. *Place in a covered container and refrigerate until ready to use. The sprouts will keep for 3-5 days under refrigeration.*

Sprouting Chart

Type of Seed or Bean	Amount of Seed or Bean	Aproximate Grow Time	Amount of Yield
Azuki Beans	½ cup	4 days	2 cups
Alfalfa Seeds	2 tablespoons	5 days	1 quart
Beans (fava, pinto, kidney)	1 cup	3-5 days	1½ cup
Garbanzo*	1 cup	3 days	3 cups
Lentils	1 cup	3 days	6 cups
Mung Beans	1 cup	3-5 days	4 cups
Radish	1 tablespoon	4 days	1 quart
Sunflower seeds	1 cup	24 hours	3 cups

*Garbanzo beans need to soak for 36 hours to soften before starting Step 3.

Side Dishes

Side Dishes

Side Dishes

Please refer to 'Vegetarian Dishes' for further recipes that may
    be used as side dishes.

⌐   Indicates recipe created by Monique Hill

Adele's Zucchini Boats

Serves 2

Ingredients:

2 medium zucchini
4 cloves garlic, minced
¼ cup olive oil
8-12 mushrooms, cleaned, and diced
½ cup dry red wine

Directions:

1. *Preheat oven to 350.°*

2. *Cut zucchini lengthwise, scoop out the inside and set aside.*

3. *Sauté minced garlic in olive oil, stir in mushrooms and sauté further. Add scooped out zucchini and sauté further.*

4. *Add wine, stir and cook until most of the liquid is evaporated. Remove from heat, and stuff this mixture into the scooped-out zucchini.*

5. *Place zucchini in a greased ovenproof dish, and bake covered for 30-35 minutes.*

Antonia's Zucchini

Serves 4

Ingredients:

2 medium zucchini, thinly sliced
½ teaspoon garlic powder
½ cup white wine
Salt and pepper to taste
3-4 thin slices of white onion (optional)

Directions:

1. Place zucchini slices in a saucepan.

2. Add garlic, white wine, salt and pepper. (Add onions if desired.)

3. Mix all together, cover pot and cook on medium heat about 10 minutes until soft.

April's Sweet Potato Bake

Serves 3-4

Enjoy as a healthy snack or a great side dish.

Ingredients:

> 1 large sweet potato
> 2 tablespoons olive oil

Directions:

1.   *Preheat oven to 375.°*

2.   *Thoroughly scrub then thinly slice the sweet potato.*

3.   *Grease a cookie sheet with two tablespoons olive oil. Place sliced sweet potatoes on sheet and bake for about 20 minutes.*

Baked Sweet Potatoes

Serves 4 to 6

Ingredients:

4 medium sweet potatoes
1¾ cup low fat yogurt
3 tablespoons chives, fresh or frozen
Sea salt and pepper to taste

Directions:

1. Preheat oven to 450.°

2. Place yogurt in a sieve lined with cheesecloth over a bowl to drain for 1 hour.

3. Scrub sweet potatoes well and prick in a couple of places. Place on a baking sheet in the oven and bake for about 50 minutes or until tender.

4. Mix drained yogurt with chives and serve with potatoes.

   Note: Baked sweet potatoes are also delicious served with yogurt-honey dressing.

Barbara's Broccoli Dip and Vegetables

Serves 8-10

Ingredients for Dip:

1 bunch broccoli stems, peeled and cut
   in chunks
4 scallions
8-10 sprigs of fresh parsley
6-8 sprigs fresh dill
2 cups lowfat mayonnaise
2 tablespoons extra virgin olive oil
1 teaspoon lemon juice
½ teaspoon sea salt
¼ teaspoon black pepper

Ingredients for Vegetable Platter:

1 green zucchini, sliced diagonally
1 bunch broccoli florets
¼ head cauliflower, florets separated
3-4 carrots, peeled and sliced diagonally
¼ pound fresh green beans, cleaned and halved

Directions:

1. *Place all dip ingredients in blender. Blend on grate or other coarse setting for several minutes. Chill for two hours before serving.*

2. *Arrange cleaned and sliced vegetables attractively on a platter. Serve with chilled broccoli dip.*

Braised Carrots and Celery

Serves 4

Ingredients:

4 carrots, cut into chunks
2 cups celery, cut into 2" pieces
1 small onion, chopped
¾ cup water
1 tablespoon butter
½ teaspoon corn oil
1 tablespoon fresh parsley, chopped

Directions:

1. Cook carrots in boiling water until crisp and tender; about 8 minutes. Drain.

2. Lightly brown carrots, celery and onion in butter and oil for a few minutes. Add water, cover and cook vegetables until tender.

3. Uncover and cook to evaporate liquid. Sprinkle with parsley.

Broccoli with Black Olive Sauce

Serves 2 to 4

Ingredients:

2 cloves garlic, crushed
¼ cup olive oil
½ cup finely chopped pitted black olives
1-2 teaspoons lemon juice
½ teaspoon salt
¼ teaspoon pepper
1 bunch broccoli

Directions:

1. *Sauté garlic in oil in small saucepan over medium-low heat, about 3 minutes. Do not let brown. Add olives, lemon juice, salt and pepper. Cook about 1 minute. Remove from heat.*

2. *Steam broccoli, drain. Pour hot oil over broccoli. Toss and eat.*

Brussels Sprouts with Sesame Seeds

Serves 4 to 6

Ingredients:

2 10 oz. packages fresh Brussels sprouts
½ teaspoon butter
3 tablespoons sesame seeds, toasted

Directions:

1. Toast sesame seeds on top of the stove in a heavy ungreased skillet over medium/low heat. Stir them often for even browning. This should take 1-2 minutes. Watch carefully. Do not let them burn! Remove at once and place into small bowl.

2. Trim the Brussels sprouts, wash and slice crosswise in half. Put into salted boiling water, add butter, and cook uncovered until tender. Do not overcook. They are done when just cooked through, but still slightly crunchy and bright green.

3. Drain well, add the sesame seeds, toss and serve.

Cauliflower with Garlic

Serves 4 to 6

Ingredients:

1 large cauliflower, trimmed
  and divided into florets
6 tablespoons fresh lemon juice
3 tablespoons olive oil
1 garlic clove, chopped very fine
Pinch sea salt

Directions:

1. Boil the cauliflower florets in salted water until crisp and tender.

2. Drain well and place in a large bowl, add garlic.

3. Mix lemon juice and oil, pour over cauliflower, tossing well to coat. Season to taste. Serve at room temperature.

Cauliflower Polish Style

Serves 4 to 6

Ingredients:

 1 large cauliflower, divided into florets
 1 tablespoon butter
 2 tablespoons bread crumbs
 2 tablespoons corn oil
 1 hard-boiled egg, chopped fine, for garnish
 1 teaspoon fresh parsley, chopped, for garnish

Directions:

1. *Boil the cauliflower florets in lightly salted water until crisp and tender. Drain well and keep warm.*

2. *Heat oil and butter in small skillet, add bread crumbs to brown. (Watch carefully as they brown quickly.)*

3. *Spread the mixture over the cauliflower.*

4. *Garnish with chopped egg and parsley.*

Chick Pea Nada

Serves 6

Ingredients:

1 pound dried chick peas
2 teaspoons baking soda
2 large garlic cloves
1 teaspoon sea salt or to taste
3 tablespoons olive oil
Fresh parsley to garnish

Directions:

1.   *Soak chick peas overnight with baking soda in about 6-8 cups water, no salt.*

2.   *Rinse chick peas and add fresh water to cover. (It will bubble when you add the water because of the baking soda left in the peas, but that's fine.) Cook until tender, it will take 1-2 hours. Reserve 1 cup of the cooking liquid and drain peas. Place in a large bowl.*

3.   *Put garlic through a garlic press, add to the peas with the olive oil and salt. It requires quite a bit of salt since it was cooked without it. Add some reserved liquid, about ½ to 1 cup, tossing all the ingredients well, garnish with parsley. Serve at room temperature for lunch, or, as a side dish with a light main course.*

Note: You can adjust the amount of garlic, salt and oil to your taste. This dish is also good with some fresh lemon juice added before serving.

Helpful Hint

You can use three 19 oz. cans of chick peas, drained, rinsed and heated thoroughly, but dried peas taste better.

Cleopatra's Carrots in Orange Sauce

Serves 4

Ingredients:

4 cups of thinly sliced carrots (or baby carrots)
3 tablespoons honey -or- ¼ cup brown sugar
1 cup orange juice
Salt and pepper to taste

Directions:

1. Place sliced carrots in a saucepan.

2. Add orange juice, honey or brown sugar, salt and pepper.

3. Mix all together, simmer over medium heat about 10 minutes, or until done to taste.

Couscous with Ginger and Lemon

Serves 4 to 6

Ingredients:

2 cups couscous
4 cups water
1 cup diced celery
5 tablespoons fresh lemon juice
¼ cup canola oil
2 medium garlic cloves, minced
3 tablespoons fresh ginger root, minced
1 teaspoon lemon zest, minced
2 tablespoons fresh parsley, chopped
1 tablespoon fresh cilantro, chopped
Sea salt and pepper to taste

Directions:

1. *Boil water in a sauce pan with a tight-fitting lid. Stir in couscous.*

2. *Remove from heat, cover and set aside for 5 minutes or until all of the water has been absorbed.*

3. *Fluff with a fork and place in a large bowl to cool, uncovered. Add celery.*

4. *In a medium bowl, whisk together lemon juice, oil, garlic, ginger, lemon zest, parsley and cilantro. Toss into couscous. Season with sea salt and pepper to taste. Refrigerate for at least 3 hours or overnight before serving.*

Note: Great with grilled salmon!

Dr. John's Jerusalem Artichoke Pasta with Olive Oil and Garlic

Serves 4

Ingredients:

16 oz. pkg. Jerusalem Artichoke pasta
(linguine, spaghetti, or angel hair)
Sea Salt to taste
4-5 fresh garlic cloves
1 cup olive oil
1 cup water
Fresh parsley, chopped (optional)

Directions:

1. Heat olive oil on low flame in small saucepan. Add chopped garlic and cook until light brown. Set saucepan aside so sauce can cool while pasta is being prepared.

2. Boil 4 quarts of water. When water is actively boiling, add pasta and a little salt if desired. Cook approximately 10-12 minutes or according to package instructions for al dente.

3. Just before pasta is cooked, remove a cup of water from the boiling pasta and add it to the olive oil-garlic mixture and re-heat the sauce. Add chopped parsley if desired.

4. Drain pasta, place in heated platter and toss with sauce. Serve immediately.

Fragrant Indonesian Rice

Serves 2 to 3

Ingredients:

½ cup soy milk, plain
½ cup water
1 teaspoon almond butter, smooth*
Pinch freshly ground black pepper
1 bay leaf
Pinch nutmeg
½ teaspoon grated lemon rind
¾ cup uncooked brown rice
1 tablespoon fresh lemon juice

Directions:

1. *Mix soy milk and water. Dissolve the almond butter in this liquid.*

2. *Add black pepper, bay leaf, nutmeg and lemon rind. Bring to a boil.*

3. *Add rice and cover tightly. Reduce heat to medium-low and cook until all liquid is absorbed, about 25-30 minutes. Serve warm.*

*Almond Butter is available in health food stores, or you can make your own by following the recipe on page 38.

French Style Peas

Serves 4 to 6

Ingredients:

2 10 oz. packages frozen peas,
  partially defrosted
1 tablespoon butter
¾ cup frozen pearl onions, partially defrosted
1 Boston lettuce, washed, dried and shredded
¼ teaspoon fructose
½ cup water
Pinch of dry thyme
Pinch of salt (optional)

Directions:

1. *Parboil the onions in boiling water for 2 minutes. Drain and set aside.*

2. *In a saucepan, melt the butter. Add the peas, onions and thyme; sauté for a few minutes.*

3. *Add the fructose and the lettuce. Pour in the water, cover and simmer until the peas are tender, about 15 minutes. Add salt if you wish.*

Green Beans with Garlic

Serves 4 to 6

Ingredients:

1 pound green beans, trimmed
1 garlic clove, chopped
2 tablespoons olive oil
1 teaspoon dried mint
Pinch of sea salt (optional)

Directions:

1. *Cook green beans in lightly salted boiling water until crisp and tender. Drain.*

2. *While the beans are cooking, cook the garlic in the oil using a small skillet. Cook over low heat until garlic is pale golden.*

3. *Toss the garlic and mint together with the drained green beans.*

Grilled Portabella Mushrooms

Serves 4 to 6

Ingredients:

3 Portabella mushrooms, stems discarded
¼ cup olive oil
2 garlic cloves, minced
1 teaspoon balsamic vinegar
Pinch dried thyme leaves

Directions:

1. Wipe dirt from mushrooms with a damp paper towel.

2. In a bowl, mix together oil, garlic and thyme. Add mushrooms and mix well to coat. Marinate at room temperature for about 1 hour.

3. Cook the marinated mushrooms in one of the following ways:
   Grilled: Grill on an oiled rack set about 4-5 inches over coals, about 10 minutes on each side.
   Pan roasted: Heat a well-seasoned ridge grill pan on moderate-high heat for 3-4 minutes. Roast the mushrooms for about 4 minutes each side, or until tender.
   Oven roasted: Set oven at 400° and roast for 20-25 minutes, or until tender.

4. Slice to serve.

Linguine with Parsley and Garlic

Serves 4 to 6

Ingredients:

1 pound Jerusalem artichoke linguine
5 large garlic cloves, sliced thin
4 tablespoons olive oil
Pinch of dried lemon-pepper flakes
1 cup white wine
1½ cups fresh parsley, washed,
   dried and finely chopped
Sea salt to taste
Low fat grated Parmesan cheese

Directions:

1. *In a large kettle, bring 5 quarts of water to a boil.*

2. *In a heavy skillet, cook garlic in 3 tablespoons oil over medium heat, stirring until pale golden (do not let them get brown, they will become bitter). Transfer with a slotted spoon to a small bowl.*

3. *To same skillet, add pepper flakes, wine and salt and boil until reduced to about ¼ cup. Set aside.*

Directions continued on the following page

Linguine with Parsley and Garlic Directions continued:

4. Boil linguine until al dente. Drain linguine, reserving 1½ cups of the water. Stir 1 cup reserved pasta water and parsley into wine mixture and add linguine, garlic and remaining tablespoon oil. Toss pasta over moderate heat until combined well, about 1 minute, adding more pasta water if necessary to keep mixture moist. Serve with cheese.

Helpful Hint

You can find Jerusalem artichoke pasta in specialty supermarkets or health food stores. You can also use spinach pasta, but do not use tomato based pasta.

Mashed Sweet Potato

Ingredients:

1½ pound sweet potatoes
½ teaspoon safflower oil
½ cup orange juice
1-1½ cup fat-free, low sodium,
   warm chicken broth
1 teaspoon orange rind,
   very finely chopped, optional
Sea salt to taste

Directions:

1. Peel and cut sweet potatoes into large chunks. Place the potatoes in salted water and cook until tender, about 10-15 minutes. Drain and mash with a potato masher.

2. Add oil and mix well. Add orange juice, stirring to mix well, then add the warmed broth slowly, mixing until you obtain the right consistency. Add orange rind and salt to taste.

3. If the sweet potatoes are not warm enough, reheat on low heat, mixing constantly with a wooden spoon.

4. Some raisins and nuts can be added before serving during the holidays. Good with turkey or chicken.

Minted String Beans

Serves 4

Ingredients:

1 pound string beans, washed and trimmed
2 sprigs fresh mint, chopped
2 tablespoons olive oil
½ teaspoons garlic, minced
2 teaspoons apple cider vinegar

Directions:

1. In a large pot, bring water to a boil. Place string beans in the boiling water and cook for 6-8 minutes, or until tender. Be sure they retain their bright green color!

2. Rinse under cold water for a minute to stop the cooking process.

3. In a blender, place the mint, oil, garlic and vinegar and process until smooth.

4. Pour mint mixture over string beans and serve.

Mushrooms, Tofu and Snow Peas

Serves 4

Ingredients:

2 small onions, halved and sliced thin
2 tablespoons corn oil
½ pound mushrooms, sliced
2 garlic cloves, minced
2 teaspoons fresh ginger, minced
1½ teaspoons cornstarch
   [dissolved in ¼ cup cold water]
5 tablespoons low sodium soy sauce
1 pound tofu, drained
½ pound snow peas

Directions:

1. Dry tofu well with paper towels and cut into ¼ " thick slices.

2. Heat oil in a large skillet or wok; add onions and brown for 2-4 minutes. Add mushrooms, sauté 1 minute, stirring. Add garlic and ginger, cook for 1 minute, stirring.

3. Stir in the soy sauce, tofu, and cornstarch/water mixture. Simmer, stirring gently and turning tofu to coat with the sauce until the sauce is thickened.

4. Stir in the snow peas and cook, stirring for 1 minute. Wonderful served over brown rice!

Mixed Vegetable Kugel

Serves 6 to 8

Ingredients:

20 oz. (1 bag) French cut frozen string beans
20 oz. (1 bag) frozen mixed vegetables
  (without nightshades)
3 tablespoons flour (spelt preferred)
1 cup soy milk (original flavor)
6 eggs
⅓ cup mayonnaise (Spectrum Natural
  Canola, preferred)
½ teaspoon low sodium vegetable bouillon
  (dissolved in 2 tablespoons hot water)
1 teaspoon onion powder
Pepper to taste
2-3 tablespoons corn flake crumbs
  (to sprinkle on top)

Directions:

1. *Preheat oven to 350.°*

2. *Prepare a 9"x13" casserole dish by either lining with parchment paper or by spraying with canola oil.*

3. *Thoroughly defrost all frozen vegetables, place in colander, squeeze out excess liquid, set aside.*

4. *In a large mixing bowl, thoroughly hand mix all other ingredients (except corn flake crumbs).*

5. *Add vegetables to bowl, mix thoroughly, then transfer to prepared casserole dish.*

6. *Lightly sprinkle kugel with corn flake crumbs.*

7. *Bake in prepared oven for 45 minutes, or until kugel appears lightly browned and of a custard-like consistency. Best if eaten after cooling for 10 minutes.*

Mr. Wok's Vegetable Packages

Serves 2

Ingredients:

¼ cup carrots, finely chopped and diced
¼ cup celery, finely chopped and diced
2-3 pieces water chestnuts
2-3 pieces Chinese black mushrooms
    (or any other mushroom)
2-3 pieces Japanese mushrooms
    (or any other mushroom)
4 lettuce leaves

Ingredients for stir-fry:

½ teaspoon olive oil
¼ teaspoon fresh garlic, minced
¼ teaspoon salt
¼ teaspoon sugar
¼ teaspoon Hoi-sin sauce (plum sauce)
2 medium whole scallions, cut into ½" lengths
1 teaspoon soy sauce

Directions:

1. Steam all the vegetables with very little hot water in the wok for 1 or 2 minutes. Remove and set aside.

2. Put olive oil into the wok along with the fresh minced garlic, then add the vegetables and start stir-frying in the wok.

3. After about 30 seconds, add the stir-fry ingredients listed above. Sauté in wok for 1 or 2 minutes.

4. Wrap the stir-fried vegetables in the lettuce leaves and serve.

Purée of Carrots

Serves 6

Ingredients:

2 16 oz. packages small frozen carrots
½ cup low fat, low sodium chicken broth
½ teaspoon honey
Pinch salt

Directions:

1. Boil the carrots until they are very tender, using a little more water and cooking longer than recommended on the package.

2. Drain thoroughly and purée in a food processor or mash them as you would do potatoes. For the hand method–add the broth gradually, whisking constantly. Stir in honey, salt, and mix well. For the food processor method–add broth slowly, then add honey and salt, and process until smooth.

3. Return puréed carrots to the empty pan. When ready to serve, stir constantly over moderate heat until hot.

Purée of Carrots and Yellow Turnips

Ingredients:

1 yellow turnip, peeled and cut into chunks
8 carrots, scraped and cut into 1" slices
½ cup fat-free, low sodium chicken broth
Pinch of salt to taste

Directions:

1. Boil the carrots and turnips separately until very tender; about 12-15 minutes.

2. Purée the carrots and turnips separately until smooth. Mix together in a saucepan.

3. Warm up on low heat, adding chicken broth slowly, stirring until desired consistency is reached. Season to taste.

Note: Yellow turnip is also called rutabaga.

Purée of Green Peas

Serves 4 to 6

Ingredients:

2 10 oz. packages frozen peas
1 teaspoon butter
⅓ cup fat-free, low sodium chicken broth
¼ teaspoon dried mint leaves
Sea salt and black pepper to taste

Directions:

1. Cook peas according to package directions. Drain.

2. Purée peas in food processor using metal blade. Process until smooth, adding broth and butter slowly until desired consistency is reached.

3. Transfer to serving dish, correct seasoning and sprinkle with mint leaves to garnish.

Quick Broccoli Rabe

Serves 4

Ingredients:

1 bunch broccoli rabe
½ cup water
3 cloves garlic
1 chicken bouillon cube
¼ cup olive oil

Directions:

1. Cut off stems of broccoli rabe. Soak in cold water to clean it thoroughly. Place in pot.

2. Add water, bouillon cube and garlic.

3. Cook on medium heat until tender. Remove broccoli rabe to a serving bowl.

4. Pour olive oil over broccoli rabe, toss, and serve hot.

Quick and Luscious Zucchini

Serves 4

Ingredients:

2 cups zucchini, shredded
1 teaspoon corn oil
1 teaspoon butter
3 scallions, thinly sliced
Pinch sea salt

Directions:

1. Heat the butter and oil in saucepan. Add scallions and sauté for a few minutes to soften.

2. Add zucchini and a pinch of sea salt. Cook, stirring often, until zucchini is tender, about 3-4 minutes. Do not overcook, they should be just tender. Correct seasoning.

Red Cabbage with Apples

Serves 4 to 6

Delicious as a side dish with turkey.

Ingredients:

2 tablespoons safflower oil
2 large onions, chopped
1 tablespoon butter
1 red cabbage, finely shredded
½ cup water
½ teaspoon cinnamon
3 cloves
2 tablespoons fructose
2 tablespoons apple cider vinegar
3 apples, peeled, cored and chopped
Sea salt and pepper to taste

Directions:

1. *Cook onions in oil and butter for a few minutes. Add red cabbage, water, cinnamon, cloves, fructose, vinegar and a little salt and pepper. Stir well.*

2. *Cover and cook over low heat for 20 minutes, stirring occasionally. If cabbage gets too dry, add a little water from time to time.*

3. *Add apples, stir and adjust seasoning with fructose and vinegar to taste. Simmer covered until tender. Correct seasoning if needed.*

Roasted Carrots and Parsnips

Serves 6

Ingredients:

2 pounds parsnips
1 pound carrots
½ teaspoon rosemary leaves
3 tablespoons olive oil
Sea salt and black pepper to taste

Directions:

1. Preheat oven to 375.°

2. Peel parsnips and carrots and cut into ¾" slices. In a large bowl, toss the vegetables together with the oil and rosemary.

3. Spread in one layer in a shallow baking dish and season with salt and pepper. You may need to use two baking dishes if one is not large enough.

4. Roast vegetables in the oven, stirring occasionally until brown and crisp, for about 25 minutes.

Roasted Fennel

Serves 4

Ingredients:

3 large fennel bulbs
2 Spanish or Vidalia onions
4 tablespoons olive oil
1 tablespoon balsamic vinegar
¼ cup black olives
Celery Seed

Directions:

1. Preheat oven to 400.°

2. Trim fennel stalks flush with bulb and remove the tougher outer leaves. Cut each bulb into 4 wedges.

3. Peel and cut onions into 8 wedges. Put into a large bowl together with fennel, olive oil and celery seed.

4. Roast vegetables in a roasting pan for about 25 minutes or until cooked through.

5. Put in a large serving bowl. Add balsamic vinegar and olives and toss well.

Roasted Vegetables

Serves 4 to 6

Ingredients:

3 zucchini, cut crosswise into ½" thick slices
2 red onions, cut into ⅓" thick slices
2 Belgian endives, split vertically
2 Portabella mushrooms, stems discarded
2 heads radicchio, cut into 4 wedges
¼ cup olive oil
1 garlic clove, cut in half
Fresh rosemary sprigs (or ¼ teaspoon dried
rosemary)

Directions:

1. *Preheat oven to 450.°*

2. *Several hours before beginning this recipe, place garlic in olive oil to marinate. Remove garlic before using oil.*

3. *Wipe off mushrooms with a damp towel. Mix all vegetables in a large bowl with the garlic-flavored olive oil and rosemary and toss well to coat them.*

4. *Brush a baking sheet with oil, or use a non-stick baking sheet. Spread vegetables in one layer on the baking sheet. Roast until lightly browned, turn on the other side and roast until tender. [If all the vegetables didn't fit at once, repeat the procedure.]*

5. *Season to taste with a little salt or sprinkle with some fresh lemon juice.*

   Note: You don't have to use all these vegetables at once. Make your own selections and cook the same way.

Steamed Vegetables

Serves 2

Ingredients:

1 pound fresh asparagus
(or any other vegetables)
Lemon Vinaigrette or dried mint leaves

Directions:

1. Wash asparagus and snap stalks. Place vegetables on steamer rack over boiling water. Cover and steam 5-8 minutes, depending on the vegetable you are using.

2. When ready, drizzle with a little lemon vinaigrette or sprinkle with some dried mint leaves.

The dentist extracted a severely abscessed tooth from a patient, and presented her with a bill for seventy-five dollars.

"What?" said the patient, "Seventy-five dollars for two minutes of work?!"

"Well, would you rather I had pulled it out more slowly?" replied the dentist.

Sweet Potatoes and Fennel Gratin

Serves 4 to 6

Ingredients:

1 pound fennel bulbs (2 medium)
1 tablespoon olive oil
1-1½ pounds sweet potatoes,
   peeled and thinly sliced
½ teaspoon celery seed
Sea salt and pepper to taste

Directions:

1. *Preheat oven to 425.°*

2. *Cut off upper stalks and shoots from fennel. Discard the tough or discolored outside leaves and slice into thin lengthwise slices. Place in a baking dish, add salt and pepper lightly and toss well with oil. Cover the dish tightly with heavy duty aluminum foil and place in the oven. Bake 15 minutes, until fennel is almost tender.*

3. *Take out of oven and arrange the sliced sweet potatoes on top of the fennel. Salt lightly and sprinkle with celery seed. Cover and return to the oven. Bake 20-30 minutes until the potatoes are tender.*

Vegetable Corkscrew Pasta

Serves 4 to 6

Ingredients:

2 cups Jerusalem artichoke pasta
3 cups broccoli, steamed
3 cups cauliflower, steamed
1 small can sliced black olives (about 6 ounces)
3 tablespoons extra virgin olive oil
1 tablespoon lemon juice
1 tablespoon low sodium soy sauce
1 teaspoon Italian seasoning
1 teaspoon garlic powder
1 teaspoon crushed black pepper
1 small onion, very finely chopped
Dash sea salt, optional

Directions:

1. Boil pasta until al dente.

2. Toss pasta with broccoli, cauliflower, olives and onions.

3. Add olive oil, lemon, soy sauce and all other spices. Mix well and serve.

Viva Broccoli Rabe

Serves 4

Ingredients:

1 bunch broccoli rabe, washed and trimmed
1 tablespoon olive oil
4 cloves garlic, minced
1 cup water
Sea salt and pepper to taste

Directions:

1. In a medium saucepan, heat oil over medium heat. Add garlic and sauté until soft.

2. Add water and oil to the garlic and bring to a boil. Simmer 2 minutes and add broccoli rabe. Cover and bring to another boil.

3. Reduce heat and simmer for 3 minutes.

Note: As a serving suggestion, add cooked pasta and sprinkle with low fat Parmesan cheese. Also, if you cannot find broccoli rabe, regular broccoli may be substituted.

Wild and Brown Rice

Serves 4 to 6

Ingredients:

½ cup wild rice
1 cup short grain brown rice
4 cups boiling water
½ teaspoon salt
1 tablespoon canola oil
Dried parsley to garnish

Directions:

1. *Place wild rice and brown rice in heavy sauce pan and pour boiling water over. Add salt and oil. Bring quickly to a boil, cover, reduce heat, cook slowly until liquid is almost absorbed, about 20 minutes. Turn off heat and let stand for 15 minutes. Serve sprinkled with parsley.*

2. *It is delicious as cooked above, but for variation try the following:*
   While the rice is cooking, sauté ¼ cup finely chopped onions in 1-2 teaspoons canola oil, add ½ teaspoon cumin seeds (optional) and toss well with rice. Sprinkle with parsley and serve.

   Note: It is important to use only short-grain brown rice in this recipe. This dish can be made ahead of time and reheated.

Wild Rice with Mushrooms

Serves 4 to 6

Ingredients:

3 tablespoons safflower oil
¼ cup chopped onions
¼ cup chopped celery
1 cup sliced carrots
¼ teaspoon thyme or oregano
1 cup mushrooms, sliced thickly
1⅓ cups (about 3 oz.) wild rice
3 cups fat-free, low sodium chicken stock
Sea salt and pepper to taste
Fresh parsley to garnish

Directions:

1. *Preheat oven to 350.°*

2. *In a heavy saucepan or heat-proof casserole, warm up oil for a few seconds, add onions and celery. Sauté on medium heat until tender but not brown. Stir in the mushrooms and carrots. Continue cooking, coating them with the oil. Add thyme or oregano.*

3. *Add the rice, stir well, then add the stock. Bring to a simmer. Season to taste. Cover and bake in the oven for about 1¼ hour. Check rice from time to time to make sure liquid does not evaporate too fast. If it does, add a little more stock.*

4. *When ready, the rice grains will have split open somewhat. After baking, set aside covered for 15 minutes before serving. Fluff with a fork and correct seasoning.*

Veggie Melt

*This can be prepared with any
permitted vegetable.*

Serves 1

Ingredients:

1 whole-wheat pita bread, sliced
1 medium carrot, sliced thin
¼ cup broccoli florets
2 tablespoons celery, diced
2 slices low fat Swiss cheese

Directions:

1. *Preheat oven to 350.º*

2. *In a medium-sized saucepan, bring water to a boil and cook vegetables until tender.*

3. *Strain vegetables and place in cold water. (This method is called "shocking" vegetables. It prevents further cooking.)*

4. *Place par-boiled vegetables on the sliced pita and top with Swiss cheese.*

5. *Place pita on a baking sheet and place in the oven for 4-6 minutes or until the cheese has melted.*

Yellow Squash and Onion Casserole

Serves 4 to 6

Ingredients:

6 medium yellow squash, trimmed, cut in chunks
2 medium yellow onions, coarsely chopped
⅓ cup water
½ teaspoon salt
¼ teaspoon freshly ground black pepper
¼ teaspoon freshly grated nutmeg
3 tablespoons butter (unsalted)
2 large eggs, beaten until frothy
¾ cup coarse soda cracker crumbs
1 teaspoon sugar

Topping:

½ cup fine soda cracker crumbs
4 teaspoons melted butter (unsalted)

Directions:

1. Preheat oven to 350.° Grease a 1½ quart casserole and set aside.

2. In a large covered saucepan on moderate heat, simmer the onions and squash in the water for half an hour.

3. Drain the squash well, then add the salt, pepper, nutmeg, and butter. Mash with a potato masher.

4. Mix in the eggs, cracker crumbs, and sugar. Transfer to prepared casserole dish.

5. Toss together topping ingredients, and spread onto casserole.

6. Bake uncovered 45-50 minutes, until top is browned.

Snacks

⌐🗁　**Indicates recipe created by Monique Hill**

Snacks

- *Fresh or dried fruit (unsulphured)*
- *Fresh vegetables: carrot, celery, broccoli florets, etc. (plain lowfat yogurt as dressing)*
- *Chopped fruit or vegetables in a plain gelatine mold*
- *Frozen fruit bars or pops (100% natural)*
- *Lowfat frozen yogurt*
- *Baked apple with honey and cinnamon*
- *Baked fruit, i.e. apples, pears, bananas, peaches, etc., with some raisins and almonds, sprinkled with some nutmeg, cinnamon, grated lemon or orange rind*
- *Frozen grapes (seedless)*
- *Fresh or frozen blueberries with plain lowfat yogurt and a teaspoon of honey*
- *Breadsticks (fat free varieties are best)*
- *Cottage cheese, lowfat*
- *Canned tuna, salmon, or sardines (salt removed) on whole-grain rice cakes or pita*
- *Almonds (4-12 a day) or 100% natural almond cookies*
- *Raisins*
- *Stewed fruit (figs, prunes, apricots, etc.)*
- *Applesauce (homemade or commercial 100% natural)*
- *Cookies, crackers (whole grain/natural)*
- *Rice cakes (whole grain, with a little honey or 100% natural fruit preserves)*
- *Toasted shredded wheat squares with a little grated Parmesan cheese*
- *Frozen pulp of cantaloupe or honeydew melon (make it a sorbet)*
- *Whole wheat or sourdough pretzels, unsalted*
- *Green leafy salad with olive oil and lemon juice dressing*
- *Fruit salad*
- *Tortilla chips, baked not fried*
- *Bagel chips (whole grain with Silken Tofu spread)*
- *Popcorn (plain, air popped) 1 cup*
- *Baked sweet potato or vegetable chips*
- *Roasted, unsalted soy nuts*
- *Almond butter on whole grain crackers*

Haricleea Pena's Homemade Yogurt

Ingredients:

½ gallon organic milk (1%, 2% or whole)
3-4 tablespoons plain commercial yogurt

Directions:

1. You will need the following:
   - A thermometer graded from 110°-200°F / 40°-95°C
   - 2-3 quart double boiler (or two pans which fit inside each other)
   - ovenproof casserole with lid, or, yogurt maker

2. Boil the milk in a double boiler or warm bath to avoid scorching it. It is important that you use a stainless steel, glass or enamel container. Heat the milk to 180°-190°F (82°-88°C), and maintain at that temperature for 20-40 minutes, if you have time, for best results. If using lowfat or nonfat milk, it must be heated for the full 40 minutes. DO NOT USE A MICROWAVE TO HEAT THE MILK! [To make the yogurt faster, bring the milk up to 190°-200°F (88°-93°C) and keep it there for 5-10 minutes. Watch it carefully to avoid boiling the milk!] This step is done to break down the protein molecules in the milk, while also evaporating a lot of the water, and to kill any bacteria. When the milk is allowed to cook longer, the yogurt becomes thicker and tastier. [If you are using anything other than whole milk, you may want to stir in ¼ cup of dry powdered milk into your quart of milk before heating it.]

3. Allow the milk to cool to 110°-115°F (43°-46°C) before adding the yogurt starter. You can accelerate the cooling of the milk by placing the entire pot in a cool water bath, taking care not to splash any water into the milk.

Directions continued on the following page

Haricleea Pena's Homemade Yogurt continued:

4. Take the 3-4 tablespoons of starter yogurt and stir into it a little bit of the cooled milk. I recommend Stonyfield Organic Plain, or Stonyfield Lowfat Plain, if these are available to you. Or use Colombo or Dannon or any other good plain yogurt. After diluting the starter with a bit of the cooled milk, stir the starter into the container of cooled milk.

5. If your double boiler is ovenproof and has a tight-fitting lid, cover the cooled milk to which you have added the yogurt starter, and place it in the oven to incubate. Or, transfer the cooled milk with the added yogurt starter to an ovenproof casserole with a lid and place it in the oven. The oven is kept OFF but provides an insulated place for the yogurt bacteria to ferment. If your oven is electric, wrap the pan in a towel. If you have a gas oven with a pilot light, place the pan on the top rack at the back of the oven. This is best prepared in the evening, then the yogurt can incubate all night, and in the morning, the yogurt will be ready. If it is not ready when you check it in the morning, leave it in for a few more hours. Then, remove and refrigerate until needed.

Stewed Apples

Ingredients:

6-8 apples, peeled, cored, sliced
Water to cover
¼ cup brown sugar
1 teaspoon cinnamon
¼ teaspoon nutmeg

Directions:

1. *Place apples in pot, cover with water and remaining ingredients.*

2. *Cover partially and cook until apples are softened. Test and make adjustments for sweetness according to your taste. Add a pinch of salt.*

   Note: *Although Red Delicious or Golden Delicious are normally preferred in the regimen, it is permissible to use Granny Smith for this recipe since they are better cooking apples.*

Power Spread

Serves 1 to 2

Ingredients:

3 tablespoons olive oil
1 garlic clove, crushed
1 round slice of onion, finely minced
Juice of ½ a lemon
¼ teaspoon salt

Directions:

1. *Mix all ingredients together thoroughly.*

2. *Spread on whole grain crackers or pita bread. Enjoy!*

Easy Sweet Potato Fries

Serves 4

Ingredients:

4 medium sweet potatoes
3 teaspoons corn oil
Sea salt to taste

Directions:

1. Preheat oven to 450.°

2. Peel potatoes and cut into strips, like medium sliced french fries. Place in a medium bowl and drizzle with oil. Toss to coat evenly.

3. Place potatoes on a nonstick baking sheet, in a single layer. Bake 15 minutes. Turn potatoes and bake about 15 minutes longer or until desired crispness is reached. They taste good this way, but you may salt if you desire.

Veggie Wedgey

Serves 1 to 2

Ingredients:

1 6" round pita bread
8 ounces low fat cottage cheese
2 tablespoons fresh parsley, finely chopped
2 tablespoons spinach leaves, finely chopped
1 tablespoon scallions, finely chopped

Directions:

1. Stir vegetables into cottage cheese.

2. Toast pita bread lightly, cut into 4 wedges, open pockets and spread cottage cheese mixture inside. Enjoy as a healthy snack or a light lunch.

Sweet Potato Crisps

Serves 2

Ingredients:

1 medium sweet potato, scrubbed
1 tablespoon olive oil
Sea salt to taste

Directions:

1. Preheat oven to 375.°

2. Thinly slice sweet potato into ¼ " slices.

3. Oil a baking sheet. Place slices in single layer on the sheet and bake for 20 minutes or until tender and golden brown. Add salt if desired.

Toasted Almonds

Ingredients:

1 package almonds

Directions:

1. Preheat oven to 325.°

2. Spread almonds in a single layer on a heavy flat baking pan. Place in oven. Bake, but roll them around with a spatula every 3 to 4 minutes, until they are light brown. Watch carefully not to burn them. They should take about 15 minutes. They will taste bitter if burned.

3. Remove and cool.

4. You can also toast them in a frying pan over low heat, tossing frequently.

Tofu Triangles

Ingredients:

Sliced whole grain bread
Tofu spread
Spinach
Cilantro

Directions:

1. Cut several slices of whole grain bread into triangular sections.

2. Mix tofu spread with finely chopped, lightly steamed spinach and finely chopped cilantro. Mix all ingredients together as a spread.

3. Spread the tofu mixture on triangular pieces of whole grain bread and serve as a snack.

Tofu Wedges

Serves 1 to 2

Ingredients:

1 6" round pita bread
4 tablespoons Silken Tofu
2 teaspoons honey

Directions:

1. Cut pita into four wedges, do not open pockets.

2. Toast the wedges and arrange pita on a flat plate. Spread one tablespoon of tofu on each wedge. Top each wedge with ½ teaspoon honey. Enjoy as a healthy snack or a light lunch.

Harry was invited to a catered affair and found himself standing next to an attorney while waiting to be served. Harry turned to the attorney and said,

"You know, last week I was at a party and was sitting next to a doctor. All I did was ask him a simple question about my health, and the next day he billed me for $100. Can he do that?"

The attorney answered, "Yes, he can!"

"Oh," said Harry, "Thank you very much."

"You're welcome," said the attorney.

The next day the attorney sent Harry a bill for $150.00.

Desserts and Beverages

Desserts and Beverages

Desserts

🖰   Indicates recipe created by Monique Hill

Apple Mousse

Serves 4

Ingredients:

1 pound McIntosh Apples
5 tablespoons honey
3 tablespoons water
1 tablespoon fresh lemon juice
3 large egg whites
¼ teaspoon cinnamon (optional)

Directions:

1. Peel and core apples. Cut into ½" pieces.

2. In a heavy saucepan, cook the apples together with water and honey until they reach a "compote consistency"–about 25 minutes. If apples stick to the bottom, add a little more water to the pan. Cool and add lemon juice.

3. In a large bowl, beat egg whites until stiff peaks form. Fold egg whites into the apple mousse mixture until smooth.

4. Pour mousse into individual glass dishes and refrigerate. Before serving, sprinkle with cinnamon or garnish with fresh blueberries.

Apricot Dessert Sauce

Ingredients:

¾ pound dried apricots
Water
3 tablespoons frozen unsweetened
orange juice concentrate
Fructose (optional)

Directions:

1. Soak apricots in water to cover, overnight.

2. Drain and place apricots in small saucepan. Add water to just cover. Simmer until tender.

3. Drain, reserving the juice. Purée apricots and orange concentrate in blender or food processor. Add enough of the cooking liquid to obtain desired consistency.

4. Sweeten to taste with fructose if necessary.

Aunt Tina's Honey Carrot Cake

Serves 12

Ingredients:

2 cups unbleached all-purpose flour
1 teaspoon baking powder
1 teaspoon baking soda
1 teaspoon salt
1 teaspoon cinnamon
1 large egg
2 large egg whites
¾ cup canola oil
1 cup honey
2½ cups carrots, grated
¼ cup raisins
¼ cup almonds, sliced and toasted

Directions:

1. Preheat oven to 350.° Lightly oil and flour a 9" x 13" x 2" pan.

2. In a large bowl, combine flour, baking powder, baking soda, salt and cinnamon. Set aside.

3. In a large bowl, with a wire whisk, beat egg, egg whites, oil and honey until well blended.

4. Stir flour mixture into egg and honey mixture until well blended.

5. Using a rubber spatula, fold in carrots and raisins. Pour into prepared pan.

6. Bake for 50 minutes, or until a toothpick inserted into the center comes out clean. Cool on a wire rack. Remove from pan and cut into 12 squares. Serve sprinkled with almonds.

Baked Apples

Serves 4

Ingredients:

4 Golden Delicious apples
4 tablespoons honey
4 teaspoons seedless golden raisins
1 tablespoon sliced almonds
1 cup 100% pure apple juice
¼ cup white wine
1 teaspoon cinnamon

Directions:

1. *Preheat oven to 375.°*

2. *Sprinkle a shallow baking dish with no-stick cooking spray. The dish should be just large enough to hold the apples. Core and peel a one-inch strip from the stem end of the apple. In each cavity put 1 tablespoon honey, 1 teaspoon raisins, and a few almond slices. Place in prepared baking dish, add apple juice and wine. Sprinkle with cinnamon.*

3. *Bake for about 45 minutes uncovered, basting frequently with the syrup in the bottom of the dish until apples are tender.*

Baked Bananas

Serves 4

Ingredients:

4 bananas
¼ cup honey
4 teaspoons fresh lemon juice

Directions:

1. *Preheat oven to 400.°*

2. *Peel bananas and cut into halves lengthwise. Place in a shallow baking dish.*

3. *Mix honey and lemon juice together and pour over bananas.*

4. *Bake for 10-12 minutes.*

Baked Pears

Serves 4

Ingredients:

4 pears (Anjou or Bosc)
1 cup pure white grape-peach juice
2 tablespoons fresh lemon juice
¼ teaspoon dried mint (optional)

Directions:

1. *Preheat oven to 425.°*

2. *Peel pears and cut in half lengthwise. Scoop out core. Place pears cored-side down in a shallow baking dish. Pour juice over pears. Drizzle with lemon juice.*

3. *Bake for 25 minutes or until pears are tender. Sprinkle with mint. They are delicious served warm or cold.*

Cheese Cake Pie

Serves 6

Ingredients:

1 cup Kamut flakes
2 tablespoons soya granules
3 tablespoons pure white grape juice
8 ounces no-fat cream cheese
1 cup fat free ricotta cheese
⅓ cup fructose
1 egg
2 egg whites
2 tablespoons fresh lemon juice
1 teaspoon vanilla

Directions:

1. Preheat oven to 350.°

2. Spray a 9" Pyrex glass pie plate with no-stick cooking spray. Crumb the Kamut flakes in a blender or food processor, then transfer to a mixing bowl. Add soya granules, stir in the grape juice and mix well. Distribute evenly in pie plate bottom and press firmly. Chill in freezer for about 10 minutes.

3. Place cream cheese and ricotta in mixing bowl, beat with electric mixer until smooth and well blended. Add fructose, egg, egg whites, and lemon juice. Beat until soft and creamy. Stir in vanilla. Pour into prepared pie plate. Bake until set, about 40 minutes.

   Note: Kamut is an organic wheat kernel and pear juice cereal. It is a fat free, low sodium cereal available in health food stores.

Chunky Apple Sauce

Serves 4

Ingredients:

3 pounds McIntosh Apples
½ cup fructose
⅔ cup water
Cinnamon or nutmeg (optional)

Directions:

1. *Peel and core apples, cut into ¾" pieces. In a large, heavy sauce-pan, bring apples, fructose and about 3 tablespoons of the water to a boil. Simmer, stirring often and adding more water as necessary. Make sure apples do not stick to the bottom of the pan.*

2. *Cook until apples are soft and starting to fall apart, about 20 minutes. Cool, cover with plastic wrap and refrigerate.*

3. *Flavor with cinnamon or nutmeg to taste.*

Creamy Topping

Ingredients:

1 cup fat free cottage cheese
½ cup fat free plain yogurt
2 tablespoons honey (optional)

Directions:

1. *Place cottage cheese in food processor and process until smooth and creamy.*

2. *Remove cottage cheese to a mixing bowl and whisk in yogurt. If you want a sweet topping, add honey and mix well with a whisk. Refrigerate.*

   Note: *Serve with fresh fruits, or mix with any fruit purée to make a nice refreshing dessert.*

Yogurt Cream

Ingredients:

4 cups nonfat yogurt
⅓ cup fructose
1 teaspoon vanilla

Directions:

1. *Drain yogurt through a cheese cloth overnight in the refrigerator.*

2. *Transfer into a mixing bowl, add fructose and vanilla. Whip with hand electric mixer to give it a creamy texture.*

   Note: *This is a very good substitute for whipped cream. It is delicious with fresh fruit.*

Date Mousse

Serves 4

Ingredients:

1½ cup pitted dates
1½ cup natural unsweetened apple sauce
1 bag orange flavor herb tea
6 ounces boiling water
¼ cup plain yogurt (optional)

Directions:

1. *Place tea bag in boiling water for several minutes. Remove bag and let cool.*

2. *Soak dates in cooled tea overnight in the refrigerator. Put dates in food processor and process until puréed. Mix in the apple sauce and refrigerate.*

3. *If using the yogurt, mix it in just before serving.*

Fall Fruit Compote

Serves 4 to 6

This is a traditional fall dessert that you can enjoy all year round!

Ingredients:

16 ounces of unsulfured dried fruit, such as
  peaches, prunes, apples, pears and apricots
Spring water to cover
1 cinnamon stick
2" piece of vanilla bean
  -or- 1 teaspoon pure vanilla extract
2-4 tablespoons honey
½ cup slivered almonds, toasted

Directions:

1. *Rinse and soak fruit in spring water for ½ hour.*

2. *Drain and place in saucepan with cinnamon stick, vanilla and 4 cups spring water.*

3. *Simmer for 30-40 minutes or until tender, adding spring water as needed to keep liquid several inches above fruit. Stir in honey, adjusting to tartness of fruit.*

4. *Serve warm or cold with toasted almonds. Delicious as a topping for frozen yogurt.*

Fruit Compote

Serves 4 to 6

Ingredients:

1 16-oz. package frozen mixed fruit*
1 12-oz. package frozen blueberries
1 12-oz. package frozen raspberries
⅓ cup fructose

Directions:

1. *Preheat oven to 375.°*

2. *Place the mixed fruits and blueberries in a shallow baking dish. Let them defrost partially for 15 to 20 minutes. Sprinkle with fructose. Place in the oven and bake about 40 to 45 minutes. Fruit should be tender but still firm.*

3. *Meanwhile, defrost the raspberries in a colander set in a bowl.*

4. *Remove fruit from the oven and gently stir in the raspberries, basting with the hot juices. Add some of the raspberry juice, to taste. Cool and chill in the refrigerator.*

*Psoriasis and eczema patients should remove any strawberries.

Note: Good served with Creamy Topping.

Papaya-Mango Sorbet

Ingredients:

1 large papaya, peeled and pitted
2 large mangos, peeled and pitted
¼ cup honey
½ cup water
2 tablespoons lime juice
½ cup mint leaves (optional)

Directions:

1. Place papaya and mango chunks in blender, purée until smooth. Add honey, water, and lime juice. Purée.

2. Pour purée into a shallow pan and place in freezer. When the sorbet starts to freeze around the edges, stir it well, and return it to freezer.

3. In another hour, stir it again and refreeze. Repeat this step after another hour, and again an hour later, until the sorbet has frozen solid.

4. Cover and freeze overnight.

5. Let the sorbet thaw for 10 minutes before serving. Cut the sorbet in chunks, purée quickly in blender then scoop into serving bowls. If you wish, garnish with mint leaves.

Party Fruit Terrine

Serves 6 to 8

Ingredients:

7½ cups mixed fruits (raspberries, blueberries,
 peaches, seedless green grapes, etc.)
2 cups Welch's white grape-peach juice
2 envelopes Knox gelatine
1 tablespoon fresh lemon juice
2 tablespoons fructose

Directions:

1.   *If using grapes, cut them in half. If using peaches, cut them in chunks.*

2.   *Remove ½ cup of the grape-peach juice and sprinkle gelatine over it. Let stand for 5 minutes. In a small pan, bring ½ cup of the remaining juice and the fructose to a boil. Slowly pour into the gelatine mixture and stir until dissolved. Add lemon juice. Pour into remaining cup of juice and stir. Using a 9 x 5¼ x 3 inch loaf pan, pour in a thin layer of liquid gelatine, chill until firm.*

3.   *Add the mixed fruit to the mold. Next, pour all except ⅔ cup of the liquid gelatine over the fruit. Cover with plastic and press the fruit down. Cover with a double layer of heavy foil and place two full cans on top to act as weights. Refrigerate until set, about 2 hours.*

4.   *Warm up the remaining gelatine liquid and pour over the fruit terrine. Cover with plastic wrap and refrigerate over-night. To serve–unmold by dipping mold in hot water for 1 or 2 seconds and invert onto a plate. Dip sharp knife into hot water to cut slices.*

Peach and Yogurt Gelatine

Serves 4

Ingredients:

2 envelopes Knox unflavored gelatine
1 cup pure peach juice
1 cup plain, nonfat yogurt
1 fresh peach, peeled and cut up
1½ teaspoons fructose

Directions:

1. Dissolve the 2 envelopes of gelatine in ½ cup of cold peach juice, set aside.

2. Heat ½ cup of peach juice in small saucepan.

3. Stir dissolved gelatine and the fructose into saucepan of heated juice.

4. Place peach and yogurt in blender and whip until smooth

5. Add the heated gelatine to the yogurt/peach combination in the blender. Whip up.

6. Pour into large mold or 4 individual dessert cups and chill until set.

Pineapple Sorbet

Serves 4 to 6

Ingredients:

2½ cups fresh pineapple chunks
1½ cups sliced bananas
¼ cup pure unsweetened white grape juice

Directions:

1. *Place pineapples and bananas in the bowl of a food processor fitted with the steel blade, and process until puréed. Add grape juice and process again until very smooth. Transfer the mixture to a shallow square Pyrex dish. Cover with heavy foil and freeze until hard.*

2. *Remove from freezer and let rest for 10 minutes at room temperature. Break into chunks. Place half of chunks into food processor and purée until very smooth and creamy. Place in a plastic container and repeat process with remaining chunks. Cover and freeze.*

   Note: When hardened, sorbet can be mounded into pineapple shells and frozen again for a festive presentation.

Pumpkin Chiffon

Serves 4 to 6

Ingredients:

1 package Knox gelatine
¼ cup cold water
1⅓ cup cooked or canned pumpkin
½ cup brown sugar
2 teaspoons cinnamon
½ teaspoon ginger
½ teaspoon allspice
½ cup skim milk
3 large egg yolks

For Meringue:

3 large egg whites
¼ teaspoon cream of tartar
6 tablespoons sugar

Directions:

1. *Dissolve package of gelatine in ¼ cup water, set aside.*

2. *In saucepan, place pumpkin, sugar, spices, milk and egg yolks, stir constantly over low heat until mixture bubbles. Remove from heat, stir in softened gelatine, place in refrigerator and chill about 2 hours until partly set.*

3. *Remove pumpkin mixture from refrigerator and beat until smooth.*

4. *To make meringue, beat egg whites with cream of tartar, gradually adding sugar, until stiff peaks form.*

5. *Fold pumpkin mixture into meringue. Transfer to serving bowl, chill until set. Serve. [If you wish to use it as a pie filling, place it into a pre-baked pie crust or a graham cracker pie shell, then chill until set.]*

Pumpkin Muffins

Makes 6

Ingredients:

¾ cup whole wheat flour
¼ cup honey
¼ teaspoon salt
1 teaspoon baking powder
¼ teaspoon cinnamon
¼ teaspoon nutmeg
2 tablespoons milk
¼ cup cooked mashed pumpkin
⅛ cup butter
1 egg

Directions:

1. Preheat oven to 400.°

2. Mix together the first set of ingredients, from flour to nutmeg.

3. Add milk, pumpkin, butter and egg to mixture. Pour into muffin tins and bake for 20 minutes.

Helpful Hint

The best way to cook pumpkin is to get small pumpkins in the fall. Cut them in half and take out the seeds. Steam the pumpkin until it is soft (between 30 and 45 minutes depending on the size.) Scrape the pumpkin from the skin and purée in a food processor. This can be frozen and used at a later date. Each small pumpkin yields about 3-5 cups of puréed pumpkin.

Pumpkin-Orange Custard

Serves 6

Ingredients:

1 cup unsweetened pumpkin purée
¼ cup fructose
2 tablespoons honey
2 tablespoons unsweetened frozen
   orange juice concentrate
½ teaspoon cinnamon
Pinch ginger
Pinch salt
2 eggs
1 cup lowfat milk

Directions:

1. Preheat oven to 350.°

2. Combine pumpkin with remaining ingredients <u>except</u> eggs and milk.

3. Place eggs in a mixing bowl and beat slightly. Stir in the pumpkin mixture, then the milk, mixing well with a whisk.

4. Pour mixture into 6 custard cups. Set in a shallow pan (such as a Pyrex rectangular dish). Add enough boiling water to the pan to come halfway up the sides of the cups.

5. Bake for 45 to 50 minutes. Allow to cool, then refrigerate before serving.

Raspberry-Peach Delight

Serves 6

Ingredients:

1 package sugar-free raspberry gelatine
1 cup boiling water
1 package frozen raspberries (12 ounces)
1 tablespoon fresh lemon juice
6 canned peach halves
Creamy Topping (see page 412)

Directions:

1. Take berries out of freezer and let stand at room temperature for 10 minutes, just to separate them.

2. Drain peaches well and wipe with paper towels. Place peach halves, rounded side up in a shallow dish just large enough to hold them.

3. Dissolve gelatin in boiling water, add lemon juice and raspberries, stirring gently until thawed. Pour over peaches and chill in the refrigerator until set. Serve with Creamy Topping on the side.

Note: For a nicer presentation, you may place a peach half, rounded side up, in bottom of 6 individual custard cups. Unmold when ready to eat, and put some creamy topping in the peach cavity.

Raspberry Yogurt Gelatine

Serves 4

Ingredients:

2 envelopes Knox unflavored gelatine
1 cup pure raspberry juice
1 cup plain, nonfat yogurt
1½ teaspoons fructose
½ cup fresh raspberries (optional)

Directions:

1. *Dissolve the 2 envelopes of gelatine in ½ cup of cold raspberry juice, set aside.*

2. *Heat ½ cup of raspberry juice in small saucepan.*

3. *Stir dissolved gelatine and fructose into heated juice.*

4. *In blender, mix yogurt and raspberries (if using), then add the gelatine/juice mixture.*

5. *Pour into large mold or 4 individual dessert cups and chill until set.*

Whole Wheat Applesauce Cake or Cupcakes

Serves 12

Ingredients:

½ cup canola oil
¾ cup brown sugar
1 cup natural applesauce
1½ cups unsifted whole wheat flour
1 teaspoon baking soda
1 teaspoon cinnamon

Directions:

1. *Preheat oven to 375.° Spray muffin tin or loaf pan with oil spray and set aside.*

2. *Cream together the oil and the sugar. Mix in the applesauce and baking soda.*

3. *Add flour and cinnamon and blend thoroughly.*

4. *Pour batter into prepared pan. Yields 12 cupcakes, 18 miniature cupcakes, or 1 loaf. Bake for 20 minutes for cupcakes or 30 minutes for loaf.*

Whole Wheat Fruit Tarts

Makes 6

Ingredients for Crust:

2 cups whole wheat flower
½ cup warm water
½ cup safflower or canola oil

Ingredients for Filling:

4-5 apples, peaches, pears or papaya,
   thinly sliced
¼ cup honey
Dash of cinnamon or nutmeg

Directions:

1. Preheat oven to 400.°

2. Mix crust ingredients and roll dough out flat. Using an upside down cereal/soup bowl (5-6 inches in diameter), cut out round circles. Place on a flat tray or pizza stone.

3. Top each tart with fruit arranged neatly in a circular pattern. Bake for 20-30 minutes, or until the edges are just a bit brown.

4. Meanwhile, heat honey in a small bowl. Remove tarts from oven and brush on the honey while warm. Sprinkle with a dash of cinnamon or nutmeg. Cool and serve.

Wild Berry Dessert

Serves 4

Ingredients:

1 large package frozen mixed berries
 -or- 12 ounces mixed fresh berries
1 teaspoon natural honey
4 cups All Natural frozen vanilla yogurt
4 tablespoons sliced almonds

Directions:

1. *If using frozen berries, first defrost. Remove strawberries.*

2. *In a medium saucepan, warm the berries along with the honey and a little water. (Adjust water according to the amount of sauce you would like.)*

3. *Scoop ½ cup of frozen yogurt into each of four serving bowls.*

4. *Pour warm berries and sauce over yogurt; sprinkle 1 tablespoon almonds over each serving. Serve immediately.*

Beverages

⌐🗁   **Indicates recipe created by Monique Hill**

Almond Delight

Serves 4

Ingredients:

3 cups hot water
⅓ cup raw almonds, ground to powder
1 tablespoon flaxseed oil
1 teaspoon lecithin granules
2 tablespoons honey
⅛ teaspoon almond extract
⅛ teaspoon vanilla extract

Directions:

1. *Place all of the ingredients in a blender along with 1 cup of the hot water. Blend on low speed until a smooth purée is formed.*

2. *Add remaining water and blend on low speed. Transfer to a bottle and refrigerate. Drink chilled.*

The Apple Orchard

Serves 1

Ingredients:

1½ cups of 100% pure Apple Juice
1 apple* cut up into small sections

Directions:

1. Put ingredients into blender and whip initially on "grate" setting.

2. After apples are somewhat reduced in size, set blender to "High" and whip until it becomes smooth and rich.

* Red or Golden Delicious apples are preferred–but any will do. Leave skin on if organically grown; if not, scrub thoroughly first or peel. The skin of the apple carries the pectin and is rich in fiber.

Mango or Papaya Yogurt Shake

Serves 1

Ingredients:

1½ medium mango or papaya
1 cup plain low fat yogurt
½ teaspoon honey, optional

Directions:

1. Place all ingredients in a blender and blend until smooth.

2. Serve in a tall glass over crushed ice.

Grape Juice Smoothie

Serves 1

Ingredients:

1 cup 100% pure grape juice
1 handful of grapes, red or white
½ pear, cut in chunks

Directions:

Place all ingredients into blender and whip until smooth and frothy.

Caution: Since all "Smoothies" are high in sugar fructose, they must be consumed with caution if you have diabetes, hypoglycemia, candida or anything in which the blood sugar content must be monitored. If it is too sweet for your palate, dilute with water according to taste.

Tropical Smoothie

Serves 1

Ingredients:

1 cup Orange-Pineapple Juice
1 cup fresh chunks of pineapple
   (canned will do if fresh is not available)
Juice of 1 fresh lemon

Directions:

Put all ingredients into blender and whip until smooth & frothy.

Soy Milk Smoothie

Serves 1

Ingredients:

8 oz. vanilla soy milk
1 ripe banana
Drop of pure vanilla extract
Dash of nutmeg
½ cup crushed ice
Sprig of mint

Directions:

1. *Place ingredients in blender.*

2. *Whirl until ice is completely blended into liquid form.*

3. *Pour over additional cracked ice and garnish with mint.*

Peach Shake

Serves 2

Ingredients:

2 cups frozen or fresh peaches
1½ cups skim milk
Pinch cinnamon (optional)

Directions:

1. *Place tall glasses in the freezer to frost.*

2. *Place peaches in blender container and purée until smooth. Add milk and blend until frothy. Serve in frosted glasses.*

   Note: This shake is also good made with fresh pineapple.

Orange-Peach-Mango "WOW"

Serves 1

Ingredients:

2 cups Tropicana Orange-Peach-Mango Juice
1 cup freshly cut mango
4-5 dried apricots

Directions:

Place all ingredients into a blender and whip up to a smooth creamy drink.

Oriental Juice Drink

Ingredients:

1 pound of carrots, juiced
2 stalks bok choy
1 clump parsley

Directions:

1. *Cut the bok choy into 1" pieces. Take a small handful of parsley (roughly equivalent in size to a broccoli floret), and chop it up.*

2. *Place all ingredients in a blender and whip until smooth. Drink immediately.*

Orange Blossom "WOW"

Serves 4 to 6

Ingredients:

> 1 quart Tropicana Orange-Peach-Mango
> 100% Juice
> 1 large California Seedless Navel Orange
> 3 apricots

Directions

1. *Pour three full cups of the Orange-Peach-Mango juice in a blender.*

2. *Peel the thick-skinned orange, saving half of the peel. Cut the saved half of the orange peel into 1" pieces and put them in the blender. Separate the peeled orange into its segments and place them in the blender. Turn the blender on and whip the mixture, first on "grate" for a few seconds, then on "liquefy" until creamy.*

3. *Pour into glass, add ice cubes if you wish, drink and say "Wow!"*

Fourteen Day Sample Menu

Fourteen Day Sample Menu

Fourteen Day
Sample Menu Plan

**These menus have been carefully compiled
in collaboration with
Rona S. Weiss, M.S., Ph.D., Nutritionist
Teaneck, New Jersey**

How to Use the Fourteen Day Menu Plan

The following menus have been designed based on the permitted food list and using the specific recipes included in this book. The primary guide is to try to be sure the alkaline foods dominate the acid forming foods. The ideal ratio is 70-80% alkaline formers to 20-30% acid formers, or, simply stated, 3 alkalines to 1 acid. (This of course is subject to change in cases of very active children or adults engaged in heavy labor. In such cases, more acid forming foods are permitted.) The ratio need not be adhered to strictly at every meal, but significantly more alkalines than acids should have been consumed by the end of the day. Using this sample menu as a guide, you can plan your own future daily menu according to your liking.

You can see that the fourteen day menu offers nutritious and varied meals that are consistent with your present health requirements. Your new food habits can be fun too! Try new recipes and use your imagination. Get out of the breakfast rut, sample a cold soup and toast for breakfast in the warm weather or enjoy a baked sweet potato and warm tea for breakfast as the snow falls. Sip freshly squeezed carrot juice for a snack. You may not have time to do all the cooking suggested by these plans, however, you may use them as a guide when ordering a meal at a restaurant or purchasing a takeout meal from a restaurant or catering store.

The program includes 6-8 glasses of bottled spring or filtered water each day along with your daily teas. This is quite a lot of fluids. Try to take most of your fluids between meals.

In a Nutshell:

- Raw green leafy salads, especially using Romaine lettuce, every day
- Cooked permitted vegetables, every day
- Fish, three or four times a week
- Poultry (chicken, turkey, wild game), two or three times a week
- Lamb (if desired), once or twice a week
- Pure water, six to eight glasses per day
- The herb teas, five days out of the week
- Extra virgin olive oil: for children, three teaspoons per day; for adults, three tablespoons per day (if there is no gallbladder problem)
- Grains (whole grains only) are part of the 20-30% category, they are all acid forming with millet and spelt the least acidic.

DAILY REMINDERS

6-8 glasses of bottled spring or filtered water
(one glass 30 minutes before each meal)

REQUIRED TEAS

A.M. Tea—Slippery Elm Bark Powder
P.M. Tea—American Yellow Saffron or
Chamomile, Mullein or Watermelon Seed Tea
Note: These "tea times" may be reversed if found
to be more practical.

LECITHIN (granular preferred)

1 tablespoon 3 times a day for 5 days out of the week for
adults; 1 teaspoon 3 times a day for children

BETWEEN MEAL SNACK SUGGESTIONS

Fresh or Dried Permitted Fruits
Fresh Permitted Vegetables
Low fat or Non fat Frozen Yogurt or Plain Yogurt
Almonds (5-10 per day!)
(See also list of permitted snacks)
A fresh green leafy salad is always advised

---

*Don't forget the recipe of making three
people laugh every day!*

Edgar Cayce #798-1

Day 1

BREAKFAST

Oatmeal topped with Toasted Almonds and/or Honey
(2-4 tablespoons of Skim Milk if desired)
Stewed Apricots and/or Figs
Herbal Tea, Coffee or Hot Water with Lemon

LUNCH

** Chicken and Zucchini Soup
** Chinese Broccoli Salad
Fresh Sprouts and Shredded Carrots
Whole Grain Crackers (2-3)
Spring Water or Herbal Tea

DINNER

** Broiled Salmon Fillet with Cucumber Sauce
** Steamed Asparagus and Carrots with Lemon Vinaigrette
Fresh Watercress and Romaine Salad with Olive Oil
and a splash of Apple Cider Vinegar
** Pineapple Sorbet
Spring Water or Herbal Tea

BETWEEN MEAL SNACK SUGGESTIONS

See Permitted List

REMEMBER DAILY TEAS AND LECITHIN

6-8 glasses of bottled spring or filtered water
(one glass 30 minutes before each meal)

(Note: ** indicates that the recipe is included in this volume)

Day 2

BREAKFAST

Brown Rice or Millet topped with Honey and/or
4-5 Almonds or 2 tablespoons of Wheat Germ
Fresh or Frozen Blackberries
Herbal Tea, Coffee, Hot Water with Lemon

LUNCH

* * Linguine with Parsley and Garlic
* * Quick and Luscious Zucchini
* * Arugula, Radicchio and Endive Salad
Spring Water or Herbal Tea

DINNER

* * French Lamb Stew
* * Cauliflower with Garlic
Fresh Carrot and Celery Sticks
Spring Water or Herbal Tea

BETWEEN MEAL SNACK SUGGESTIONS

See Permitted List

REMEMBER DAILY TEAS AND LECITHIN

6-8 glasses of bottled spring or filtered water
(one glass 30 minutes before each meal)

(Note: * * indicates that the recipe is included in this volume)

Day 3

BREAKFAST

2 Eggs—Poached, Hard or Soft Boiled
1-2 slices of Whole Grain Toast with olive oil or a dab
of butter or unsweetened preserves
Fresh or Frozen Blueberries
Herbal Tea, Coffee or Hot Water with Lemon

LUNCH

* * Eight Vegetable Soup or Garden Salad
* * Couscous with Ginger and Lemon
* * Grilled Portabella Mushrooms
* * Apricot Dessert
Spring Water or Herbal Tea

DINNER

* * Lemon Baked Chicken
* * Roasted Vegetables
* * Mandarin Spinach Salad
Spring Water or Herbal Tea

BETWEEN MEAL SNACK SUGGESTIONS

See Permitted List

REMEMBER DAILY TEAS AND LECITHIN

6-8 glasses of bottled spring or filtered water
(one glass 30 minutes before each meal)

(Note: * * indicates that the recipe is included in this volume)

Day 4

BREAKFAST:

* * Pumpkin Muffins (2) or whole grain cereal
* * Chunky Applesauce
    4 Roasted Chestnuts
    Herbal Tea, Coffee, or Hot Water with Lemon

LUNCH

* * Lean and Delicious Garden Soup
* * Pasta Salad with Olives and Artichokes
* * Viva Broccoli Rabe!
    Spring Water or Herbal Tea

DINNER

* * Roast Turkey Breast
* * Red Cabbage with Apples
* * Green Beans with Garlic
    Mixed Green Salad (Romaine and Red Leaf Lettuce,
        Watercress etc.) with Olive Oil and Lemon Juice
    Spring Water or Herbal Tea

BETWEEN MEAL SNACK SUGGESTIONS

See Permitted List

REMEMBER DAILY TEAS AND LECITHIN

6-8 glasses of bottled spring or filtered water
        (one glass 30 minutes before each meal)

(Note: * * indicates that the recipe is included in this volume)

Day 5

BREAKFAST

Wheatena with chopped or slivered Almonds
and Honey
2-4 tablespoons of Skim Milk if desired
Fresh Peach or Nectarine
Herbal Tea, Coffee, or Hot Water with Lemon

LUNCH

Mixed green or spinach salad with chunk white tuna or
sliced chicken or turkey breast
* * Braised Carrots and Celery
* * Steamed Asparagus with Lime-Dijon Dressing
Spring Water or Herbal Tea

DINNER

* * Poached Orange Roughy with Spinach
* * Apple-Butternut Squash Soup
* * Fresh Romaine and Mushroom Salad
Whole Grain Crackers
* * Pumpkin Orange Custard
Spring Water or Herbal Tea

BETWEEN MEAL SNACK SUGGESTIONS

See Permitted List

REMEMBER DAILY TEAS AND LECITHIN

6-8 glasses of bottled spring or filtered water
(one glass 30 minutes before each meal)

(Note: * * indicates that the recipe is included in this volume)

Day 6

BREAKFAST

* * Baked Sweet Potatoes with Yogurt Topping
  Fresh or Stewed Pears
  Herbal Tea, Coffee, or Hot Water with Lemon

LUNCH

* * Onion Soup
* * Wild Rice with Mushrooms
* * Romaine and Endive Salad with Scallion Dressing
  Spring Water or Herbal Tea

DINNER

* * Marinated Broiled Leg of Lamb
* * Red Cabbage with Apples
* * Green Beans with Garlic
  Fresh Cucumber with Dill
  Spring Water or Herbal Tea

BETWEEN MEAL SNACK SUGGESTIONS

See Permitted List

REMEMBER DAILY TEAS AND LECITHIN

6-8 glasses of bottled spring or filtered water
(one glass 30 minutes before each meal)

(Note: * * indicates that the recipe is included in this volume)

Day 7

BREAKFAST

Permitted Dry Cereal (See list of permitted cereals)
Skim Milk or Soy Milk
Herbal Tea, Coffee, Hot Water with lemon

LUNCH

* * Brown Rice with Lentils
* * Cole Slaw
* * Quick and Luscious Zucchini
Fresh Sprouts with Shredded Beets
Spring Water or Herbal Tea

DINNER

* * Baked Fish Steaks (see permitted fish list)
* * Sweet Potato Soup
Mixed Fresh Greens with
* * Creamy Lime Dressing
* * Aunt Tina's Honey Carrot Cake
Spring Water or Herbal Tea

BETWEEN MEAL SNACK SUGGESTIONS

See Permitted List

REMEMBER DAILY TEAS AND LECITHIN

6-8 glasses of bottled spring or filtered water
(one glass 30 minutes before each meal)

(Note: * * indicates that the recipe is included in this volume)

Day 8

BREAKFAST

Open Faced Melted Cheese Sandwich with a Sprouted Whole Grain Bagel and 1 oz of Low Fat or Fat Free Cheese
Fresh Cherries or Grapes
Herbal Tea, Coffee, or Hot Water with Lemon

LUNCH

* * Ten Minute Vegetable Soup
* * Easy Garlic and Onion Pasta
Fresh Sprouts and Shredded Parsnip
Spring Water or Herbal Tea

DINNER

* * Broiled Chicken with Mushroom Sauce
* * French Style Peas
Steamed Carrots and Celery with fresh or dried mint leaves
Spring Water or Herbal Tea

BETWEEN MEAL SNACK SUGGESTIONS

See Permitted List

REMEMBER DAILY TEAS AND LECITHIN

6-8 glasses of bottled spring or filtered water
(one glass 30 minutes before each meal)

(Note: * * indicates that the recipe is included in this volume)

Day 9

BREAKFAST

2 Eggs—Poached, Hard or Soft Boiled
Whole Grain Toast with olive oil or a dab of butter
or unsweetened preserves
Fresh Pear
Herbal Tea, Coffee or Hot Water with Lemon

LUNCH

* * Cold Tuna and Pasta Salad served on a bed of
Romaine Lettuce
* * Steamed Cauliflower
* * Green Beans with Garlic
Fresh Carrot and Celery Sticks
Spring Water or Herbal Tea

DINNER

* * Broiled Fish (see permitted fish list)
* * Creamy Carrot Soup
* * Grilled Portabella Mushrooms
Whole Grain Cracker (2-4)
* * Apricot Dessert
Spring Water or Herbal Tea

BETWEEN MEAL SNACK SUGGESTIONS

See Permitted List

REMEMBER DAILY TEAS AND LECITHIN

6-8 glasses of bottled spring or filtered water
(one glass 30 minutes before each meal)

(Note: * * indicates that the recipe is included in this volume)

Day 10

BREAKFAST

    **Pineapple and Sweet Potato Salad
    Whole Grain Rye Crackers
    Herbal Tea, Coffee or Hot Water with Lemon

LUNCH

    **Mushrooms, Tofu and Snow Peas on Brown Rice
    **Creamy Celery Soup
    **Red Leaf Lettuce with Creamy Lime Dressing
    Spring Water or Herbal Tea

DINNER

    **Apple Cider Lamb Stew
    Steamed Carrots with olive oil or a dab of butter and
        nutmeg
    Fresh Watercress and Cucumber Slices
    Spring Water or Herbal Tea

BETWEEN MEAL SNACK SUGGESTIONS

See Permitted List

REMEMBER DAILY TEAS AND LECITHIN

6-8 glasses of bottled spring or filtered water
        (one glass 30 minutes before each meal)

(Note: ** indicates that the recipe is included in this volume)

Day 11

BREAKFAST

Permitted Cereal
Skim Milk or Soy Milk
Whole Grain Muffin with olive oil or a dab of butter and/
or unsweetened preserves
Herbal Tea, Coffee or Hot Water with lemon

LUNCH

** Brown Rice with Carrots and Leeks
** Cabbage Soup
Steamed String Beans with Yogurt-Dill Dip
Fresh Celery Sticks
** Cheese Cake Pie
Spring Water or Herbal Tea

DINNER

** Pan Roasted Chicken Breast with Turnip and
Cucumber Sauce
** Mixed Vegetable Salad
Steamed Spinach with Olive Oil and Minced Garlic
Spring Water or Herbal Tea

BETWEEN MEAL SNACK SUGGESTIONS

See Permitted List

REMEMBER DAILY TEAS AND LECITHIN

6-8 glasses of bottled spring or filtered water
(one glass 30 minutes before each meal)

(Note: ** indicates that the recipe is included in this volume)

Day 12

BREAKFAST

    * * Pumpkin Muffins (2) with Honey and/or a dab
         of butter or olive oil
       Fresh Figs or Peaches
       4 Almonds
       Herbal Tea, Coffee or Hot Water with Lemon

LUNCH

    * * Charlton Tuna Salad on a Bed of Greens
    * * Lean and Delicious Garden Soup
       Fresh Carrot and Celery Sticks
       Whole Grain Crackers (2-4)
       Spring Water or Herbal Tea

DINNER

    * * Linguine with Parsley and Garlic
    * * Roasted Vegetables
    * * Cucumber Salad
    * * Pineapple Sorbet
       Spring Water or Herbal Tea

BETWEEN MEAL SNACK SUGGESTIONS

See Permitted List

REMEMBER DAILY TEAS AND LECITHIN

6-8 glasses of bottled spring or filtered water
       (one glass 30 minutes before each meal)

(Note: * * indicates that the recipe is included in this volume)

Day 13

BREAKFAST

Cream of Wheat Cereal with chopped or slivered
Almonds and Honey
2-4 tablespoons Skim Milk if desired
Fresh Blueberries
Herbal Tea, Coffee or Hot Water with Lemon

LUNCH

** Hearty Spinach Soup with Lamb Meat Balls
** Chinese Broccoli Salad
Steamed Yellow Squash and Asparagus with minced
garlic and a dab of butter or olive oil
Spring Water or Herbal Tea

DINNER

** Grilled Swordfish with Vegetables
** Steamed Asparagus with Lemon Vinaigrette
Fresh Watercress and Shredded Carrots
Spring Water or Herbal Tea

BETWEEN MEAL SNACK SUGGESTIONS

See Permitted List

REMEMBER DAILY TEAS AND LECITHIN

6-8 glasses of bottled spring or filtered water
(one glass 30 minutes before each meal)

(Note: ** indicates that the recipe is included in this volume)

Day 14

BREAKFAST

* * Cold Cucumber Soup
    Sprouted Grain Bagel with olive oil or a dab of
        butter and/or honey
    Herbal Tea, Coffee or Hot Water with Lemon

LUNCH

* * Easy Pasta Primavera Salad
* * Sweet Potato Soup
    Fresh Sprouts with Shredded Beets
    Spring Water or Herbal Tea

DINNER

* * Grilled Turkey Cutlets with Vegetables
* * Viva Swiss Chard! (use recipe for Broccoli Rabe, but
    simmer until chard is soft)
    Steamed Carrots with * * Creamy Lime Dressing
* * Pumpkin Orange Custard
    Spring Water or Herbal Tea

BETWEEN MEAL SNACK SUGGESTIONS

See Permitted List

REMEMBER DAILY TEAS AND LECITHIN

6-8 glasses of bottled spring or filtered water
        (one glass 30 minutes before each meal)

(Note: * * indicates that the recipe is included in this volume)

After breakfast, work a while;
After lunch, rest a while;
After dinner, walk a mile!

Edgar Cayce #3624-1

Part III
Eye on Nutrition

Part III
Eye on Nutrition

PART III

on
Nutrition

When Edgar Cayce was asked if there
was an absolute cure for psoriasis, his
answer was:
>"Most of this is found in DIET.
>There is a cure. It requires patience,
>persistence and Right Thinking also."

#2455-2

Dietary "Do's and Don'ts"–

Good for Anybody, Anywhere, Anytime!

- When taking orange juice, add lime or lemon juice. To four parts orange juice add one part lime or lemon juice (fresh).

- Orange juice and milk are helpful, but they should not be taken together. They should be taken separately, at opposite ends of the day.

- Fresh citrus fruits may be taken with any food, except whole grain cereals. (In case of Eczema and Psoriatic Arthritis however, citrus fruit is often irritating to the skin and should be avoided).

- When the body tends toward the Alkaline side, there is less tendency for colds and congestion.

- Do not take milk or cream in coffee or in tea.

- Do not eat fried foods of any kind.

- Include in the diet often—raw vegetables prepared in various ways, not merely as a salad, but grated and combined with gelatine. Knox Unflavored Gelatine, combined with the juice of a fresh lemon or lime is preferred.

- Variety and balance should be the basis of a healthy daily diet.

- Maintain the acid-alkaline in the body—the proportions of food being 70-80% alkaline formers to 20-30% acid formers—or as close to that as possible.

- Eat plenty of fresh fruits and vegetables. Most of them are alkaline. (However, avoid the nightshades).

- When eating cereals, use whole grain varieties exclusively with skim or 1% milk, but do not combine with citrus fruit or juices.

- Often eat raw vegetables such as celery, lettuce, carrots and watercress—especially combined with gelatine.

- Avoid using fat as much as possible.

- Drink plenty of water: 6 to 8 glasses full, in addition to other beverages.

- The meats should be: Fish (not shellfish), Fowl (chicken, turkey or wild game) and Lamb—one serving daily.

- Grains: Bread, cereals and flour should all be whole grain, enriched or restored and taken every day as part of the diet. Avoid white flour products. Remember, all grains (except Millet) are acid forming, therefore, should be part of the 20-30% portion of the daily diet.

A Word About...Super foods!

In 1958 seven countries took part in a study, appropriately named "The Seven Country Study," to determine what foods or types of food have a tendency to reduce the risk of developing such serious illnesses as cancer, heart disease, and other degenerative diseases. (My guess is that psoriasis, eczema, and arthritis could be numbered among them.)

Although the study began four decades ago, 1998 yielded interesting results. For instance, citizens of Italy, Greece and Japan have less heart disease than people in other countries. The study reveals a lower consumption of red meat and dairy products in these three countries, coupled with increased consumption of fish, grains, legumes and vegetables than the other four countries in the study: Yugoslavia, Finland, the Netherlands, and the United States.

Among the "Super foods" listed are:

Cruciferous Vegetables

Cabbage, kale, arugula, broccoli, Brussels sprouts, mustard greens, turnips and collard greens, all of which are on the "recommended" list in this book.

Fish

A study by the AMA found that people who eat as little as one fish meal a week cut their risk of sudden cardiac death in half! Cold water fish, such as salmon, tuna, halibut, sardines, mackerel, orange roughy and tilefish contain high levels of Omega-3 fatty acids which are known to reduce blood clotting and reduce risk of heart disease. They may also help lower blood pressure and cholesterol levels.

Olive Oil

Now, more than ever before, awareness of the beneficial qualities of olive oil is emerging. When a group of scientists began studies fifty years ago on why people of the Mediterranean countries lived long, healthy lives, olive oil came out with high honors. Olive oil contains no cholesterol. It is packed with monounsaturates, so it actually lowers blood cholesterol levels. It also has vitamin E, an antioxidant. Olive oil also has a protective effect on metabolism, arteries, stomach, liver, and biliary tract. It promotes growth during childhood and extends life expectancy in the elderly. All these are adequate reason to consume all the olive oil you safely can. The dose I recommend for most of my psoriasis patients is 3 teaspoons a day for children and 3 tablespoons a day for adults. This amount must be reduced or avoided altogether if the patient has an underlying gall bladder problem, or, in some cases, if there is an allergy to olive oil.

Soy

A member of the pea family, soy is the only vegetable source for the eight essential amino acids. One of the amino acids, tyrosine, is a building block for dopamine, a neurotransmitter that enhances alertness and a feeling of well-being. A deficiency of dopamine is associated with Parkinson's disease. Soy also contains genistein, a phytochemical that cuts the risk of prostate cancer, and phyto-estrogens that help reduce the chance of breast cancer.

Tea

American Yellow Saffron Tea, Chamomile, Mullein, and Watermelon seed Tea are the primary teas, along with Slippery Elm Bark Powder, in cases of psoriasis. There are certain teas that have proven to be powerful stimulants and many contain antioxidants and bioflavonoid which may lower the risk of cancer, heart disease and stroke. Two Chinese teas recognized for centuries as having untold beneficial effects are Green tea and Black tea. Green tea has in its makeup a great deal of vitamin K, essential for blood clotting, and is considered a powerful antioxidant. Black tea, five cups a day, reduced the risk of stroke by 70 percent in a recent study. The theophylline content of these teas dilates airways in the lungs and has helped some people with asthma and other respiratory disorders.

Wine

The French have only one-third the amount of heart attacks as Americans, yet, they consume much more fat than Americans. The French drink 21 gallons of wine per person each year compared to a yearly consumption of 3 gallons per person by Americans. Is there a connection? A report titled *The French Paradox* in 1991 concluded that moderate consumption of wine (two 4-ounce glasses of wine per day, with meals) may decrease the risk of heart disease and certain types of cancers. Wine also increases the absorption of calcium, magnesium, phosphorus, and zinc. With all the benefits attributed to wine, moderation is still the key. Too much wine can trigger allergies, migraine headache and stroke in some people. I permit my patients to consume no more than four ounces of a dry, red wine (preferably without preservatives), but only if they do not experience any adverse effects, and none at all if they are on medication.

Citrus Fruits

Citrus fruits are high in vitamin C, one of the most powerful antioxidants, along with vitamin A, vitamin E, selenium and the carotenoids, beta carotene, lycopene and coenzyme Q10. (See section on Antioxidants vs. Free Radicals)

For many years the Recommended Dietary Allowance for Vitamin C has been established as 60 milligrams. A recent report by Mark Levine of the National Institutes of Health (NIH) however encourages an increase in vitamin C from 60 milligrams to 100 - 200 milligrams. He states that this quantity is more in accordance with that recommended by the U.S. Department of Agriculture and the National Cancer Institute which recommends at least five servings of fruits and vegetables a day, yielding a vitamin C intake of 210 to 280 milligrams of vitamin C. Body cells depend on this vitamin for many biochemical reactions such as the healing of wounds and bone formation. [Source: *Tufts University Health and Nutrition Letter*, June 1999, p. 3]

Note: Keep in mind however that citrus fruits are to be avoided in cases of eczema and psoriatic arthritis. If such is the case, the necessary RDA for Vitamin C may be derived from other sources rather than citrus fruits and/or juices.

Food Allergies...Not to be taken lightly!

The word "allergy" covers a wide range of symptoms from a mild annoyance or irritation to a potentially life-threatening reaction. An allergic reaction that causes only slight discomfort for one person may send another person to the hospital. There are two basic rules for handling allergies: 1) learn what you are allergic to by medical testing or sheer experience, and 2) stay away from it!

There is a difference between *food allergy* and *food intolerance,* and it is best to understand that difference. A *food allergy* refers to a protein in your bloodstream, called an antibody, that can cause a severe reaction which can put a person into shock or cause his airways to close, leading to possible suffocation. People with this severe form of allergy should or must carry a syringe with adrenaline (epinephrine) in case they accidentally consume an offending food. Their very life may depend upon it. At times, a speedy trip to the emergency room of the nearest hospital may mean the difference between life and death. Lesser symptoms of a food allergy may include a rash, swelling anywhere in the body, itching, asthma, itchy eyes and sneezing.

To those who minimize the effects of allergy by simply stating "It's all in your head!"—I say, don't take it lightly! I have a patient who ate a tiny piece of cake containing a very small, indistinguishable amount of hazelnuts. Although she was well aware of her allergy toward hazelnuts, she did not know that hazelnuts were part of this recipe. Had she not been able to get to the hospital at a moment's notice, she might not be with us today.

Food intolerance, on the other hand, causes an uncomfortable or even miserable feeling, and the sufferer needs only to avoid the foods he knows will have this effect on him. The condition is not life-threatening and no antibody-reaction is involved. For instance, many people, especially Americans, cannot tolerate milk. Their system lacks an enzyme that can process the milk. Most of these people resort to using "lactaid." They experience symptoms such as gas, diarrhea, and stomach cramps when they ingest milk. This is called lactose intolerance, not milk allergy. Some people develop headaches after drinking red wine. Wine contains stimulants that dilate the blood vessels in the brain, put pressure on the nerves, and result in headache.

To repeat my opening statement, the way to control food allergies and food intolerance is to first know what they are, then avoid the foods which trigger them.

[Source: *United Features Syndicate, Inc.*, 1992]

What Is Behind So Many Allergies?

Life Story Of a Tomato—Any Town, U.S.A.

[Article Contributed by Harry K. Panjwani, M.D., Ph.D.]

"I begin life in a greenhouse with a starter solution of synthetic fertilizer. Then I am transplanted to a field, treated with large quantities of fertilizer. The field has been fumigated with methyl bromide gas, a very toxic ozone depleting chemical, scheduled to be banned by the Department of Agriculture in 2005!"

Some growers also use Paraquat, another very toxic herbicide. Many tomato crops are periodically sprayed with more herbicides and fungicides to control disease. These chemicals are often mixed with insecticides known to be fatal to birds. These tomatoes, however, look lovely in a supermarket produce section and may have also been sprayed with nontoxic dye to make them look healthy.

This chemical intervention affects the health of the nation's soil, waterways, wildlife and of course humans! These chemicals wind up in our ground water, rivers, food, body fat, breast milk, and often poison the farm workers exposed to them. Exposure to these pesticides forms the genesis for all kinds of allergies, resulting in other diseases, disability, impaired performance, excessive dependence on medications with problem of addiction and untold side effects. What applies to tomatoes also applies to other vegetables and fruits.

The Rodale family in the U.S.A. and Rudolph Steiner in Germany have promoted organic farming since WW I based on cosmic concepts. Many organic farmers have ecofriendly and safe substitutes for these harmful chemicals. We must recognize the difference between organic farming and conventional farming and support the former!

According To...

Reader's Digest's *The Healing Power of Vitamins, Minerals, and Herbs* [Reader's Digest, 1999, p. 193]: "People who smoke 20 cigarettes or more a day, especially women, are twice as likely to develop psoriasis as nonsmokers. A quarter of all psoriasis cases may be related to smoking."

Lawrence A. Miller, M.D., adviser to the National Psoriasis Foundation and The National Institute of Health: "As far as psoriasis is concerned, modern medicine is absolutely inadequate." [*New York Daily News*, Nov. 22, 1992]

The Department of Health and Human Services in conjunction with the **National Cancer Institute** advises that at least one of the daily portions of food be high in beta-carotene. Beta-carotene-rich fruits and vegetables tend to be deep orange, deep yellow and deep green in color and include: cantaloupe, carrots, persimmons, apricots, pumpkins, butternut squash, spinach and broccoli—all of which are recommended on this psoriasis diet!

The National Cancer Institute says we should be eating 20 to 35 grams of fiber a day. Foods rich in fiber include beans, whole-wheat products, turnips, Brussels sprouts, peas, oranges, apples. This completely conforms to the psoriasis diet recommended herein.

The U.S. Department of Agriculture, The Department of Health and Human Services, The National Cancer Institute, and the **National Academy of Sciences** all recommend that Americans eat a minimum of five servings of fruit and vegetables a day.

[A servings is: 1 cup of raw leafy greens; ½ cup of other kinds of vegetables; 1 medium apple, orange or banana, or similar size fruit; ½ cup of small or diced fruit, such as grapes or chopped pineapple; ¼ cup dried fruit, such as raisins; ¾ cup pure fruit or vegetable juice.]

The American Council on Science and Health states that "only 10 percent of Americans consume the recommended five to nine servings of fruits and vegetables per day." They provide us with a list of the best natural food sources.

Beta-carotene
- cantaloupes
- carrots
- sweet potatoes

Vitamin C
- cabbage
- citrus fruits
- tomatoes*

Vitamin E
- almonds
- mangoes
- wheat germm

- sweet potatoes
- avocados

---

* *Tomato* is the only food listed that is not permitted on the psoriasis diet.

So with all this knowledge, how do Americans stand as far as changing their eating habits? The MRCA Information Service supplies us with recent statistics (February 1999) on a survey conducted on 2000 participants.

- Only 10% of the foods eaten at breakfast are fruits, vegetables or juices.

- Americans eat an average of 3 servings a day of fruits and vegetables—two servings short of the minimum recommended amount.

- Only 15% of the participants polled chose fruit as a snack; even fewer chose a vegetable. These comprised only 3% of snacks.

- Far more popular as snacks were sweets, such as cookies, cakes and candy bars; and salty snacks, including potato chips, pretzels and crackers.

Vegetarianism—The trend of the future?

> *"An ever-increasing number of people all over the world are turning to vegetarianism as a way of life which leads to health and strength of body, mind and soul."*
>
> *–Dada J.P. Vaswani,*
> *Revered Spiritual Teacher of India*

Recently I heard a radio broadcast in which the announcer stated that the day will come when salads and raw vegetables will constitute the main course of a meal, while meats of any kind, if eaten at all, will be considered a side dish.

The trend toward vegetarianism is very real indeed and the more it is appreciated and practiced, the longer and healthier we will live. It is now well established that many degenerative diseases have their origin in the consumption of animal products, particularly in processed meats. When I was growing up, meat and potatoes were the mainstay of the American diet. It was promoted as the way to grow strong and healthy. Who really promoted that idea? Is it any wonder—the meat industry and the potato growers, of course!

A shift in man's tastebuds to fruits and vegetables and pure water, in my opinion, will not only solve many of his health related problems, but may very well be the solution to world hunger. However, that touches upon another subject which is not part of this treatise. Perhaps in some future volume I can elaborate more fully on the concept.

In 1989, after I addressed a body of 500 physicians in India at the First International Conference on Holistic Health and Medicine, I was at first at a loss to explain the several cases of psoriasis various physicians had me meet and examine. I had been under the impression that India, being basically a vegetarian culture, would be exempt from conditions such as psoriasis, eczema, arthritis, and any number of other diseases. But the fact is it is not. It has been estimated that the population of India has now reached one billion! It has long been established that psoriasis afflicts about 2% of the population of any given country. This indicates that there are about 20 million people with psoriasis in India if these estimates are accurate.

Why, in a vegetarian country? From what I experienced and observed while there, I have deduced the following reasons: 1] extensive consumption of the nightshades, found in the hot spices used in food preparation; 2] fried foods; and 3] lack of pure water (50% of the population lacks pure water).

To my astonishment, while I was in Italy speaking before the Italian Psoriasis Association in Rome, I learned that 4% of Italy's population of 55 million was afflicted. That's twice the world average. Again, the culprits may be extensive use of the nightshades (especially tomatoes and peppers), much fried food, too much pasta (starch), and rich pastries. They follow the Mediterranean Diet which keeps meat at a minimum, but *pomodore* (tomatoes), that's another story! Thank goodness they consume large quantities of olive oil. That may well be their saving grace.

The critics of vegetarianism say their dietary habits lack complete proteins (all essential amino acids) for proper growth and development. Although meat and dairy products are complete proteins, certain foods or combinations of foods constitute complete proteins as well. Some of these are:

- Corn tortillas with pinto beans and a little cheese
- Lentil soup with cornbread
- Vegetable-tofu stir fry over rice
- Navy bean soup with rye bread
- Black-eyed peas with cornbread
- Black-eyed peas and brown rice
- Brown rice and red beans
- Soybean products: tofu, cheese, soy milk, tempeh
- Whole grain bread with nuts or seeds
- Legumes with any grain
- Peanut butter on whole grain bread

(Note: peanut butter in general is not permitted, but, if it is not hydrogenated, it can be used sparingly. Natural peanut butter where the oil appears at the top of the jar is best. Hydrogenated products were once unsaturated in nature, but have been processed by adding hydrogen to them in order to solidify them. This turns them into a saturated fat, which is most undesirable. Peanut butter which is smooth throughout is hydrogenated, and should be avoided.)

These items supply the necessary proteins in the daily diet, about 45 grams, or 15% of the daily diet, but with a difference. They lack the saturated fats, chemical additives, uric acid content of meats, as well as fiber found in their substitutes.

You may not lean toward full vegetarianism, but if you meet people who do, don't mock them. They may know something you don't know. And who knows, maybe someday you will be numbered among them.

> "The vegetarian manner of living, by its purely physi-
> cal effect on the human temperament, would most
> beneficially influence the lot of mankind."
>
> –Albert Einstein

[Having said all of the above, there is, however, one essential vitamin that is available primarily from animal sources—vitamin B12. A deficiency of vitamin B12 can lead to serious health problems, especially in later years. B12 deficiency is not common in vegetarians because it is available to them in fermented foods such as miso, tempeh, brewer's yeast and sprouted beans and grains. The natural bacterial activity produces B12 in these foods.]

(Source: Braly, James, *Dr. Braly's Food Allergy and Nutrition Revolution*, Keats Publishing, Inc. 1992, p. 108)]

According to...

Harvard University's Nurses' Health Study: women need at least 109 micrograms (mcg's) of vitamin K daily to reduce the risk of hip fracture. Lettuce, especially romaine, and other dark green varieties are good sources, along with collard greens, spinach, Brussels sprouts, and broccoli.

Johns Hopkins and **Harvard** researchers found that people who eat dark green, leafy vegetables, particularly spinach and collard greens, may reduce the risk of declining vision, macular degeneration (MD) being the most common type after age 65. People with a high intake of green vegetables, high in carotenoids, had a 43 percent lower risk of neovascular macular degeneration. Research continues.

Congress of the European Society of Cardiology: their Mediterranean Diet reduces dramatically the risk of heart disease. The diet consists principally of vegetables, whole-grain cereals, fruit, berries, fish, and only small amounts of animal products.

The Journal of Clinical Nutrition shows that people can absorb folic acid when it is added to foods such as bread and cereal. Folic acid is found naturally in green leafy vegetables, Brussels sprouts and black-eyed peas. This nutrient is most important for the health and well-being of a pregnant woman as well as her developing baby and can prevent neural defects such as spina bifida.

Tufts University Diet & Nutrition Newsletter (December 1996), shows that fruits and vegetables contain insoluble fiber, as do whole wheat products and bran, which may be why they are strongly linked to a decreased risk of certain cancers. The reason fruits and vegetables appear to be deterrents to so many other cancers as well is that they contain antioxidant nutrients (beta-carotene and vitamins A and C) and dozens of phytochemicals—compounds that research suggests play a major role in preventing malignant tumors.

Pennsylvania State University: a study shows that garlic and onions block the formation of a potent carcinogen. The findings are consistent with epidemiological evidence from China that shows vegetables from the onion family can help reduce cancer risk.

The Harvard School of Public Health reveals that people who consume olive oil have a very low rate of heart disease. In addition, women who consume olive oil more than once a day have a 25 percent reduced rate of breast cancer. The study suggests that the type of fat may be more important than the total fat.

The American College of Sports Medicine and the **American Dietetic Association** say that only 10-15% of daily calories should come from protein, 50-60% from carbohydrates, and 25-30% from fat.

The Center for Science in the Public Interest suggests the top ten foods we should be eating are: sweet potatoes, whole grain breads, broccoli, strawberries, beans, cantaloupe, spinach and kale, oranges, oatmeal, and fat-free skim milk. (Note: With the exception of strawberries, all of the above are advised for the psoriasis, eczema, and psoriatic arthritic patient.)

Sugar, Sugar, Everywhere!

Most of us who read labels focus on a product's fat or cholesterol content, and rightly so. But, reader beware, keep searching the "Nutrition Facts" label on a product for its *sugar content* as well, for, in the opinion of modern day nutritionists, therein lies the origin of many ailments. Aches, pains, and overweight that eventually leads to acquired conditions such as diabetes, heart disease, kidney disease, and obesity can have their origin in excessive sugar intake. Excessive sugar consumption is the leading cause of blindness and toe and foot amputations. It happens insidiously, over a long period of time.

The advice by specialists has been to regularly check blood sugars after the age of 45, but because of the large consumption of sugar in recent years, it is recommended that the age of 45 be reduced to 25.

Nancy Appleton, Ph.D., in her excellent book **Secrets of Natural Healing with Food,** states that "...at the turn of the century, we ate approximately 40 pounds of sugar per person per year. Today we eat 139 pounds of sugar per person per year." [Appleton, Nancy: *Secrets of Natural Healing with Food,* Rudra Press c/o Sterling Publishing Co., Inc. 387 Park Ave. S., NY, NY 10016, 1995, p.23] *Tufts University Health and Nutrition Letter* of January 1999 estimated it at 20 teaspoons of sugar for the average American every day! That's 320 calories worth, and it doesn't include sugars that naturally occur in foods such as fruit, legumes or milk. It's sugar that has been **added** to foods. That's too much for just about everyone, according to the US Department of Agriculture (USDA). The agency suggests limiting added sugar to 6 teaspoons for someone who eats 1,600 calories a day, 12 teaspoons for anyone who consumes 2,200 calories, and 18 teaspoons for persons averaging 2,800 calories per day. Sugar is in practically every food item we buy, especially in processed foods.

"Sugar," says Appleton, "so upsets the body chemistry that it doesn't matter what else you put in your mouth, neither healthful food nor junk food will digest properly." Appleton estimates that the average teenage boy eats twice as much sugar as people in any other age group. This means he eats an average of more than a cup of sugar a day! Your body needs only two teaspoons of blood sugar at any time in order to function properly. This amount can be obtained easily through the digestion of unrefined carbohydrates, protein, and fats. Even if we ate no glucose or refined sugar at all, our bodies would still have plenty of blood sugar. "Every extra teaspoon of refined sugar you eat works to throw your body out of balance and compromise its health," according to Appleton. [Appleton, Nancy, *Lick the Sugar Habit,* Avery Books, 1996, p. 13]

In summary, we Americans consume far more refined sugar than we need or even suspect. When it has been estimated that 20-25% of all our calories are derived from refined sugars, "something's got to give"—and that something is your vital organs: pancreas, heart, kidneys, liver, brain, arteries, joints, eyes, and have no doubt about it, your skin! It most certainly contributes to psoriasis and eczema and, more than likely, to the most common of all skin diseases—acne! The effect the consumption of such huge quantities of refined sugar has on the skin is too overwhelming to ignore. That is why I list "sweets" as just as important to curtail as I do saturated fats or the nightshades. If the desire for sweets is overpowering, a fresh fruit or a little honey is the recommended source. Not only will such a practice help save your skin, but your internal organs as well.

As I visualize it, I look upon processed sugar in the blood as I would sand—and who wants sand circulating throughout the blood? Imagining it this way makes it easier to turn down that extra piece of cake, candy or ice cream. Sugar in itself has no nutritional value. Refined sugar is 99.4 to 99.7% pure calories—no vitamins, no minerals, no proteins—just simple carbohydrates.

A Further Word About Carbohydrates

Keep in mind that carbohydrates, both simple sugars and complex sugars commonly known as complex carbohydrates, are just as capable of raising blood sugar levels as candy bars, cookies, etc. Complex carbohydrates are found in all starchy foods, most of which tend towards acid forming. Such foods include breads, potatoes, pasta, rice, etc., thus the reason they fall within the 20%-30% range of food selection.

Diabetes—The Epidemic of our Time

"Diabetes is turning into a worldwide epidemic as it spreads from rich countries to the developing world..."
[Reuters, New York Daily News, *May 16, 1999*]

The Daily News report goes on to say that scientists expect 22 million Americans will have diabetes by the year 2025, which is up from 16 million today. The disease, which is associated with a sedentary life and inactivity, is the sixth-leading cause of death in the United States, killing almost 200,000 people a year. According to the Federal Centers for Disease Control and Prevention, diabetes is expected to climb 170% in the next thirty years. The aging, slowing down and fattening of Americans are the major factors in this alarming trend. That is understandable when statistics indicate the average American consumes 20 teaspoons of sugar per day while only 2 are needed. With these facts and figures at our fingertips, common sense tells us to curb our sugar habit. To ignore it can only lead to ill health, lowered resistance, and vital organ breakdown. To take heed to it promises good health, vitality and longer life.

Sugar Substitutes

With sucrose (table sugar) dominating the sugar consumption scene, and a growing awareness of the harmful effects it can have after long-term use, it naturally follows that sugar substitutes are a sought after item among health-minded individuals.

The following partial list of sugar substitutes is provided for your consideration:

Honey, man's first sweetener, has been a favorite since ancient times, and is advised above all other sweeteners, but again, in moderation. [To satisfy a sweet tooth, try a half teaspoon of honey on a whole grain cracker. This not only can end the craving but is nutritious as well, as long as it is not overdone.] Honey should also be used whenever possible as a sugar substitute in baking or glazing.

Fructose is fruit sugar. It is found in fruits as well as in honey. It is somewhat more expensive than white sugar (sucrose) but you use half as much. High-fructose corn sweetener is often used in food processing because in the long run it is less expensive. Nevertheless, it is still sugar and must be used sparingly.

Saccharine, known by the brand names *Sweet n' Low, Sprinkle Sweet, Twin,* and *Sweet 10,* is classed as being *300 times* sweeter than white sugar. Saccharine comes from petroleum. It was held suspect in causing bladder tumors, which prompted the FDA to propose a ban on the product, but it was left on the market by public demand.

Aspartame, also known as *Equal,* is found in a myriad of products from soft drinks to candy, under the name *Nutrasweet.* Some people claim high sensitivity to the product with some reporting headaches and even seizures. Claims that Aspartame can cause brain cancer, multiple sclerosis, Alzheimer's and other diseases is not backed up by any scientific evidence. It can, however, harm people with advanced liver disease or phenylketonuria or PKV, a rare inherited disorder, according to Patricia Bertron, RD, Director of Nutrition, Physicians' Committee for Responsible Medicine, Washington, DC. Drinking water and eating plenty of whole grains, fruits and vegetables is the better way to go for weight loss than consuming artificially sweetened sodas and desserts. [Source: *Bottom Line,* Sept. 1, 1999]

Sorbitol is an artificial sweetener used mostly in chewing gum, candy and breath mints. Sheah Rarback, Nutritionist and Assistant Professor of Pediatrics at University of Miami

Medical School asserts that in large quantities sorbitol has a laxative effect. "Even a few sticks of sugarless gum for a small child can cause problems," states Rarback. [*The Record*, April 17, 1999, p. H-3]

Stevia (honey leaf), is 100 times sweeter than sugar, has a slightly bitter aftertaste, and no calories when refined into a powder. According to one article by Marie McCullough, reported in the *Philadelphia Inquirer* on February 9, 1999, stevia is seen either as a healthy replacement for sugar and artificial sweeteners that has long been used in South America and Asia, or as an unapproved food additive that may disrupt fertility, blood sugar levels, and kidney function. Although the controversy continues, stevia is now readily available in the United States and is gaining in popularity. The bottom line is that it is really up to the consumer to decide.

FruitSource: this is a new sweetener derived from grapes and whole grain rice. It comes in both granular and syrup forms and is quite tasty. It can be used as you would honey or any other type of sugar.

To be sure there are other effective sweeteners one can use, such as barley malt, rice syrup, barley syrup, blackstrap molasses and herbal sweeteners that carry valuable essential nutrients which are often lacking in artificial sweeteners. At the present time, the jury is still out regarding the use of artificial sweeteners and the long-term effects they may have in human nutrition.

Additional Information:

Children with a sweet tooth (and most have one) often end up with dental and/or weight problems. There are some ways to counteract the problem, such as: use seltzer, not club soda, with unsweetened fruit juice in place of regular or diet soda. Serve hot cereal or whole grain waffles with cinnamon or nutmeg instead of syrup or sugar, and use ¼ less sugar than the recipe calls for. The kids will never know the difference!

Consumer groups are beginning to insist that food labels disclose the amount of sugar added to the products. They want the words "added sugar" included because there is no way the buyer can tell how much is naturally occurring sugar and how much has been added. According to Michael Jacobson of the Center for Science in the Public Interest, natural sugars supply other nutrients, including vitamins and fiber, whereas added sugars add only calories to the diet. The proposal to include the wording "added sugars" on the food label was sent to the FDA in August 1999; Jacobsen said that changing that rule will probably take about five years!

The Agricultural Department, says Jacobson, recommends that the average person on a 2,000 calorie diet include no more than 40 grams of added sugar. That's about 10 teaspoonfuls, or the equivalent of one 12 ounce soft drink!

Are Americans consuming too much sugar? It is no wonder that diabetes, heart disease, and obesity, not to mention skin diseases such as psoriasis and eczema, especially in children, are on a steady rise. The annual consumption of **added** sugar *per person* in 1984 was 51 pounds; by 1998 it had increased to 64 pounds, with no sign of letting up!

Where does this added sugar come from? Observe the following:

- Soft drinks   33%
- Table sugar and other sources   25%
- Baked Goods   14%
- Fruit Drinks   10%
- Dairy Desserts   6%
- Candy   5%

- Breakfast Cereals   4%
- Tea   3%

Common forms are table sugar (cane and beet), corn sugar, corn syrup, and high-fructose corn syrup. [Source: *Center for Science in the Public Interest,* Aug. 1999]

From what I have observed, the above are listed among the major culprits in the creation of psoriasis and eczema in children as well as adults. How do I know this? Simply by observing the positive results once the patients delete them from their daily diet.

On Fats

The Undesirable Effect Of Frying Foods

Frying foods is emphatically advised against by modern nutritionists. Ph.D. Nutritionist, **Nancy Appleton,** in her highly informative book, ***Secrets of Natural Healing with Food,*** says: "Fast foods are usually fried foods, and therefore are notoriously high in the free radicals formed in the process of frying foods. The fats used for frying fast foods are often heated over and over and become rancid. These are the fats that clog the arteries, whether they be saturated or unsaturated. Stay away from all fried foods— *they are killers."* [Appleton, Nancy: *Secrets of Natural Healing with Food,* Rudra Press c/o Sterling Publishing Co., Inc. 387 Park Ave. S., NY, NY 10016, 1995, p. 23]

Simone Gabbay, a Toronto registered nutritional consulting practitioner, further explains in her remarkable book ***Nourishing the Body Temple,*** that: "Frying requires the use of a cooking fat, which is one reason this method is warned against, and cooking meats in their own juices, with no additional fats or oils, is recommended. The chemical structure of vegetable oils used for frying, especially those that are polyunsaturated, is adversely affected by cooking at high temperatures, which promote the formation of harmful trans-fatty acids and other toxic substances. The charring of meats, which usually occurs during frying (and always in barbecuing), results in carcinogens being formed. Baking or broiling is much less destructive, and meats thus prepared are easier to digest." [Gabbay, Simone: *Nourishing the Body Temple*, ARE Press, Virginia Beach, VA, 1999 p. 57-58]

The Dangers Of Trans-fatty acids

Familiarize yourself with the term **trans-fatty acids** (also referred to as *transfats* or TFA's) for, if ever there was a destructive by-product of the modern day manner of processing foods, this is it. Simone Gabbay has done a splendid job of summarizing the problem in clear, precise language:

> *"Further damage is done when vegetable oils are artificially hardened by hydrogenation. Hydrogenated fats are found in margarines, vegetable shortenings, commercial baked goods, and processed foods and snacks. These are true junk foods, since they contain trans-fatty acids, which are chemically altered molecules that disrupt the function of enzymes and metabolic processes in the body. Medical research has shown that trans-fatty acids raise serum cholesterol levels and contribute to cardiovascular disease. In 1994, a study out of Harvard said that trans-fatty acids found in margarine could be responsible for 30,000 deaths due to heart disease in the United States each year. Unfortunately, the myth that margarine is a heart-friendly health food lives on, since its producers and marketers naturally have no interest in dispelling it."* [Nourishing the Body Temple, *p. 69-70*]

In speaking of the effects of hydrogenated fats which are found in margarine, Zoltan P. Rona, M.D., M.Sc., of Toronto cites a study conducted in India and published in 1967 in the American

Journal of Clinical Nutrition: "'The population that used margarine instead of butter had a heart disease rate that was **fifteen times greater** than that of the population that used butter. A follow-up study twenty years later reported the same statistics.'" [*Nourishing the Body Temple*, p. 70]

Research conducted at the University of Maryland found large amounts of trans-fatty acids (TFA's) in margarine, cooking fats, bread, cakes, french fries, pretzels, chips, frostings, puddings, and highly processed foods. Our bodies need more *essential fatty acids*, not trans-fatty acids!

In summary, it is best to completely avoid frying or buying fried foods. With the availability of so many other methods of cooking that are much less destructive and easier to digest, staying away from fried foods should be no big deal. *The rewards of avoidance far outweigh the benefits of indulgence.*

The increased awareness of the harmful effects of transfats as they relate to human health prompted the FDA to propose that the amount of trans-fatty acids in a product be included as a footnote to saturated fats on the Nutrition Facts label. This change would be the first since the government initially required labels on food products in 1994. Why is it important? Because research has mounting evidence that transfats are possibly the worst artery cloggers of all, even more so than saturated fat. Studies indicate that transfat increases LDL-cholesterol (bad cholesterol) which increases the risk of heart disease. As it increases the LDL level, it simultaneously decreases the HDL (good cholesterol) level that is beneficial to the heart.

Trans-fatty acids are what gives the taste to the foods most of us love: doughnuts, cookies, pastries, etc. Previously, consumers had no way of knowing how much transfat was in a food item. That is no longer the case since it has been added to the Nutrition Facts label. "It's not going to be able to slip under the radar screen anymore," says FDA Commissioner, Jane Henney.

With heart disease being the leading cause of death in the United States, taking the lives of 500,000 Americans a year, it pays to be aware of transfat content so you may possibly ward off being numbered among the fatalities.

In the past, trans-fatty acids were listed as "hydrogenated" fats in the list of ingredients. That is because the most common source of transfat is partially hydrogenated vegetable oils in which liquid oil is turned into a solid by combining it with hydrogen to retard spoilage and retain flavor over a longer period of time. In general, the harder the margarine or cooking fat, the higher the transfat content. For example, stick margarine used in deep-fried fast foods, cookies, and pastries have transfat hidden in them; whereas, spreadable margarine in a tub has little trans-fatty acids.

As of January 2, 2006, however, the Food and Drug Administration (FDA) requires that trans-fatty acids be declared in the nutrition label of conventional foods and dietary supplements (68FR41434). [For positioning in the food label, see page 493. Source: FDA] It is hoped that by requiring the amount of transfat to be included on the Nutrition Facts label, manufacturers of such products will be encouraged to replace transfats with beneficial oils that are known to promote health, particularly where the cardiovascular system is involved.

Saturated Fats (Sources)

There is an old saying "Forewarned is forearmed." In order to control, alleviate, and even cure a condition of psoriasis one must know specifically which foods cause the most problems and which foods promote healing. High on the list of foods to avoid, as already indicated, are saturated fats (those that harden at room temperature).

Tufts University Newsletter [Vol. 12, No. 11, Jan. 1995] identifies some of the most common foods containing saturated fats and provides us with the following information. Most people in the United States consume about 25 to 30 grams of saturated fat a day, whereas someone following an 1800 to 2000 calorie diet should not go beyond 20 grams. The most concentrated sources of saturated fat are ground beef; whole milk and whole milk beverages; cheese; beef steaks and roasts; hot dogs and luncheon meats; doughnuts; cookies and cakes; butter; ice cream and other frozen desserts.

Fat Substitutes

Avoiding saturated fats is not only advised for the psoriasis or eczema patient but for the general public as well. The following list provides suitable substitutes for fats that are detrimental to the body. These should be substituted whenever possible.

Instead Of:	Use:
Butter, lard, palm or coconut oil	Olive oil (extra virgin) or canola oil
Ice cream	Frozen low-fat yogurt
Regular cheeses	Low-fat cheeses
Whole milk	Skim or 1% milk
Heavy cream	Evaporated skim milk
Sour cream	Nonfat sour cream -or- nonfat yogurt
Whole milk ricotta cheese	1% fat cottage cheese
Beef, pork, veal	Fish, fowl, lamb
Hamburger (beef)	Broiled veggie, lamb or turkey burger
Poultry with skin	Poultry without skin

Fried foods	Food prepared any way *except* fried!
Potato Chips	Baked sweet potato chips
Danish pastry	Bran muffin
White rice with beef	Brown or wild rice with beans
Meat-based soup	Tofu, lentil, or bran soup
Casseroles using meats	Casseroles using beans
Pasta with tomato sauce & meatballs	Vegetable Pasta with olive oil & garlic sauce

A Word to the Wise...!

Hydrogenated (hardened) oils are almost impossible for the body to assimilate. When fat is hydrogenated (combined with hydrogen under high heat) for the purpose of extending shelf life, the essential fatty acids are destroyed. Examples of hydrogenated oils are margarine and shortening. Any oils that are solid at room temperature tend to act like saturated fat and are to be avoided. They raise cholesterol level which is a precursor to heart disease, liver disease, cancers of the breast, prostate, and colon, and obesity, all of which can be traced back to high saturated fat consumption. Partially hydrogenated soybean oil and frying foods (especially deep-frying as done in fast-food chains) also have a deleterious effect on the body by virtue of their changing the molecular structure of the oils from one of an antioxidant to a free radical. Vitamin E, a powerful antioxidant, is the ideal antidote in that it will protect the body's cell membranes from free-radical damage that occurs when oils are subjected to intense heat, such as in frying or in the hydrogenating process. All those chemicals, pesticides, etc. are consumed by the animals and stored in their fatty tissues, thus the reason for avoiding such foods.

Obesity—Something to think about

Obesity has hit epidemic levels in America! Obesity has been defined as 30 percent over ideal body weight. On October 28, 1999 the Journal of the American Medical Association released warnings from federal health officials that obesity must be treated as a serious health threat - not merely for cosmetic reasons.

One study found that almost 80 percent of obese adults suffer from diabetes, high cholesterol, high blood pressure, gallbladder disease, osteoarthritis, or heart disease (the leading killer of adults in the United States!).

Dr. Jeffrey P. Kaplan, Director of the U.S. Centers for Disease Control and Prevention, blamed the changing American lifestyle for this alarming trend. Kaplan said the problem is due in part to the growth of fast food chains, jobs that are less physically demanding, convenience devices in the home and continual use of the automobile rather than bicycles and simple walking.

Dr. Stephen H. Schneider, an endocrinologist at UMDNJ-Robert Wood Johnson Medical School in New Brunswick, NJ who specializes in diabetes said part of the problem is that physicians are simply too busy to educate and monitor their patients regarding weight. "The truth of the matter is most physicians don't treat it at all. We're lucky if they even mention it." [Source: *The Record*, Hackensack, NJ, Oct. 27, 1999]

With these facts before you, ask yourself the question: "How do I stack up?"

How Do You Stack Up?

Overweight and/or obesity are the number one killers in this country! It may be classified as heart disease, kidney disease, diabetes, etc., but in the majority of instances, overweight is the underlying basic cause of many ailments and deaths. For those who would like to live a long and healthy life, the following chart will help you see where you stand for your height, age and weight. Are you 30% over your ideal body weight?

SUGGESTED WEIGHTS FOR ADULTS

Height*	Weight in pounds†	
	19 to 34 years	35 years and older
5' 0'	97-128	108-138
5' 1"	101-132	111-143
5' 2"	104-137	115-148
5' 3"	107-141	119-152
5' 4"	111-146	122-157
5' 5"	114-150	126-162
5' 6"	118-155	130-167
5' 7"	121-160	134-172
5' 8"	125-164	138-178
5' 9"	129-169	142-183
5' 10"	132-174	146-188
5' 11"	136-179	151-194
6' 0"	140-184	155-199
6' 1"	144-189	159-205
6' 2"	148-195	164-210

*without shoes   †without clothes

Source: *The Dietary Guidelines for Americans*, US Department of Agriculture, US Department of Health and Human Services.

Calcium

New research by a New York research group reported that eating more calcium-rich foods reduced the risk of colon cancer in men prone to the disease. Another New York-based team described a 50% reduction in life-disrupting premenstrual symptoms (PMS) among hundreds of women who took daily calcium supplements. [Source: *The New York Times*, Oct. 13, 1998, p. F1]

Calcium is the key nutrient in avoiding osteoporosis. Without enough calcium, there won't be enough bone. But without enough Vitamin D, calcium cannot be absorbed. The Recommended Daily Allowance (RDA) for calcium for ages 11 through 24 is 1,200 mg. Vitamin D is manufactured by the body when it is exposed to natural sunlight. But, as one gets older, the ability of the skin to react in this manner becomes less. This can be solved by consuming foods rich in vitamin D. Fatty fish like sardines, salmon, herring, mackerel and swordfish all provide reasonable amounts of vitamin D. Eggs, and some fortified cereals contribute vitamin D as well. [Source: *Tufts University Diet and Nutrition Newsletter*, Vol. 12, No. 4, 1994]

Yogurt

Yogurt, milk fermented by lactic acid bacteria, has for centuries been recognized by physicians in the Middle East as playing a valuable role nutritionally and medicinally. However, it was not until Elie Metchnikoff, Nobel Prize winner, began his scientific study of yogurt in the early 1900's that yogurt received a wider recognition in the West. He noticed that Bulgarian people lived longer, more productive lives compared with their Western counterparts, and discovered yogurt to be a mainstay of their daily diet. Metchnikoff concluded that yogurt (lactobacilli) in large numbers in the human intestinal flora was a major factor in the successful prevention and treatment of disease. The presence of those "friendly" bacteria (naturally found in the human intestinal tract) has proven to be of great value in the synthesis of several nutrients, including B-complex and calcium, and in the reducing of serum cholesterol level and the risk of bowel cancer.

Simone Gabbay, RNCP, in her book *Nourishing the Body Temple* (ARE Press, Virginia Beach, VA, 1999, p. 48) states:

> *"Faulty diet, stress, and pharmaceutical drugs, (particularly antibiotics), can seriously deplete levels of beneficial bacteria in the intestinal tract, thus making it possible for undesirable yeast organisms, such as candida albicans, to invade and thrive. Numerous health problems, such as chronic fatigue, multiple food allergies, and hyperactivity in children, have been linked to yeast overgrowth in the intestines."*

Since our approach to psoriasis focuses attention on the health and maintenance of the intestinal tract, yogurt (as well as buttermilk) is a valuable part of this regimen and, unless there is an allergy to it, yogurt should be consumed regularly and in large quantity. Store-bought yogurt is of course readily available to most people. I suggest you buy only plain yogurt, or vanilla flavor, with active cultures. Of course you can develop a taste for the plain, and many people actually come to enjoy it. Avoid yogurt with added fruit since that raises the sugar content. If you would like to make your own yogurt, follow the recipe included in the "Side Dishes" section of this book.

Frozen Yogurt vs. Ice Cream

On November 17, 1994, Channel 7, Eyewitness News, New York, revealed the outcome of a special investigation they conducted on the amount of calories and fat found in several brands of yogurt. To the dismay of many consumers, it was found that frozen yogurt, while lower in fat than regular ice cream, contained over half, or even three times, more fat, and consequently more calories, than the public had been led to believe. The lesson is don't believe everything you read on labels unless they are approved by the FDA or some other "consumer watch" agency. I still advise my patients to substitute frozen yogurt for ice cream, but with the understanding that it may not be as fat free as we would like to believe. Keep in mind that the flavor "vanilla" contains the least amount of calories. Patients are advised to avoid all other flavors, especially strawberry and chocolate.

Pass Up The Salt!

Salt is one of the basic elements that make up the human body. The U.S. Department of Agriculture's most recent guideline (2005) recommends that a 2,000 calorie diet contain no more than 2,300 mg of sodium, equal to slightly more than a teaspoon of salt. An intake of salt over and above that could eventually lead to problems in circulation and consequently affect the vital organs, such as the heart, kidneys and liver, as well as the eyes and, of course, the brain itself. There is no question that salt does indeed enhance taste and it is the primary reason it is used. Problems arise, however, when instead of being used, it is abused. So what does one do in that case? The answer is simple, season with salt substitutes. Not only can they enhance taste, but they are actually healthier than too much salt. The following chart gives an idea of how many salt substitutes are readily available. Try them, you might like them!

When Cooking:	Use This Instead Of Salt:
Lamb	Garlic, mint, mint jelly, rosemary, pineapple, kelp
Chicken	Lemon juice, marjoram, parsley, sage, thyme, kelp
Fish	Bay leaf, lemon juice, parsley, marjoram, dill, garlic powder, kelp
Eggs (poached)	Basil, cloves, dill, ginger, lemon, onion, savory

When Cooking:	Use This Instead Of Salt:
Pasta (whole grain or vegetable)	Basil, garlic, lemon juice, oregano, caraway seed, kelp
Asparagus	Garlic, lemon juice, onion, apple cider vinegar (ACV)
Broccoli	Lemon juice, garlic, ACV, kelp
Cucumbers	Chives, dill, garlic, ACV
Green Beans	Dill, lemon juice, marjoram
Greens (in general)	Onion, ACV, lemon juice
Peas	Mint, onion, parsley
Rice (Brown or Wild)	Chives, onion, saffron
Squash	Brown sugar, cinnamon, ginger, nutmeg, onion
Soups:	
Bean	Dry mustard
Milk Chowders	Peppercorn, bay leaf, parsley
Pea	Bay leaf, parsley
Vegetable	ACV, brown sugar, kelp, allspice

Note: If a little touch of salt is needed, sea salt (fine) is preferred.

A Little Spice Is Oh So Nice!

Herbs and spices have been used to enhance the flavor of foods for as long as man has been cooking food. There is nothing wrong with adding a little zip to your cooking, the question is which spices are the best to use if you are a psoriasis, eczema, or psoriatic arthritis patient. The most important thing to avoid are the hot spices and use instead the milder more flavorful ingredients. The following is a list of the most frequently used herbs and spices and what they are best used with. There are others, but these are the favorites. (Only permitted foods are listed in the second column.)

Herb/Spice:	Best Used On:
Basil	lamb, seafood, bean soup, cucumber salad, onion, rutabaga, squash, greens
Coriander	lamb (ground, steaks, chops), beet and fruit salads
Dill	lamb, fish, bean/split pea soup, seafood salads, lamb stew
Mint	lamb, fish, pea/lentil soups, peas, celery, cabbage, snap beans, spinach, fruit, green salads, iced drinks, cranberry juice
Oregano	lamb, poultry, fish, game, lentil, bean and onion soups, broccoli, carrots, lima beans, peas, onions, squash
Parsley	fish, lamb, poultry, soups, stews, salads, vegetables, garnishes
Rosemary	fish, lamb, poultry, pea/spinach soups, lentils, peas, spinach, squash, fruit salads
Sage	poultry, lamb, fish stock, chicken stews, string beans, lima beans, Brussels sprouts, carrots, onions, peas

Herb/Spice:	Best Used On:
Savory	fish, poultry, lamb, barbecue, bean/pea/lentil soups, kasha, cabbage, Brussels sprouts, turnips, beets, in cooking water for asparagus and artichokes
Sweet Marjoram	fish (esp. broiled), stews, carrots, lima beans, peas, spinach, green beans, green salad
Tarragon	fish, poultry, lamb, pheasant, chicken soup, broccoli, cauliflower, peas, cabbage, spinach, beans, asparagus, beets, vegetable juice, mixed greens
Thyme	fish, lamb, game, onion/pea/vegetable soups, asparagus, beans, beets, carrots, onions, peas, rice

[Source: *The Herb Companion Cooks*]

Be careful to avoid the hot stuff, such as: cayenne, cumin, chili, horseradish, mustard seed, paprika, peppers of all kinds (especially hot red pepper), turmeric and curry powder.

Learning To Read Labels

How often have we heard "You are what you eat!"? As far as your physical body is concerned, it couldn't be more plain. What you ingest literally becomes a part of you. It then follows that knowledge of the food we eat and the quantity is of profound importance in determining what to eat and what to avoid.

On May 8, 1994 the Food and Drug Administration (FDA), acting on the Nutrition Labeling and Education Act of 1990, transformed forever the way Americans buy their food. It then required that "Nutrition Facts" labels be placed on all processed foods. By July 6, 1994, meat and poultry products had to follow suit. The new law requires manufacturers to clearly indicate lettered information that can help consumers limit their intake of fat, cholesterol, sodium (salt), and sugar while increasing vitamins and fiber. The labels list amount of nutrients in grams (g) or milligrams (mg).

Under the label's "Nutrition Facts" panel, manufacturers are required to provide information on certain nutrients. The mandatory components, and the order in which they must appear, are:

- Total Calories
- Calories from Fat
- Total Fat
- Saturated Fat
- Cholesterol
- Sodium
- Total Carbohydrate
- Dietary Fiber
- Sugars
- Protein
- Vitamin A
- Vitamin C
- Calcium
- Iron

[Source: *FDA Backgrounder*, pp. 3-4, May 1999. For a complete list of both mandatory and voluntary components, check the FDA Website: http://vm.cfsan.fda.gov/~dms/ -or- contact FDA, Office of Consumer Affairs, HFE-88, Rockville, MD 20857 -or- call the Food Safety Hotline at 1(800) 332-4010.]

A Sample Of Present Food Labeling

Please note the following:

Look carefully at the *serving size.* All the numbers on the food label are referring to a specific amount of food, usually not the whole box or package.

The **bold** writing on the label denotes the primary categories, i.e. total fats, total carbohydrates. The indented, non-bold categories are subcategories of the primary categories. These subcategory numbers are part of the total number.

If fat is the primary concern, note the total calories per serving and the total calories from fat per serving. The guideline is to have no more than one-third of calories from fat. If the percentage is higher, the food would be considered a *high-fat* food, and should be chosen less frequently.

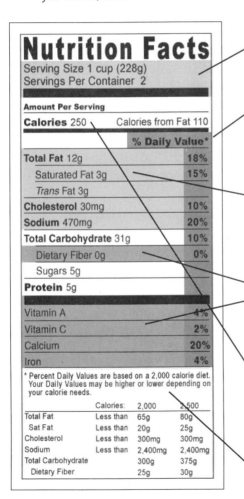

Nutrition Facts

Serving Size 1 cup (228g)
Servings Per Container 2

Amount Per Serving

Calories 250   Calories from Fat 110

	% Daily Value*
Total Fat 12g	18%
Saturated Fat 3g	15%
Trans Fat 3g	
Cholesterol 30mg	10%
Sodium 470mg	20%
Total Carbohydrate 31g	10%
Dietary Fiber 0g	0%
Sugars 5g	
Protein 5g	

Vitamin A	4%
Vitamin C	2%
Calcium	20%
Iron	4%

* Percent Daily Values are based on a 2,000 calorie diet. Your Daily Values may be higher or lower depending on your calorie needs.

	Calories:	2,000	2,500
Total Fat	Less than	65g	80g
Sat Fat	Less than	20g	25g
Cholesterol	Less than	300mg	300mg
Sodium	Less than	2,400mg	2,400mg
Total Carbohydrate		300g	375g
Dietary Fiber		25g	30g

SERVING SIZE tells you a normal portion and how many servings are in the package. Compare this portion size to how much you actually consume.

Note the **asterisk** after the heading "% Daily Value," It refers to the footnote in the lower part of the label, which tells you the percentages are based on a 2,000 calorie-a-day diet.

The **nutrients listed first** are the ones Americans generally eat in adequate amounts—or, more often, to excess. Eating too much saturated fat, trans fat, cholesterol or sodium may increase your risk of certain chronic diseases, such as heart disease, some cancers or high blood pressure.

Most people don't get enough **dietary fiber, vitamin A, vitamin C, calcium and iron**. Eating enough of these nutrients can improve your health and help reduce the rist of some diseases and conditions.

CALORIES provide a measure of how much energy you get from a serving. Many people consume more calories than they need without meeting recommended intakes for a number of nutrients. The calorie section of the label can help you manage your weight. As a general guide, 40 calories per serving is low, 100 calories is moderate, and 400 or more is high.

The **Percent Daily Value** is based on the recommendations for key nutrients as calculated for a 2,000 calorie daily diet. Many people consume more calories in a day, and most don't even know how many calories they consume. But you can still use the percentages as a frame of reference, whether you consume more or fewer than 2,000 calories. (Source: US Food and Drug Administration)

Most Important Terms To Be Aware Of

"Grams (g)" and **"Milliliters (ml)"** are the metric units that are used in serving size statements.

"Calorie free" means less than 5 calories per serving.

"Fat free" and **"sugar free"** both mean less than 0.5g per serving.

"Low cholesterol" means 20mg or less of cholesterol per serving **or** 2g or less of saturated fat per serving.

"Good source of vitamins or minerals" means one serving of a food contains 10-19 percent of the Daily Value for a particular nutrient.

"High" means this food contains 20% or more of the Daily Value (DRV) for a particular nutrient in a serving.

Serving Sizes

The Nutrition Labeling and Education Act of 1990 (NLEA) defines *serving size* as the amount of food customarily eaten at one time.

Daily Values (DRV's), comprises two sets of dietary standards: Daily Reference Values (DRV's) and Reference Daily Intakes (RDI's). Only the Daily Value (DRV's) appear on the label to make it less confusing. The NLEA has established DRV's for nutrients which are sources of energy: fat, saturated fat, total carbohydrates (including fiber), and protein; and for cholesterol, sodium and potassium, which do not contribute calories.

DRV's for the energy-producing nutrients are based on the number of calories consumed per day at a reference of 2,000 calories per day.

DRV's for the energy-producing nutrients are calculated as follows:

- fat based on 30 percent of calories
- saturated fat based on 10 percent of calories
- carbohydrate based on 60 percent of calories
- protein based on 10 percent of calories (The DRV for protein applies only to adults and children over 4. RDI's for protein for special groups have been established.)
- fiber based on 11.5 g of fiber per 1,000 calories.

Because of current public health recommendations, DRV's for some nutrients represent the uppermost limit that is considered desirable. The DRV's for total fat, saturated fat, cholesterol, and sodium are:

- total fat: less than 65 g
- saturated fat: less than 20 g
- cholesterol: less than 300 mg
- sodium: less than 2,400 mg

Note: The above applies to psoriatic/eczema patients as well, but in the case of "sugars" keep it at an absolute minimum or none at all.

It is not within the scope of this volume nor is it practical to go into every detail regarding food labeling. Those readers who are interested in greater depth on this subject may consult the FDA Website at the address given above. Furthermore, it should be mentioned that there are certain foods that are exempt from nutritional labeling under NLEA. For a more detailed account of such foods and rules, please contact the FDA at either their Website or mailing address given above.

Supplement Facts

A dietary supplement refers to products made of one or more of the essential nutrients, such as vitamins, minerals, and proteins. The *Dietary Supplement Health and Education Act* (DSHEA) of 1994 requires manufacturers to include the words "dietary supplement" on product labels. Starting on March 23, 1999 a "Supplement Facts" panel was required on the labels of most dietary supplements. It appears as follows:

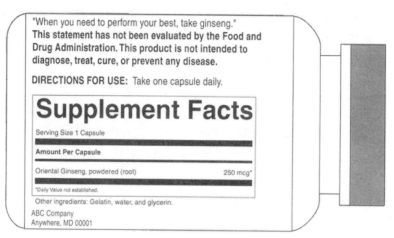

> "When you need to perform your best, take ginseng."
> **This statement has not been evaluated by the Food and Drug Administration. This product is not intended to diagnose, treat, cure, or prevent any disease.**
>
> DIRECTIONS FOR USE: Take one capsule daily.
>
> # Supplement Facts
>
> Serving Size 1 Capsule
>
> **Amount Per Capsule**
>
> Oriental Ginseng, powdered (root)   250 mcg*
>
> *Daily Value not established.
>
> Other ingredients: Gelatin, water, and glycerin.
>
> ABC Company
> Anywhere, MD 00001

Dietary supplements (with some exceptions) now include any products intended for ingestion as a supplement to the diet. This includes vitamins, minerals, herbs, botanicals, and other plant-derived substances, amino acids (the individual building blocks of protein), as well as concentrates, metabolites, constituents, and extracts of these substances. They come in the form of tablets, capsules, powders, softgels, gelcaps and liquids.

Since dietary supplements are not drugs, the FDA does not authorize or test dietary supplements as they do drugs prior to marketing. Consumers spend over $6.5 billion on dietary supplements annually, and the law essentially gives dietary supplement manufacturers freedom to market more products as dietary supplements and provide information about their products' benefit.

Dietary supplements should first be approved by your personal physician or health care professional. This is especially important for people who are:

• pregnant or breast-feeding

- chronically ill

- elderly

- under 18

- taking prescription or over-the-counter medicines (some combinations can prove to be extremely hazardous!)

[Source: *An FDA Guide to Dietary Supplements* by Paula Kurtzwell.]

For more information on this increasingly popular subject, contact the FDA at the address previously provided.

Antioxidants vs. Free Radicals

One cannot help but come upon the terms *antioxidants* and *free radicals* in modern day nutritional terminology. You may be asking, what do these terms mean? Very simply stated, you may look upon antioxidants as the "good guys" in nutrition—the elements that construct, build up and regenerate. On the other hand, you may view the free radicals as the "bad guys"—the forces that break down, damage and destroy. Both antioxidants and free radicals are primarily derived from the foods we eat. I say "primarily" because some can have their origin in our external environment.

To be more specific, antioxidants help protect and repair the cells from free radical damage. Free radicals are unstable oxygen molecules that can damage cells. It is true that the cells of the body are dying and being generated every moment of every day. This is a continuous cycle found in all of nature. It is part of what we call *life.*

Oxygen is an integral part of our being, but it could have adverse effects on the cells of the body. Just by using oxygen, chemical changes occur that can create oxygen molecules which are unstable and reactive. These are the ***free radicals*** which can cause havoc with the cellular membrane, cell structure and all components of the cells including the DNA. Free radicals can be produced by certain external stimuli such as cigarette smoke, alcohol, environmental pollutants, enzyme reactions, inflammations, UV light, and radiation. They can weaken arterial walls and cause fat deposits that can lead to heart disease.

However, the body has agents to protect itself. These are the highly desirable **antioxidants.** These fight the free radicals and bring the body into a state of homeostasis (equilibrium). They also repair the damage to the body cell structure caused by the free radicals.

Classified as antioxidants are: vitamins A, C, and E; Selenium; Carotenoids, such as beta carotene and lycopene; Coenzyme Q10; fruits and vegetables; milk thistle (silymarin). Since the purification of the liver is vital to the well-being of the psoriatic/eczematic patient, keep in mind that milk thistle (silymarin) and vitamin E in particular are believed to act as protectors of liver cells against the damage caused by free radicals. They also promote growth of liver cells and improve liver function. Herbs such as green tea, grape seed extract, and ginkgo biloba are all believed to have antioxidant qualities. [Source: *The Healing Power of Vitamins, Minerals and Herbs,* The Reader's Digest Association, Inc., 1999]

With this knowledge, one can choose wisely what to consume and what to avoid, and know the reason why. Modern nutritionists not only see it as a key to obtain and retain optimal health, they also believe it may play a part in the aging process. In other words, to use an old adage, your wise food choices can "Add years to your life, and life to your years!"

Antioxidant supplements—to take or not to take

The question now before us is should we double-up on antioxidant supplements as a safeguard against free radicals? Surprisingly, the experts suggest "no!" *Tufts University Health and*

Nutrition Letter (June 2000) reports that some three dozen distinguished scientists, after examining hundreds of studies on antioxidants and disease risk, concluded that most Americans get enough antioxidant vitamins from the food they eat. In a 500-page report for the Institute of Medicine that sets new RDA's for antioxidants, these scientists noted that there is insufficient evidence to support the claim that antioxidants taken in large doses prevent chronic disease or improve health.

Actually, the answer to the question should we or shouldn't we is simple. We should know what the antioxidants are, then obtain them by correctly selecting the foods we consume. It is not only healthier, it is also profoundly cheaper.

The following is a list of antioxidants and some fruits and vegetables where they are found. [Only foods acceptable for the psoriasis/eczema diet have been included.]

Vitamin C	Broccoli, citrus fruits
Vitamin E	Almonds, sunflower seeds, whole wheat
Lutein, Zeaxanthin	Spinach, kale, parsley
Lycopene	Ruby red grapefruit
Beta & Alpha Carotene	Carrots
Allyl Sulfides	Garlic
Proanthocyanadins	Grapes
Anthocyanadins	Blueberries
Mixed flavanoids	Sunflower seeds
Catechins	Green tea
Gingerols	Ginger

The Apple Diet
(Three Day)

The three day apple diet has been classified as the most effective way to clean the toxins out of anyone. No other foods should be consumed during the apple diet. Before beginning the diet, check with your personal physician to see if there is any contraindication. If you are allergic to apples, do not follow this diet!

If at all possible, purchase organic apples. The Delicious are the easiest of the recommended varieties to find. Both the red and yellow may be used, although most people prefer the yellow, which contain the most pectin, a substance that helps to reduce cholesterol and moves waste matter through the alimentary canal because of its fiber content.

Try to get a colonic on the first day, if that service is available in your area. If after the first or second day you have feelings of weakness or dizziness, discontinue this diet and begin to follow the regular psoriasis/eczema diet as outlined in this book.

Day 1

Eat as many apples as you like, and as much pure water as you can drink. Most people consume between 6 and 8 apples on the first day, 4 to 6 on the second day, and 2 to 4 on the third day. Some people continue to eat 8-10 apples a day, while others eat as few as one.

If the apples are organic, they may be washed and eaten with the peel. If they are not organic, then peel them. If for some reason you don't like the whole apple, you can mix it in a blender for uncooked "applesauce." This way they are quite palatable and easy to consume. Preferably near the end of the day, have your first colonic, although it can be taken at any time during the first day.

If there is no colonic service available in your area, you must have an enema at the end of the first day or during the second day, otherwise you may begin to reabsorb the toxins you are throwing off from the lower colon. If possible take a steam bath, and try to get a massage and do some general exercise.

You may have one ounce or two of **extra virgin olive oil** each night of the Apple Diet, and if you prefer, you may mix it in hot water or apple juice, which makes it easier to take in case you don't like oil. Or, you may take two tablespoons of olive oil at the end of the third day. [If you have a history of gallbladder problems or a liver condition, take one tablespoon of olive oil each day, or none at all if there is an adverse reaction to olive oil.]

Day 2

Have a colonic or an enema and eat any number of apples. Drink as much water as you can.

Day 3

Continue eating the apples, and, if at all possible, have another colonic or enema in the evening. Have all the water you can drink.

Natural Cathartics

Since internal cleansing is a vital part of the regimen, it is helpful to know what is available in the form of natural cathartics (eliminants) to help purge the large intestine of accumulated wastes. The following should be a help:

Fruits

Raw and stewed fruits should be eaten as often as possible, especially prunes, figs, apples, raisins, apricots, pears, and peaches. They may be mixed together if desired, and are to be eaten until a complete evacuation takes place. Diabetics however should beware of the high sugar content of stewed fruits. *(Remember, fruits are the cleansers of the body.)*

Vegetables

Raw and steamed vegetables make the best vegetable cathartic, particularly because of their high fiber content. Romaine lettuce, celery, rhubarb, Brussels sprouts, onion, and carrots are the best. *(Remember, vegetables are the builders of the body.)*

Foods Rich in Vitamin B

Wheat germ, brewer's yeast, whole raw barley, soybean flour, whole wheat flour, buckwheat, raw peas, egg yolks, rye bread, almonds, fish, poultry, honey, turnips, beets, dandelions, leafy green vegetables, and broccoli. Vitamin B and other factors in the B-complex tend to increase the tone of the intestinal musculature, which enhances proper evacuation.

Effective Combinations

- *Senokot* mixed in a glass of warm prune juice or, in the case of a diabetic, use warm water.

- *Fletcher's Castoria* combined with syrup of stewed figs.* From a 6 oz. bottle of Castoria remove one teaspoon of it, and replace it with one teaspoon of syrup of stewed figs. A half-teaspoon of this mixture is taken every half hour until there is a complete evacuation.

- *An Orange Juice "Sandwich"*—a combination of orange juice and castor oil. In a 6 oz. glass pour in 2 ounces of orange juice, then tilt the glass and add one ounce of castor oil, then, while the glass is still slightly tilted, add another two ounces of orange juice. (The castor oil "sandwiched" between layers of orange juice makes it more palatable.) Drink down and wait!

- *Castor oil* followed by a cup of American Yellow Saffron, green, or black tea. A patient swallows a teaspoon of castor oil but immediately follows it with a cup of hot tea void of cream or sugar.

- *Psyllium Husks* in water or juice, as directed on the bottle.

- *Eno Salts, Upjohn's Citrocarbonates*, and *Milk of Magnesia* are natural laxatives that are alkaline in nature.

- *Olive oil*. The importance of taking pure olive oil on a regular basis cannot be overstated. My patients take 3 tablespoons of olive oil a day. It not only lubricates the entire alimentary canal, but is an intestinal food and a powerful antioxidant. (Pure, extra virgin olive oil is preferred.)

* Fresh figs (when in season) may be heated and eaten immediately with great effectiveness. For syrup of stewed figs, place 5 or 6 dried figs in a cooking pot, and add enough water so the water level is approximately 4-5 inches above the figs. Soak the figs for several hours. After soaking, begin cooking figs by bringing water to a boil. Cover the pot and cook over a very low flame—simmer thus for about 50 minutes. After first 15 minutes, check to see if too much water has evaporated. If so, add enough water to keep the figs submerged. When figs are fully cooked, you may use some of the syrup in the recipe above. [Note: You

can follow the procedure for making syrup of figs to make stewed prunes.]

Apple cider vinegar—Beyond Taste!

Apple Cider Vinegar (ACV) is the only type of vinegar recommended on this regimen since it is the only one that is alkaline reacting. Apple cider vinegar, olive oil and lemon juice, with some mild spices if desired, is the salad dressing of choice. But there are other uses for apple cider vinegar of which few people are aware; uses that can help the psoriatic condition externally as well as internally. The following uses of apple cider vinegar demonstrate its versatility above and beyond pleasing the palate.

As a scalp rinse:

Pour two ounces of ACV into a measuring cup, then add six ounces of lukewarm water. After shampooing and rinsing the scalp, the vinegar solution is gently poured over the entire scalp and tenderly massaged into the scalp for about 30 seconds. The solution is left on for two minutes, then it is rinsed out with cool, or even cold water. Pat dry, or use a blow dryer set to "cool". This procedure however is *not* recommended when hair coloring is used.

As a skin softener:

A simple and effective preparation can be made by mixing a 20% solution of ACV and water in a spray bottle and spraying the affected areas, such as knees, elbows, or other dry areas with the solution. It may sting a bit if lesions are open, but it is not harmful. If bothersome at first, wait until the skin has healed over before applying.

As an ACV bath:

To a tub full of tepid water, add one cup of ACV. The patient then gets in the tub, up to his/her neck and relaxes for about twenty minutes. This will not only soften the skin, but will be a great comfort when the itch is intolerable. I have seen it work time and time again. One patient reported to me that after using the ACV in a bath three times a week for three months the psoriasis/eczema condition he was plagued with for years completely cleared up. If psoriasis of the scalp is a problem, while in the tub, saturate a small Turkish towel and set it on the scalp, renewing every few minutes, but not if hair coloring is used.

For hands and feet:

To a small basin of lukewarm water, add ½ to 1 cup of ACV. Immerse affected hands and/or feet in the basin and massage gently for 3-5 minutes. Pat dry and add a moisturizer if desired. It will leave the hands or feet soft and pliable and consequently more comfortable.

For psoriatic arthritis:

Great when getting up in the morning is a cup of hot water to which has been added a tablespoon of ACV and a tablespoon of honey. This is not only a very effective internal cleanser, it is also rich in potassium, and is very tasty! D.C. Jarvis, M.D., author of the ever popular book, **Vermont Folk Medicine,** has for decades recommended drinking ACV mixed with water and honey for cases of arthritis. It can also be a great aid for cases of constipation, which can in turn benefit an arthritic condition.

For the genital region:

Psoriasis and/or eczema of the genitals, with men or women, is perhaps the most agonizing, irritating, and embarrassing area of the body to be afflicted; yet, I have seen these areas completely clear up to the great joy and relief of the patient by a simple procedure. In conjunction with the regimen, I recommended a sitz bath using a diluted solution with the mouthwash Glyco-Thymoline in my book **HEALING PSORIASIS: The Natural Alternative.** If Glyco-Thymoline is not readily available, the mouthwash Lavoris may be used instead. Just as effective, however, is using ACV in a basin of lukewarm water placed in the bathtub. To a basin large enough for the patient to sit in, add about ½ cup of ACV to the water. The patient then simply squats in the water enough to submerge the genitals, and remains there 10-15 minutes. The patient then pats him/herself dry. A moisturizer may be used if deemed necessary. This not only relieves the itch, it also helps heal the lesions.

As a Laryngitis remedy:

Actors have long known about the healing properties of apple cider vinegar. When you find yourself with a case of laryngitis, fill a tall glass ½ full of warm water and ½ full of apple cider vinegar. Gargle until you finish the whole glass. Swallow your last mouthful. Repeat every hour until your voice fully returns.

Killing the Itch— Before it Kills You! (Pruritis)

You cannot talk about psoriasis or eczema without mentioning one of the most irritating, miserable, agonizing aspects of the disease, the incredible itch that often takes place. It is an itch that a patient feels will never go away. Most patients could deal with the psoriatic or eczema lesions if it weren't for the often generalized itch that goes with it. This constitutes the most difficult period a patient goes through during the "healing crisis," when the body is purging the toxins through every pore of the skin surface. As hard as it is to believe, it is a good thing that is happening. But getting through this period is the order of the day. To do it without resorting to scratching or having to take systemic drugs is the challenge each natural doctor and patient faces, but the rewards are well worth it once it is achieved.

Several anti-itch measures are covered in my book **HEALING PSORIASIS: The *Natural Alternative*** but since it is such a troubling aspect of the disease and since many of the remedies may be found right in your pantry, I feel it apropos to repeat them here. One or more may prove to be a godsend when and if the itch becomes unbearable. The following is a list that I have recommended to my own patients, advising discretion in their application. Remember, however, that hot tub baths are not recommended for patients with high blood pressure or any cardiac ailment.

Oatmeal and Cornstarch

Place 2 cups of old fashioned oatmeal, and 1 cup of cornstarch in a blender, whip about 15 seconds. This makes a powder of 3 cups, enough for 3 applications. Add 1 cup to a bathtub of lukewarm water. Immerse up to the neck and relax for 20-30 minutes. Add hot water if it gets too cool.

Apple Cider Vinegar or Witch Hazel or Glyco Thymoline

Add a cup of one of these to a bathtub of warm water and immerse for 20-30 minutes.

Olive Oil/Peanut Oil (50/50 mixture)

½ to 1 cup to a bathtub of water and immerse for 20-30 minutes. Be careful, it is very slippery. Get assistance with getting in and out of the tub!

Baking Soda

Add a one-pound box to a tub of comfortably hot water and immerse for 20-30 minutes.

Flax Seed Oil

Add ½ to 1 cup to a bathtub of comfortably hot water and immerse for 20-30 minutes.

Dead Sea Salts

Add 10-12 oz. dead sea salts to a tub of water and immerse for 20-30 minutes.

Epsom Salts

Add entire 4 lb. box to a tub of warm water and immerse for 20-30 minutes.

Warm, wet towels

Draped around the inflamed areas and allowed to cool. This will pull the heat out of the inflamed areas. It is best done on the bed with a sheet of plastic (such as a shower curtain liner or a tablecloth) under the patient.

Alka Seltzer

Taken internally with warm or cold water if there is no contraindication.

Sodium Bicarbonate (baking soda)

A level teaspoon in a glass of warm water taken internally unless not advised by your family physician.

A high colonic irrigation

or home enema.

A cold, wet application

to the irritated zones, especially in cases of eczema.

An ice cube

applied to the inflamed area, rather than scratching in cases of eczema.

Crisco (regular cooking)

applied to irritated areas of eczema.

Avoid drinking all fruit juices

during the itch cycle, especially citrus juices or eating citrus fruit.

Of course, there are several other anti-itch formulas or procedures on the market, but the above are the ones I have used successfully on patients. One may work better for one person than another. Having such a list to refer to may help a patient hit upon the right one for which they will be eternally grateful.

Caution—All of the above remedies should be used with discretion. Remember, patients with a heart problem of any kind should avoid hot baths. If, however, the water is kept on the lukewarm side, there should be no problem. It is best to check with your personal physician first.

Cooling The Flames

Some health practitioners call it "The Detox Period," others refer to it as "The Healing Crisis," still others label it "The Purge Cycle," while scientists know it as "The Herxheimer Reaction," and I simply call it "The Terrible Time," because that's exactly what it is—both to the patient and to the doctor. Whatever you call it, it is the same frightening experience: when the body is throwing off toxins through every pore of the skin in the form of flare-ups. In every case, I have seen these flare-ups soon begin to disappear when the patient sticks to the regimen. This is when drinking several glasses of distilled water per day will help prevent dehydration and speed up the cleansing process as well. The flare-ups may last for a week or a month—every patient is different—but usually the longer you've had psoriasis or eczema the longer it will take for this severe reaction to pass. Anything the patient can do to ease the discomfort of the skin surface is encouraged, such as the procedures outlined above in "Killing the Itch."

During this period, the patient must always keep in mind that the body is ridding itself of toxins, therefore no matter how difficult it may be to get through, it is a welcome sign of eventual healing. Let your body do what it is trying to do—clean up your insides! Only then can you expect true healing. Even if it takes a year to clean up your skin, what difference does it make as long as the job gets done? Ask yourself how long have you been going to doctors up to this point—a month, a year, 5, 10, or 20 years? This "terrible time" (and it may occur more than once) is as necessary as changing your diet—it is an integral part of the healing process. Your body must go through this before it can move on to the next stage—a gradual, but steady new skin formation.

A Word About Nail Psoriasis

Psoriasis of the fingernails or toenails is surely one of the more embarrassing forms of the disease to live with. Not only is it difficult if not impossible to cover up, it can be very painful. Psoriasis may attack the nail folds or the nail bed and cause pitting and dimpling of the nail plate. Debris builds up under the distal end and sometimes the palms of the hand and soles of the feet are affected. Yet, I have seen such conditions clear up and nails regenerate beautifully by following a few simple procedures. However, nails do take longer to heal and regrow than any other area of the body.

I must reiterate the importance of following the high alkaline/low acidic diet as outlined in my regimen. It is the key that I have found to heal and prevent recurrence of psoriasis regardless of its location, be it nails, scalp or body. Having said that, the following are external applications and procedures that will offer help along the way.

- Keep fingernails and toenails trimmed to prevent too much build up under the nail forcing the end of the nail to slant upward.

- Soak affected hands or feet in a basin of comfortably hot water with about a full cup of Epsom salts dissolved in it for 15 to 20 minutes. This will help soften the nails.

- Gently rub two or three drops of castor oil in and around each nail, then place each hand or foot in a white cotton sock and leave on overnight. At times, I advise a paste or poultice of castor oil combined with baking soda applied generously in and around each fingernail. If it proves to be too caustic, it is washed out in favor of using only the castor oil. This procedure can also be carried out using Vaseline instead of castor oil. They are then washed out in the morning.

- Take one packet of Knox Gelatine, 5 days out of the week.

Again it is realistic to expect treatment to take a minimum of three to six months. Here is a case where patience is truly a virtue!

The Regimen in Real Life

Can A Patient "Bend" A Little?

The question inevitably arises as to how strict one must be on the regimen, especially the diet. Can you fall back now and then—can you have that occasional glass of cold beer or a lobster tail or a steak, or a slice of pizza or an ice cream cone? Let's face it, food is a source of pleasure as well as nourishment, as well it should be. I have found that to deprive a patient completely and totally of one or more of his favorite foods is not only inadvisable, it is also unnecessary and counterproductive. Past experience has convinced me that total deprivation can act in the reverse of what we are trying to accomplish. It can cause frustration on the part of the patient which in itself doesn't help matters. So, I have found no harm in bending the rules *on occasion* and allowing a patient to relax and have his favorite dish now and then. But here is where control comes into play. Control does not mean every other day—it means just what it implies—perhaps once a month. Patients have proven to me that most can live with that.

My suggestion is that once a patient has been on the regimen for about three months, he may indulge in his favorite foods occasionally without "blowing it." In other words, the rare treat will not nullify all past efforts. In one of my classic cases, little Andrew Senson (now Dr. Andrew Senson) cleared up in three months at age five. Seventeen years passed during which he broke all the rules before he had a slight recurrence. He went back on the diet and quickly cleared again. He and I appeared together on the popular TV series, NBC's "Unsolved Mysteries," in 1991 to tell our story. Another of my patients craved a dish of ice cream but was afraid to try it for fear of destroying all her past efforts. I suggested she have it. Once she had it, she knew she was "good" for several months!

More often than not, however, patients feel so much better that they may not want to break the diet! I have seen this happen quite frequently.

To the question, therefore, can patients break the diet if they choose to now and then, my answer is "yes"—and if a reaction takes place afterwards, don't panic, just get back on the diet again! The overall picture is not broken. The contentment a patient feels afterwards may very well act in his or her favor. It goes without saying however, that if the patient continues to have an adverse reaction to a certain food item, it is foolhardy to continue eating it. Avoid it completely, not even indulging on occasion. It is their body telling them something, and to ignore the warning is to invite trouble.

Attitude and Emotions At the Dinner Table

Did you know that if you sit down to eat with anger, resentment, frustration or anxiety on your mind, you actually poison the food you eat? Better to go without eating than to partake of food you have just cursed.

In the same way that we have become conscious of fats, cholesterol, sugars, grams and milligrams, we are now zeroing in on the part that emotions play in our healthy eating agenda. Physiology gives us an answer.

The autonomic (automatic) nervous system consists of two neurotransmitters—the Sympathetic Nervous System and the Parasympathetic Nervous System. They both have opposite functions to one another. The Sympathetic Nervous System, which consists of twelve spinal segments, has often been called the "flight or fight" mechanism, and activates and prepares your body for a hostile or dangerous confrontation, thus the "fight or flight" concept. It is in action when action is needed; the blood diverts itself from the internal viscera such as the stomach, digestive tract, colon, etc. and floods where it is needed most, in the muscles and brain.

The counterpart to the sympathetic nervous system is called the Parasympathetic System. Originating in the cranium, it exists primarily as the vagus nerve and supplies all the organs of the viscera, when the body is in a relaxed state. The digestion and assimilation of food as well as proper eliminations through the colon and bladder is the function of the Parasympathetic nerve supply. Therefore, pure logic and physiology assure us that the digestion of food is normally done in a relaxed, comfortable manner. If a person sits down to eat with the opposite mental environment, the Sympathetics take over, discharge abnormal amounts of adrenaline and in general cause digestive disturbances which can lead to ulcers, intestinal spasms, constructive or ulcerative colitis and undoubtedly a large number of similar maladies.

When Dining Out

I have often heard from patients whose jobs take them on the road, or who are traveling as tourists, or are just dining out, that "there simply is nothing to eat!" This is an exaggeration of course; there is plenty to eat. The difference is now you have to pick and choose rather than eat anything placed before you.

The following chart has been prepared for you to see at a glance, foods you can order when you're out. Soon the list will become automatic and you will be able to select your food without hesitation. *Be wise—focus on what you can eat, not on what you cannot!*

What To Order When Eating Out

Beverages: Water, herb tea, seltzer (lemon or lime may be added). Coffee: decaf, black, maximum 3 cups per day. Skim or 1% milk, soy or goat's milk. Fruit juices. A little dry red wine. No citrus, fruit or juice, in eczema or arthritis cases.

Appetizers: Fresh fruit cup, broth/bouillon/consommé, vegetable or fruit juice, raw vegetables (no tomatoes/ peppers), tossed salad.

Grains or Breads: whole grain hard rolls, slices, bread sticks, or crackers. Breakfast cereals, whole grains with skim or 1% milk.

Salads: Romaine, spinach, or mixed raw garden salad. Dress with lemon juice & olive oil. Fresh fruit salad, with low-fat cottage cheese.

Entrees: Fish (no shellfish), poultry (without skin), or lamb, that is broiled, steamed, grilled or roasted (any way but fried), with raw or steamed permitted vegetables.

Desserts: Fresh fruit, low-fat frozen yogurt, sugar-free Jello.

Snacks: Raw almonds, mixed nuts on occasion, whole grain crackers, baked sweet potato chips, whole grain rice cakes,

100% natural fruit jelly, low-fat cottage cheese, honey and olive oil (to eat with crackers), fresh or dried fruits, bottled water.

Avoid: red meats, processed meats, the nightshades, too many sweets and starches, alcohol, soda, hot spices, vinegar, fried foods, junk food and fast foods.

Note: *This is but a "thumbnail" sketch of foods to consider when dining out. Once you master and identify the proper food selections you will be able to expand your choices.*

A Story Worth Sharing (Anti-Perspirants)

[Although this account does not involve diet, I think it is so profound that I feel obliged to include it here.]

A patient of mine whom I had not seen for many years called recently to share an experience she had had. This woman had psoriasis on various parts of her face. It goes without saying that this is one of the most embarrassing places to have psoriasis. Patients will do anything to get rid of it on the face.

In addition to the facial psoriasis, this particular patient also had a severe problem for many years with foul-smelling underarm odors. The only thing that curtailed it was heavy use of antiperspirants. Never suspecting that this second problem could in any way be connected to the facial psoriasis, this patient had used antiperspirants extensively for years. One day this woman went on vacation some distance away. After settling in her vacation home, she realized that she had forgotten to pack her antiperspirant, and there was none to be bought where she was. Mortified at her smelly perspiration, and lacking the only remedy, she resorted to vigorous washing with plain soap and water several times daily in an effort to neutralize the odor. **To her great amazement, the psoriasis of her face soon disappeared completely!** She offered the following explanation:

"I feel the antiperspirant sealed off the sweat glands under my arms and prevented the toxins from being emitted from my body. These toxins had to go somewhere—so they made their way up and out on my face!"

This is a perfectly logical explanation as far as she and I are concerned. The use of a deodorant rather than an antiperspirant is the answer. Better yet, simply clean the area with soap and water and keep it dry, then the sweat glands will be able to function normally. I do not claim that this is the answer to every case of psoriasis of the face, but, in this particular case there definitely appears to have been a direct link.

[**Note:** A growing number of people feel there may be a connection also between breast cancer and the use of antiperspirants. I am not aware of any scientific studies on this subject, but in my opinion the idea is not remote for the very reason discussed above: i.e. the antiperspirant blocks the toxins from escaping and they then build up in the lymph glands under the arms. It is at least something to think about for the health-minded individual.]

A Story That Needs Telling

Eight-year-old J. J. came to me with his parents in November of 1999, suffering from a severe degree of plaque-type psoriasis (common vulgaris). Lesions the size of quarters covered his entire body. He had been treated extensively by orthodox methods for five years with no appreciable results. His parents decided to try the natural approach after finding my website on the Internet. An appointment was made and since they had to travel a great distance by car, they decided to consult with me on two consecutive days, learn all they could, then go home and follow through.

After examining the boy, I knew from past experience that he might very well have a severe flare-up in the process of detoxifying. I warned them of this possibility and also that it could be followed by others, not unlike the aftershocks of an earthquake. They all agreed to go this route anyway simply because young J. J. had no place else to go. As far as orthodox management was concerned—he'd been there!

It wasn't long before my predictions came true. For the next four months, the boy went through living hell! Anything and everything from an external point of view was tried to help calm down the skin's inflammatory reaction. It was one of the worst reactions I ever encountered with a young person. His family doctor insisted he be hospitalized, which he was for a very short period, but J. J. and his parents soon reverted back to my regimen in order to "ride it out!," which was a difficult decision to make under the circumstances.

Their faith in the process finally began to pay off after about four months. Finally by May 2000, six months from the start of the regimen, J. J. was practically free of all lesions. Many areas of his skin that were once covered with thick, scaly lesions were now as smooth as the day he was born! I have witnessed this on several patients in the past. His mother took a photographic account of the various stages he went through. Not only was he free of pain and disfigurement, but he was back in school with all his friends and into sports again. When I spoke to J. J. last, I asked what he thought was the key factor in his healing. Quick and to the point, his answer was, "The Diet!"

Understandably, they couldn't wait to share this wonderful news with their family doctor. They wanted to show him, firsthand, the remarkable results J. J. had attained and that if it worked for him, it could work for many others. The doctor's reaction was anything but what they expected. Instead of being enthusiastic about the boy's recovery, he was indifferent, smug and derisive. He said to J. J. and his mother, "You don't really think the diet had anything to do with this, do you?" J. J.'s mother was speechless, as was the boy himself.

She was so appalled at the doctor's attitude that she did not even attempt to persuade him otherwise. Young J. J. was in tears all the way home. But, being the trooper he is, he remains on the regimen and continues to heal a few remaining lesions every

May 2000

Dear Dr. Pagano,

What can I say?
I look at these pictures and cannot believe the heartbreak is almost over. J. J. is doing great. His spirits are picking up almost every day —he is playing sports and smiling again. What do you say to a man who saved our child's life? I can't believe how you were there for us, and put up with my hysterics! I will be forever grateful.

J.J.'s Mom

A letter from J. J.'s mother
(Reprinted by permission)

See Photographic Portfolio, Page 74, to see remarkable pictures of J. J. during his healing process.

day. He is no longer restricted in his activities, his skin is as smooth as silk. His mother contacted Oprah Winfrey, Rosie O'Donnell and other network personalities in an attempt to share this story with them. As of this writing, there has been no response. Perhaps in time...!

It Could Happen To You

I would be remiss if I did not share this story because *it could happen to you!* Unless your dermatologist is an independent thinker and a true physician who recognizes the truth when he sees it, and more importantly, acknowledges it, you may very well be met with a similar reaction from your dermatologist and/or family physician. I am not exaggerating, it has happened many times. Be ready for the well-worn phrases: "It has never been proven scientifically that diet has anything to do with psoriasis." Or "It's all in your head." And the ever favorite, "It is nothing more than in a state of remission."

So—if you have success in following this regimen and wish to convey your experience to your doctor, be prepared to receive a rejection slip, or at least an attitude of indifference. Clearly, this does not hold true for all dermatologists. If he acknowledges the results, fine, but don't count on it. You've been through enough anguish, you don't need any more. You know what you've been through, as did J. J. with the undaunted efforts of his mother and father. *That's all that really matters.*

Have faith in yourself and the healing process. Remember, your body is *always* trying to heal you. The best results are obtained when you give it the right tools to work with. J. J. did it to an outstanding degree. He is truly an inspiration to all psoriasis sufferers, especially young children. What he did was prove that if orthodox medicine fails, all is not lost—*there is another way!*

Diet and Acne?

According to an Australian study, there may be a link!

Why is acne common in the industrialized Western world and relatively uncommon in developing countries? Australian researchers went a bit further than just asking this question—they formed a research study, the results of which might change the way dermatologists think about diet.

The small study they conducted consisted of 50 people between the ages of 15 and 25 all having mild to moderate acne. The participants were divided into two groups of 25 each. The researchers instructed one group to eat a diet of lean meat, poultry, fish, fruits, vegetables, and whole grain breads and cereals. The second group was given a typical Western diet.

After twelve weeks, the results were staggering: "The acne of the boys on the higher-protein, low glycemic index diet improved dramatically by more than 50 per cent, which is more than what you see with topical acne solutions," wrote senior author Neil Mann, an associate professor at the Royal Melbourne Institute of Technology.

A Western teenager's typical diet appears to raise hormone levels, which have long been linked to acne. "A diet high in processed foods pushes glucose and insulin levels higher, exacerbating the problem, but low-glycemic foods do the opposite. The mechanism and the results are clear as day," says Mann.

The American Academy of Dermatology has typically denied that there is any link between diet and acne. It seems that more studies should be conducted.

[Source: An article printed in The Record, Hackensack, NJ, 12/04/07, by Linda Shrieves of The Orlando Sentinel.]

Dr. John's Final Comments

Having been in clinical practice for over forty years, I have deduced the existence of some fundamental principles in the healing process. Although these are simple, they often evade the patient and the practitioner in their efforts to bring about healing of whatever kind.

It has sometimes been said that all things come in "threes." Whether or not this is true is not for me to say, but I have found some validity in the statement. Some examples that come to mind are: It takes three to make a happy marriage - the man, the woman, and God; the Holy Trinity; the Three Wise Men; Three Coins in the Fountain; and, Three strikes and you're out! The list is virtually endless, but I for one believe there is some truth in it.

Over the years I have found it can apply to the aspect of healing in that I look upon healing as a triangle, a three-sided structure that is classified as the strongest geometric shape in nature. In applying this concept to healing I see three essential components that make up the triangle—the *patient,* the *therapy,* and *time*!

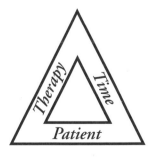

The **patient,** of course, constitutes the basic foundation of it all for without a patient there would be no procedure to consider and time would be of no consequence.

The **therapy,** whether it be allopathic, natural, spiritual or tea leaves is the avenue the patient decides to follow in his attempt to get well. And, depending on the patient's inner belief, they *all work* to one degree or another.

Time, however, the third side of the triangle, is what I have observed to be the weakest link on the part of most patients to keep the healing triangle in balance. Mind you, if I had a devastating condition, such as psoriasis, I too would like to have overnight healing, but such is not the case in the natural order of things. It takes time to get sick; it will take time to get well. It is as simple as that. Or, to put it more succinctly, "Give time a chance!"

I do believe that the fastest way to make healing a reality is: 1) See yourself, in your mind's eye, as being well; as if the healing had already taken place; 2) Visualize the chosen procedure as working; that you have been guided to the right procedure and/ or doctor; and 3) Do not put a time limit on the invisible inner workings of the creative process. Allow it to happen in its own time. All you have to do is keep your mind centered on the healing, not on the disease. Be satisfied with little signs of improvement on the path to healing, for it is the direction you are going in that matters, not the speed at which you are traveling.

This is what I feel applies to all types of healing, whether it be medication, surgery, homeopathy, nutritional or spinal manipulation. They all have worked on one patient or another— but—since we live in a three-dimensional world, they all require the element of time to bring about a more permanent healing.

To all psoriasis, psoriatic arthritic and eczema patients, I repeat—follow the procedure, visualize the healing, and above all give time a chance!

May you live all the days of your life in sound, radiant health, which is your God-given right—your spiritual heritage!

Customer Reviews

★★★★★**No question that it works**

Reviewer: A reader named Bill, October 16, 2006

"I found this book after googling a bunch of different things, and came across these reviews. Lots of good reviews, a few negative ones. Well, I noticed that all the negative ones were either people who hadn't actually tried it or people who didn't really stick with it. You can't rate a book negatively if you don't follow the program. Anyways, the diet simply works. When all the drugs I was prescribed stopped working, I turned to this. After a few weeks, there was a definite change. It has taken a little longer than the 2-3 months he writes about in the book, but that's because I still drink beer once a week or so. If I cut that out, it would be gone by now (about 4 months). In total, half of my spots are completely clear, and the others are completely clear in the middle with a ring around the outside. Lastly, a more moderate version of the diet should be called "how Americans should eat." I am almost happy I have psoriasis and found this book as it is so much more healthy. It takes a little bit for the body to assimilate, but if you have some discipline, it works wonders."

★★★★★**Thank you Dr. Pagano**

Reviewer: A reader from Washington, January 14, 2000

"Finally, after 15 years of battling psoriasis there is hope and a cure. I've tried every topical, own my own light machines, and have even tried the dreaded oral medications. None of them worked, much less made much of a difference. I have been treating the symptoms for 15 years. Thanks to Dr. Pagano, I am now treating the cause of my psoriasis...poor elimination. After only three weeks of following Dr. Pagano's diet and cleansing recommendations, I have noted a remarkable improvement..."

★★★★★Miserable in Hawaii
Reviewer: A reader from Chicago, December 7, 1999

"I have struggled with mild psoriasis since I was 16 but two weeks before our 30th anniversary trip to Hawaii, I broke out with guttate psoriasis literally from neck to my toes. Only my face was spared. What timing! I found John Pagano's book when I returned and immediately began the full program in Feb. of 1999. I was completely clear by August of 99. Even my scalp became pink and healthy again...I highly recommend this book. Your skin will improve as well as your general health."

★★★★★A life-changer.
Reviewer: A reader from New York, November 9, 1999

"I bought Dr. Pagano's book in August, 1999, inspired by other reader reviews on Amazon.com, and followed most of his guidelines. I tried to be optimistic, but was sure the flare-up of my moderate-to-severe psoriasis that I'd come to expect every autumn would hit me soon. Three months later–no flare-up, and I'm almost clear! After 27 years of enduring the discomfort and depression of psoriasis, this is really amazing..."

★★★★★Buy copy for your dermatologist
Reviewer: A reader from Washington, DC, November 5, 1999

"John Pagano says it all in this book. DIET, DIET, DIET is the key. Stop eating tomato! NIGHTSHADES! Don't listen to your dermatologist. Mine told me that he had to sign off on me, it was incurable. John Pagano says it is curable. Have to go now, sending a copy of this book to my doctor...John."

★★★★★I Read, I Believe & I'm On My Way To A Healing!
Reviewer: A reader from Pennsylvania, September 16, 1999

"...After suffering for 36 years with psoriasis, and applying expensive 'rub-on' medications...I came to the realization that something had to be wrong inside, but no one (doctor) could help

me because they didn't have a clue. Now Dr. John Pagano, he had more than a clue, and his book is proof! I bought this book July 23rd. I read it in 3 days, cover to cover. Immediately I gave up the nightshade foods....on August 16th, I was ready, and began the cleansing regimen. I have been following it as closely as I can, and on Saturday, last, I realized that the psoriasis on my scalp was totally gone! It's wonderful! The rest of my body is responding, and realizing that it took me 36 years to get to this point, I've got as long as it takes to heal myself completely!...Thanks Dr. Pagano! You are one very compassionate person."

★★★★★This totally worked for me!!!
Reviewer: A reader from California, May 14, 1999

"If you have psoriasis, buy this book. I had a moderate to severe case of psoriasis, followed these simple instructions, and the psoriasis almost totally cleared in a few months. Don't waste money on external medications. This book explains how to clear psoriasis and become much healthier in the process."

★★★★★A must-have book for anyone with psoriasis.
Reviewer: A reader from Baltimore, Maryland, April 28, 1999

"I've had psoriasis for 29 years, and this book has changed my life. The diet detailed in this book is a challenge to follow, but the truly dedicated (desperate) will get used to it, and the results are well worth the effort. My skin has never been as clear as it is today, and for the first time I am really looking forward to the summer and all of the skimpy clothing! If there was a 10 star rating on Amazon.com, this book would deserve it."

★★★★★It just made so much sense... and it's working!
Reviewer: A reader from Kanata, Ontario, Canada, April 25, 1999

"It's a natural, chemical-free way to treat your condition. Patience and persistence are required (some faith, too). After 5 months, my psoriasis is fading. And I've noticed improvements to several other health problems as well. I haven't felt this good in a long time!"

★★★★★Relief at long, long last!!!
Reviewer: A reader from Kitty Hawk, NC, February 28, 1999

> *"My Dad suffered with psoriasis for 25 years. I've been fighting it myself for about 15 years. Between us, we've tried every salve, ointment and cream known to man (including Dermatologists). I even went the methotrexate route which isn't a very healthy thing to do. During the summer of 1997 as I went through the stress of a divorce the condition just got worse and worse. Finally, a Chiropractor suggested Dr. Pagano's book. The diet is a challenge, let's be honest. But the results (6 mos. and 90% clear) are worth every bit of effort. Stop the insanity and get your life back; buy this book. By the way you'll save hundreds of $ in the process."*

★★★★★A must get book if you have psoriasis
Reviewer: A reader from Hong Kong, February 9, 1999

> *"This is a very comprehensive book which includes a very effective program to heal psoriasis. I never thought I could heal my psoriasis until I bought this book."*

★★★★★WHY YOU NEED THIS BOOK.....
Reviewer: A reader from Connecticut, February 6, 1999

> *"This book will shock you! There is a solution for this illness and you'll find it in the pages of this fabulous book! There are great photos of "before" and "after"–these are no gimmicks, these are real. The case studies are real too. It worked for me!"*

★★★★★buy it, read it, follow it and kiss your psoriasis good-bye
Reviewer: A reader from New York, NY, January 21, 1999

> *"One terrific read. Do yourself a favor and follow the regimen for 3 to 6 months and then decide whether this really works...I've been following it for 6-9 months and have cleared about 90%. You will lose weight and feel healthier. More importantly, you will be in control and not the disease."*

The following are excerpts from customer reviews posted by *barnesandnoble.com*.

★★★★★Lost Hope: Found
A reviewer, on November 8, 1999

> *"As a psoriasis sufferer I have tried a variety of treatments. Dr. Pagano's book is the only thing that has offered any sense of relief in ten years. He is totally sympathetic and understanding of the psoriatics emotional and physical needs. I strongly recommend this book to anyone who has the will power to carry through his regimen."*

★★★★★I'm hoping It Works!
A reviewer, on August 18, 1999

> *"The book makes so much sense! I've had the disease for 36 years and nothing has worked for any length of time. I knew that it had to be a problem on the inside, but I could never find any doctor who could give me any info to get me started on the right track....The book is written with enthusiasm and hope, chapter by chapter, touching all aspects of the disease that need to be treated...."*

We Get E-Mails
(Excerpts from unsolicited e-mail responses to Dr. Pagano's book)

> *I would like to share my success story after reading your book. My name is G.B and I live in Austria. I was diagnosed with eczema at the age of six months. I received several treatments with cortisone creams. The condition didn't go away instead it deteriorated with each passing year. In the first 10 years it was seasonal (mainly in winter) and afterwards it become steady and eventually part of my life. Since the condition was mainly on my hands it was a very humiliating experience because my environment didn't know why my hands were fire-red (with bleeding cracks) and I had the pressure that I must hide my hands from the people. After 30 years of suffering I have eventually found your book and read it at once.*

I immediately began applying the steps in your book. After 4 months putting only the recommended diet into action I am finally symptom free! I now have the feeling that I have the upper hand over the condition. The keys in my healing were: eliminating all milk products, vinegar, tomato, sugar, white potato and fried items from my menu. Thanks again for your blessed service!

–G.B., Dec. 9, 2006

"I am so amazed!" For 15 years I have put up with this most annoying ailment. I have been to doctors, dermatologists, and never once did I hear one of them say don't eat this or that! ... I just knew that someone had answers. That is you Dr. Pagano. I am filled with gratitude and can barely read the keyboard through my tears. Thank you is not enough! God's richest blessing to you Doctor.... I'm finally looking forward to summer clothes!!!!"

–With Gratitude, E.L.B.

"Your book is wonderful. After three weeks my skin is almost clear. After having psoriasis for 16 years no doctor ever recommended this approach. I am glad you have a web site or I would still be suffering."

–Thank You, C.M.

"I have suffered from pustular psoriasis on the soles of both feet and the palm of my right hand for over 22 years. I can't thank you enough. Your book **HEALING PSORIASIS: *The Natural Alternative*** *has been a revelation. I found tomatoes to be the worst thing I could have been eating. I haven't eaten them since and the psoriasis on my right palm has cleared up, my feet have improved greatly (no more redness and some areas have cleared up completely). I am so happy with what I have managed to do myself."*

–Yours sincerely, J.H.

"Two years ago, my seven year old daughter J. was diagnosed with Guttate psoriasis. Her entire body was covered with hundreds of scaly red patches. Her scalp sores were so bad that by this time last year, she had lost 50% of her hair. She looked awful. The psoriasis had taken over half her face, and the piles of scales were well visible above her hair. The flakes were everywhere. A well loved teacher at the school got me your book, I read it in two days. J. Started the diet on the third day. In one week we noticed a difference in the severity of the redness, the second week the skin seemed to soften, but we still held our breath. Today, one month later she is 95% cleared!!! I've never met you, Dr. Pagano, but I just wanted you to know how you've changed one little girl's life and how much we love you for it."

–God bless you. D.S.

"I have had psoriasis for 63 years of my 68. Every method has been tried from tar baths to puva. The disease always came back more severe–sometimes over 80% of the body. I ordered **HEALING PSORIASIS:** *The Natural Alternative on 2/27/97 after reading about it on the Internet. I really started the diet, etc., in the latter part of March, 1997. Now, three months later, I can't believe the results. I have followed the regimen/diet, etc. I even stopped smoking. My skin is almost completely healed."*

–C.S.

"My name is C.K. I am a certified colon hygienist who practices on Manhattan's Upper East Side. Over the last several months I have had the pleasure of treating several patients who have read your book, followed your diet and received colonics. It brings me great joy to see their lesions get smaller and smaller every follow-up session and then eventually disappear. I have seen cases of complete recovery occur in patients suffering previously 10-20 years. I commend your work and I will continue to give my patients your phone number."

–All my respect, C.K.

"I am not sure if you remember us. My name is J.K., and my son S. has psoriasis. We participated in the beginning of the Psoriasis Study Conference in November, 1995. We started your treatment in October, 1995. 60% of my son's body was covered with lesions at that time. In 10 days after we started the treatment, my son was 100% clear....We had about 5 flare-up waves like this before he cleared completely. He was cleared completely by March, 1996. In May we lifted the diet, and it not cause any reaction. The only reaction we had, was when S. had bronchitis (summer 1996), and his doctor prescribed antibiotic for him (Amoxicillin). In a couple days after starting on antibiotic, the lesions started to appear in all the old places. It was scary. They have never reached the stage of redness, they had a pale pink color, but we were upset just as well. As soon as we stopped antibiotics his skin was clear again. Right now, S. is completely off the diet (with some exceptions) and stays clear. Thank you Dr. Pagano. You and your book have really made a difference for us."

–Best Regards, J.K.

"I just wanted to write a thank you letter to you for the help you've given me, personally, through the recommendations in your book. The book has changed my life. I'm a 36 year old woman with psoriasis for 15 years with 5-10% coverage and the diet and other lifestyle changes you recommend have not only improved the psoriasis but have improved my overall health and feeling of well being physically, as well as emotionally. For this I thank you so much. If I may ever provide a more formal testimonial I would be honored. Thank you again."

–B.L.

Ordering

The following suppliers carry the most important items required in the Psoriasis, Psoriatic Arthritis and Eczema regimen, including:

- Slippery Elm Bark Powder
- American Yellow Saffron Tea
- Aura Glow (Olive oil/Peanut oil Mixture)
- Glyco-Thymoline
- Castor Oil

Baar Products, Inc.
P.O. Box 60
Downington, PA 19335

(800) 269-2502
(610) 873-4591
www.baar.com

The Heritage Store
314 Laskin Road, Box 444
Virginia Beach, VA 23458

(800) 862-2923
(757) 428-0100
heritage@caycecures.com

A.R.E. Bookstore and/or Press
215 67th Street
Virginia Beach, VA 23451

(757) 428-3588 x 7231 (Bookstore)
(800) 723-1112 (Press)
bookstore@edgarcayce.com
www.edgarcayce.org

A.R.E. (New York)
150 West 28th Street, Suite 1001
New York, NY 10001

(212) 691-7690

A.R.E. Clinic (Cayce Corner)
4018 N. 40th Street
Phoenix, AZ 85018

(602) 955-9206 (tel)
(602) 956-8269 (fax)

Most other items such as Hydrophilic Ointment, Epsom Salts, Witch Hazel, etc. can be easily obtained at or ordered from your local pharmacy.

To Order Supplies Internationally

Sweden
Sockerskrinet
[Ingrid Bergman or Gunnar Olsson]
Box 120 03
Russvägen 20
SE-850 12 Sundsvall
Tel: 060-552-780
Fax: 060-552783
sockerskrinet@telia.com

Germany
Renate Werner
Regional Representative der A.R.E.
Halker Zeile 158
12305 Berlin
Tel: 030 745 97 75
Fax: 030 745 38 79

Japan
Naoko Mitsuda
Temple Beautiful
3-30-17-B1 Okusawa Setagaya -ku
Tokyo
Japan 158-0083
Tel: 03-5499-6264
Fax: 03-5499-6268
www.caycegoods.com
templebeautiful@neti.com

England
The Edgar Cayce Centre: Durham
John Walsh
13, Prospect Terrace
New Kyo, Stanley
Co. Durham,
England DH9 7TR
Tel: 01207 237696
Fax: 01207 236398
cayce.walsh@virgin.net

To order Dr. John Pagano's award-winning book **HEALING PSORIASIS:** *The Natural Alternative* or additional copies of **Dr. John's Healing Psoriasis Cookbook...Plus!** [$35.00 plus $8.00 shipping and handling in the USA]:

By Website: www.psoriasis-healing.com

By Phone: (800) 919-4001 or (201) 947-0606
(Monday-Friday 9:00-5:00 E.S.T.)

By Fax: (201) 947-8066
(24 hours a day)

By Mail: 35 Hudson Terrace
Englewood Cliffs, NJ 07632

[enclose check, money order or credit card information]

If ordering by credit card you must give your name, complete shipping address, telephone number and credit card number with expiration date.

Contact & Ordering Information
Dr. John O.A. Pagano
Chiropractic Physician
The Pagano Organization, Inc.
35 Hudson Terrace, Englewood Cliffs, New Jersey 07632
Phone: (201) 947-0606 (9:00-5:00 E.S.T.)
Fax: (201) 947-8066
Website: www.psoriasis-healing.com

[Editor's Note: Dr. Pagano regrets that he cannot answer personal questions unless the caller is his actual patient. For him to do so would not be in the best interest of the caller or the doctor. You are invited to call (201) 947-0606 to make an appointment for a personal consultation with Dr. Pagano in his New Jersey office.]

The Ancient Wisdom

READ the Classics

STUDY the Philosophers

LISTEN to the Masters

OBSERVE the Enlightened

ABSORB True Knowledge

MEDITATE on Life

SEARCH the Scriptures

PRAY to the Gods

then bask in the glory of
The Ancient Wisdom
of simply
Being Yourself!

John O.A. Pagano

Index

W

water 14, 15, 20, 34, 39, 40, 41, 42,
    45, 49, 50, 53, 55, 56, 58, 60,
    61, 458, 467, 475, 500, 501,
    502, 503, 504, 505, 506, 507,
    508, 509, 510, 514, 515, 516
watermelon seed tea 21, 39, 460
web sites
    amazon.com iii, 523, 524, 525
    barnesandnoble.com iii, 523, 527
    http://vm.cfsan.fda.gov/~dms/ 492
    www.baar.com 531
    www.caycegoods.com 533
    www.edgarcayce.org 531
    www.onzedirect.com 532
    www.psoriasis-healing.com 534
weight 52, 55, 59, 476, 484, *See also*
    overweight
weight loss v, 18, 50, 475, 526
weight, Suggested for Adults 485
Why Me? Syndrome, The 14
wine 6, 18, 40, 49, 58, 460, 461,
    463, 514
witch hazel 507, 532
wok cooking 59, 60

Y

yeast 18, 469, 487, 502
yogurt 17, 23, 36, 48, 103, 104, 113,
    114, 139, 141, 145, 148, 168,
    169, 181, 184, 188, 189, 190,
    194, 211, 212, 239, 246, 247,
    253, 289, 303, 311, 331, 354,
    395, 396, 397, 412, 413, 414,
    418, 424, 427, 432, 482, 486,
    487, 514
yogurt, homemade 396–397

Z

zest 115
zest, lemon 363
zest, orange 113

zucchini 98, 219, 254, 322, 351,
    352, 380